LITTLE GREGORY

LITTLE GREGORY

by

Charles Penwarden

FOURTH ESTATE · *London*

First published in Great Britain in 1990 by
Fourth Estate
289 Westbourne Grove
London W11 2QA

British Library Cataloguing in Publication Data
Penwarden, Charles
Little Gregory
1. France. History, Crimes
I. Title
364.10944

ISBN 1-872180-31-0

Typeset by York House Typographic, London W7
Printed by Bookcraft Ltd, Midsomer Norton

The photographs in this book were
taken by J. Alexandre, G. Curien and
P. Gless, and are reprinted with their
kind permission.

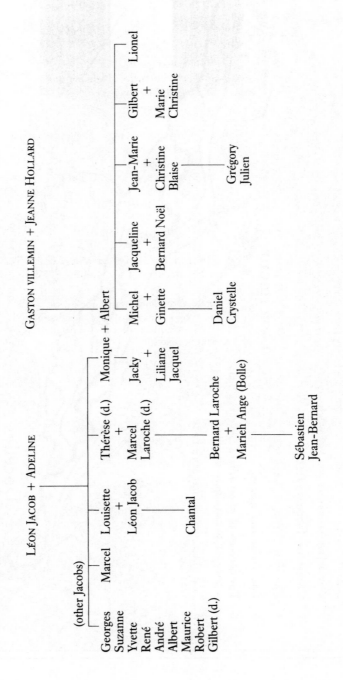

JACOB

VILLEMIN

LÉON JACOB + ADELINE

GASTON VILLEMIN + JEANNE HOLLARD

(other Jacobs)

Marcel   Louisette   Thérèse (d.)   Monique + Albert
          +   +
          Léon Jacob   Marcel   Jacky
                       Laroche (d.)   +
                                         Liliane
                       Chantal   Jacquel

Georges
Suzanne
Yvette
René
André
Albert
Maurice
Robert
Gilbert (d.)

Bernard Laroche
+
Marieh Ange (Bolle)

Sébastien
Jean-Bernard

Michel   Jacqueline   Jean-Marie   Gilbert   Lionel
  +   +   +   +
Ginette   Bernard Noël   Christine   Marie
                             Blaise   Christine

Daniel   Grégory
Crystelle   Julien

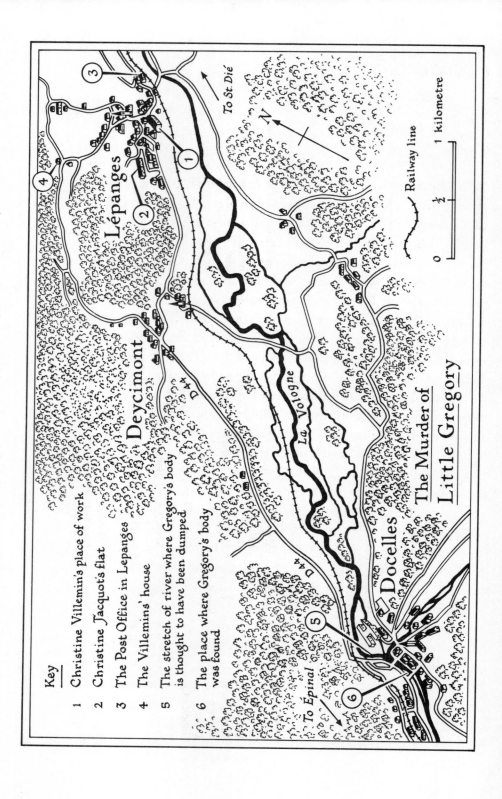

Key

1 Christine Villemin's place of work
2 Christine Jacquot's flat
3 The Post Office in Lepanges
4 The Villemins' house
5 The stretch of river where Gregory's body is thought to have been dumped
6 The place where Gregory's body was found

Lépanges

Deycimont

Docelles

La Vologne

To St. Dié

To Épinal

N

Railway line

0   ½   1 kilometre

The Murder of
Little Gregory

Introduction

In 1986 I was asked by a French magazine to make some enquiries into the 'Little Grégory' case – the brutal murder of four-year-old Grégory Villemin in a remote and desolate region of France. Because Little Grégory's mother Christine was under suspicion of having committed the crime, and because of violent developments in the wake of the murder, this case has apparently captivated the imagination of the French public ever since it happened.

I went over to the Vosges region of France, studied statements and evidence, spoke to the Examining Magistrate and some of the police involved in the murder hunt, and examined the scene of the crime. It is without doubt one of the most intriguing and complex I have come across in thirty years as a Detective. The business of unravelling it would make an excellent test for Scotland Yard Detectives – a test which I am sorry to say the French police have failed.

Both from the point of view of the crime itself, and of the investigation that followed, the 'Little Grégory' case illustrates many of the problems that can beset a murder enquiry.

First of all, the whole atmosphere of the tightly-knit community in which the murder took place was poisoned by 'Le Corbeau' – an anonymous writer of vicious hate-mail who bombarded local residents with threats, curses and abuse. Le Corbeau clearly knew in the minutest detail the movements of all who received the letters. There seems little doubt that Le Corbeau was also the murderer of Grégory.

This atmosphere was rendered even more claustrophobic and impenetrable by the fact that the area is dominated by a small number of closely inter-related families – of which Grégory's father was a leading member. Have these families closed ranks and concealed crucial evidence that could direct the police to the killer?

Add to that a key witness who retracts her testimony; a mass of forensic evidence, some of it significant, some of dubious value; the violent murder of a suspect; a host of witnesses to various circumstantial events; and a judicial system that allows – in my view – too much room for speculation and not enough for assessment of the value of individual witnesses – take all that together and you have a real quagmire of a case.

Despite all that, it should not be beyond the wit of readers to work out for themselves who murdered Little Grégory and dumped his body in the River Vologne. Here are a few clues to look out for as you read.

Firstly, consider the circumstances of the murder. While Grégory was still alive, a letter was posted by Le Corbeau announcing his death: 'I hope you die of sorrow. Not all your money can give you back your son.' Did Grégory's mother have time to leave work, post that letter, and kill her son before raising the alarm? I believe the timing is crucial, and offers the key to the crime. And why were all the windows of the Villemin house shut tight and the radio turned up loud?

Then look at evidence gathered when the body was discovered and at the post-mortem. How is it that Grégory showed no sign of having struggled against his attacker? Why were the knots that bound his little body so loosely tied, despite having been immersed in water for several hours? And why was so little water found in Grégory's lungs – as if he had been breathing only lightly when thrown in the river?

Finally, consider the motives. Who had reason to kill an innocent and likeable little boy? If it was not Christine, who could have hated the comparatively successful Villemin family so much as to have killed their son? If it was Christine, why should she commit such an unnatural crime? It has been argued that she felt imprisoned by the dreary circumstances into which her marriage had forced her. Was Grégory, for her, the symbol of that imprisonment? And did she see his death as her only means of escape?

Blunders committed in the crucial early days of the investigation mean that there may never be enough evidence to bring the case to trial – and without a full trial it is impossible to say for certain who killed Little Grégory. But my own enquiries into the case lead me to believe I know who committed this most bizarre and horrible of crimes.

The evidence presented in this book should lead you to the same conclusion.

Jack Slipper

1

'In this river pearls have been found.' The words were written in Latin, in the sixteenth century. In those times, the Vologne was known for a rare, pearl-bearing variety of freshwater mollusc. It was a source of finery for the nobility of Lorraine. But no one talks about the pearls now, and the tourist or incidental traveller would have little reason to stray into this corner of the Vosges; certainly, he would have none to stop there. It is an in-between sort of place, a patchwork of villages tucked away among forest-covered foothills. The *Michelin Guide* shows it as a greenish blank between Epinal to the west, Bruyères to the north and Gérardmer to the east. Gérardmer is close to the Vologne's source. It is a tourist town, the modern-day pearl of the Vosges. It even has a casino. Its clustering holiday homes and hotels attest to the drawing power of its lake, the biggest in the region. And then there are the panoramic views and skiing facilities offered by the nearby heights.

From the Höhneck, a peak of more than 4,000 feet, you can see as far south as the Alps if the weather is right. And historically-minded tourists can look down to the Schlucht pass. Now the sight of a popular skiing station, it marks the frontier that Bismarck's new Reich imposed on its humiliated neighbour in 1870 after Germany's crushing victory in the Franco-Prussian War. The spot is still popular with Germans today, although their tourism now takes more peaceful forms.

Such a mixture of tourism and history is far removed from the daily cares of the Vologne. The people are too busy with their homes and work. For some, Gérardmer is a source of employment. Saint-Dié and Epinal are the limits of their horizon, centres for shopping or perhaps legal transactions. Epinal, half an hour away by train, is the administrative centre of the Vosges *département*; a town of some 50,000, straddling the Moselle river as it makes its way north to the Rhine.

Mention the name Epinal to any Frenchman and he will reply *Imagerie d'Epinal*, referring to the illustrations produced by the town's printing presses in the nineteenth and early twentieth centuries.

These brightly-coloured, popular images used to accompany anything from nursery rhymes to accounts of First World War battles. Nowadays, though, the term has taken on a negative resonance. The naïve pictures symbolise a stereotyped and outdated view of reality. 'Imagerie d'Epinal' suggests cliché, simplification, and perhaps a dose of childish innocence – the sort expressed by brightly-coloured drawings.

Life, so any French adult will tell you, is not like an image from Epinal, even if we might want it to be. After all, there is something comforting about simplicity.

Such then is the fame of Epinal. But, in 1984, who had so much as heard of the Vologne? It belongs to that shadowy world known as *La France profonde*: deepest France: a world of small towns or villages and closed communities. In Britain, the popular, representative, mode of feeling and thinking is expressed by the mythical 'man in the street'. *La France profonde* serves the same purpose, but it is much more than that. It is both a place and a person. The idea expresses the height of ordinariness, an ordinariness which is also a deep sea full of potential monsters. Its inhabitants are assumed to be basic, inarticulate and beyond the reach of modernity: primitives. With them, social intercourse is at its roughest and human passion at its most brutal. Theirs is a world that both fascinates and repels: the roots from which we have all grown, and the primeval mud we hope to have washed from our lives.

You cannot really visit deepest France although you may, perhaps unwittingly, live there. Most of the time, it is a quiet, unspectacular place: average, dormant. But when this elusive entity does manifest itself to the public mind, it is usually through crime. Any kind of aberration is permitted, but murder is the prime felony, the confirmation that obscure and volcanic passions are at work. It was murder that lifted the mantle of obscurity from the Vologne in the autumn of 1984. So effectively, indeed, that the whole of France took an interest. You would only have to mention the place for someone to comment: 'Isn't it terrible, what happened to that little boy Grégory? Do you think the mother did it?' The heart of *la France profonde* was found beating in the Vologne: violently.

An affair fit for Epinal to illustrate, the cynics would say.

2

On the maps, the roads that follow the Vologne are marked with the green fringe that signals 'scenic route'. Not that such pleasant byways are unusual in this part of the Vosges, where there are few major settlements to break into the calm if monotonous beauty of river, hill and forest. Local communities rarely count more than 1,000 or 2,000 inhabitants. Certainly, if you drove along the D44 as it heads upstream from the Vologne's confluence with the Moselle, you would not pay much attention to the small, undistinguished villages that punctuate the valley at regular intervals of two to three miles. Cheniménil, Docelles, Deycimont, Lépanges, Laveline-sur-Bruyères, Aumontzey; so many permutations of the drab working communities that grew up or expanded to the rhythm of the textile mills established here in the nineteenth century.

With its abundant supply of wood and water, the Vosges was one of France's first industrialised regions. Textiles have remained the main employer in the region, along with subcontractors to the motor industry and the odd paper mill. Almost the only employer, in fact. In spite of redundancies here and closures there, the industry has survived the onslaught of Asian competition in the seventies and the depression of the early eighties. It continues to pay modest, often minimum wages to a population that has never learnt to expect more. Besides, those who have a secure job can consider themselves lucky. The textiles industry has halved its work-force since the beginning of the century, and unemployment in the Vosges is well above the national average.

For neither nature nor nurture have been kind to the inhabitants of the Vologne. Winter in the Vosges can last anything from four to six months. As a local joke has it, here there are only two seasons, winter and 15 August. The region has a history of alcoholism and illiteracy, of inbreeding and poverty, of illness and malnutrition. On the positive side, its inhabitants are also reputed to be hard-working and upright, toughened by their conditions. To make a decent living you have to work hard and many of the locals combine two activities: worker and woodcutter, farmer and craftsman. They belong to a kind of rural proletariat of factory employees who cultivate small allotments, or rent plots of woodland for firewood. In pre-revolutionary days, most were landless peasants – no better than serfs to the lord of the manor or to land-owning ecclesiastics. Their lowly condition is reflected in the surnames of their descendants: Bernard, Noël, Jacques, Robert, Philippe; the simple christian-name patronyms of the non-possessing classes.

Come Liberty, Equality and Fraternity, many of these down-trodden peasants became agricultural labourers, scraping to supplement the meagre produce of their inadequate land. As late as 1900, young boys were being sent to mind wealthier neighbours' cattle in exchange for the proverbial, and sometimes literal, crust of bread.

Such was the work-force tapped by the mill-owning families who colonised the region in the 1850s and 1860s, families like the Kieners, the Hattons, the Seites, who built the redbrick workers' terraces near their factories, just like the blocks that grew up in the mining towns to the north. The houses are still inhabited today, and the region still has a tradition of respect for the boss. Other workers have moved to more recent council estates, whose concrete slabs bear the bright names of municipal good intentions: Vraichamp, Gaichamp, Tranche-Million.

And then there is the third category, those who have managed to get their own detached home or *pavillon*. To an English ear, the word carries an association of regal grandeur; but it is soon deflated when you see the characterless constructions put up by the industrial builders on the outskirts of towns and villages all over France. Decent enough, but hardly palatial. A Parisian may laugh about *pavillons* in the suburbs, but in Lépanges or Docelles, owning a *pavillon* was the first sign that you were moving out of the underclass of mill labourers. You were your own man. What with a smart car and a collection of sophisticated goods from the mail-order catalogues, there was not much further you could go: unless you left the valley.

Few did. Like so many other isolated districts of France, the area is characterised by its social immobility. Generations have gone through school knowing that their only realistic prospect was a job at the mill. What was the point of learning? Besides, there was the economic pressure, the need for an extra income in the family. Consequently, few stayed on after obtaining the minimal school-leaving certificate. Anyway, family often exerts an almost magnetic force in these small villages. It has formed a dense tissue of intermarriages and more or less distant relationships. The Villemins were a typical example.

3

Records of the Villemin family went back as far as the early eighteenth century. Members had fanned out all through the valley and one of them, Jean-Antoine, even achieved fame. There is a statue commemorating him in Bruyères: to the distinguished colleague of Pasteur who demonstrated that tuberculosis is contagious.

The discovery had been of little use to Antoine's distant relative, Albert Villemin. Albert contracted the disease in his forties while working at the Boussac Saint Frères textile mill.

To compensate for his ill health, Albert had neither fame nor fortune. But Albert could consider himself happy. From his marriage to Monique Jacob in 1953 he had six healthy children: Jacky, Michel, Jacqueline, Jean-Marie, Gilbert and the youngest, Lionel, born in 1973. Of course, it had been a struggle bringing them up. He and Monique had spent thirty years on alternate shifts at the same factory, seeing each other only at weekends. Neither rose above the minimal wage of 4,200 francs a month, but they were determined: by scraping and sacrificing, they earnt enough to put down a payment on their own house. It was a large place with extensive gardens from the days when the textile industry was thriving. A house befitting heads of a large family. On the lawn outside the white, metal-shuttered building, they set an old cart, painted with black varnish – the noble agricultural symbol of their escape from the rural proletariat.

Life had tired Monique and Albert Villemin. Although only fifty, Monique had that grandmotherly look that comes suddenly to women who have spent all their lives working and rearing children. Her hair was beginning to go white at the brow. Albert had left Boussac Saint Frères at the age of fifty-three, compelled by a mixture of depression and illness. He was a short bespectacled man with a typically French, sideburn-free beard. It emphasised his schoolmasterly looks.

Parents do not like to distinguish between their children. For them, ideally, each one has his merits and the weaker are loved for their vulnerability. Monique and Albert liked to see their family as a whole, a joyous democracy where each child had his place, and sought to justify it, carrying with him just that pinch of resentment at having to share and to compromise. But if Monique and Albert had to say who was the most successful, they knew they would choose Jean-Marie.

You could see it in the liveliness of his expression, in the poise of his body: Jean-Marie liked to boast of his ten years of body-building, five years of football and two years of karate. And you could hear it at family get-togethers. For some years now, Jean-Marie's nickname had been *Le Chef*, the chief. He had acquired it because of his outspoken, headstrong personality. Jean-Marie was free with his opinions, and generally delivered them to other members of the family in the bluntest possible manner. The chief knew what he wanted, and he had little tolerance for those who got in his way. He was a foreman at the Autocoussin car accessories factory in La Chapelle-devant-Bruyères. In itself, this was enough to set him apart from the other members of the family. His sister Jacqueline and his brothers Jacky, Michel and Gilbert were all *ouvriers*, unskilled manual labourers. For the fourth and youngest brother, Lionel, born in the mid seventies, it was still early days. But then the mills hadn't been taking on too many new people recently.

The chief was different in other ways too. In 1979, at the age of twenty-one, he had got married and moved out of his parents' home in Aumontzey to set up his own household in the Gaichamp council flats in Lépanges. A few months later, he and his wife Christine bought a plot of land in Paremont, on the slopes above Lépanges. In August 1980, Christine gave birth to a boy, Grégory. It was an unusual name, with an American ring to it, but then Christine and Jean-Marie were attracted to the out of the ordinary. The name Grégory bore their dream of a richer, more ambitious life.

The first step was their own house. Jean-Marie and Christine Villemin could not content themselves with council accommodation, however spacious, nor would they settle for second best in the construction of the chalet on Paremont. Jean-Marie was a perfectionist. He chose his design and materials with care and inspected the building work with vigilance. By June 1981, Christine and Jean-Marie Villemin were ready to give the child they doted on his own house. Their efforts, now, were for Grégory.

It had all gone very fast. Christine was coming on twenty. She had met her husband to be when she was sixteen, and still a student at Bruyères secondary school. Christine had come to Laveline with her mother when she was eleven. Perhaps that was what made her attractive to Jean-Marie – that she was different from the other girls. The relationship had soon become serious, and they pursued it in spite of any reticence felt by other members of the family, or by Christine herself. Marriage, Christine knew, did not always simplify things, the experience of her own family could tell her that. Still Jean-Marie was not like other men, and certainly not like the second husband who beat her older sister, or the husband her mother had lost no time divorcing from – the one who just wanted her to look after his kids.

The marriage was a simple ceremony, attended only by the parents on each side: Monique and Albert Villemin, and Gilberte Chatel. This simplicity was unusual in the Vosges, where weddings were always the occasion for great family gatherings. Still, it was not as if the couple had just met. They had more practical priorities.

Now, three years later, Jean-Marie and Christine had everything: a handsome, energetic child, success at work, and a spacious home of their own. They had escaped the dingy lower part of Lépanges, with its glum workers' housing along the main road, and they had built at the top of the village, where the better houses were – where you could get a bit of privacy, and magnificent views over the Vologne valley. Behind them lay only the hills and the deep green woods of Scots pine, spruce and beech.

An exceptional couple? Perhaps they were, for the region. By its standards, certainly, they were successful and forward looking, the most successful and forward-looking couple in a family that counted at least 70 members, and more than 300 relations in Lépanges and the outlying villages. You could hardly expect them not to be envied. After all, it is never good policy to be conspicuously happy, especially in a small village. It doesn't take much to inflame an ancient grudge. Any member of the Villemin family could have told you that. Especially Monique and Albert, in Aumontzey.

The first sign was a letter. It arrived in 1980. It bore the postmark of Bruyères, the biggest of the Vologne towns. Albert opened the envelope and saw a few lines of big block capitals, crudely formed with the help of a ruler, on grey, blue-chequered paper:

YOUR WIFE IS A SLUT. YOUR SON IS A BASTARD, AND YOU ARE A CUCKOLD.

This was a surprise that Monique and Albert would have time to get used to. For there would be other letters, all of them stuffed with obscenities, and in the same, awkward hand. But above all there were the phone calls. Hundreds of them. At first, they were no more than breathy silences. Then, the insistent stab of insults: slut, whore, cuckold, bastard, repeated scores of times. Every man and woman in the family was forced into these coarse moulds. But it was Albert Villemin who came in for the worst treatment: 'Albert, your house will be burning tonight!' warned the voice. 'Albert, you'll be hanged!' Monique's final tally of calls was 700.

The author of these letters and calls soon became known as *Le Corbeau*, the Crow. In France, this is the generic name for poison-pen letter writers. It entered usage after 1941, when Henri Clouzot made a film about a particularly venomous outbreak of anonymous letters in the south-western town of Tulle. His model was a woman called Angèle Laval, who baffled local police from 1917 to 1920. Laval even killed one of her victims, albeit indirectly. The man died from a heart attack after reading that his wife had been identified as the Crow. In Clouzot's film, the arch penman had become a male, but he still signed each of his missives with a crudely drawn representation of a crow.

Soon, everyone in or around the Villemin family was receiving calls. If you had a new car, then your wife was playing the whore to pay for it. Alone in your house? Perhaps we'll come round and flay you alive. The Crow peopled the area with sluts, cuckolds and bastards. Children became mentally retarded. And there was always the past to draw on, with its ample reservoir of quarrels over money, theft and illicit affairs.

The Crow was thorough. Gilbert Villemin did not have a phone, so messages were left with a neighbour.

Directly or indirectly, Jean-Marie and Christine were also favourite targets. The Crow seemed to know everything that was going on. 'I see you were working on your masonry all day', he or she would observe. The tone was familiar, insolent. 'Hallo,' said the voice to Jean-Marie, 'it's me. Come on, I can describe your house by heart.' One night, Monique and Albert Villemin were round at Paremont for dinner. When suspicious noises were heard near the house, Albert went outside to take a look. Nothing. And then the phone rang. 'I saw everything,' said the voice. The Villemins were being watched. More than watched. There were malevolent night-time visits. Gun shots were heard around Paremont, a newly-built wall was knocked down, a freshly-dug trench caved in. The front-door window was smashed.

It was a long and insistent war of nerves. Jean-Marie and Christine came to feel that their every movement was observed. The Crow told them he or she was watching with binoculars. The Crow kept insinuating there was something they didn't know: 'There's a secret in your family, and I may be the only one who knows about it. Your mother, she knows too. Yes, she knows, but she's afraid of the truth, but you can't talk to her about it, your mother, 'cos there's no proof. She's the only one who records.'

The Crow knew that he or she, too, was being watched, or at least monitored. But the taunts continued, accompanied by threats: there was the secret, and death – an obscure revenge with a missing link and with Albert or Jean-Marie as its object. 'I'll stick a bullet between your shoulders,' the Crow told Jean-Marie during a long call to his workplace in 1982. 'Then again, maybe I won't. I'll get your kid instead. That'll hurt you more. Don't leave him outside. You'll find him below.' Below, from Paremont, or from anywhere in the valley, was the Vologne.

And then there was the note that Christine Villemin said she found against the window one morning. It had been slid between the shutters: 'I'll get you, Villemins.'

Individually, reactions to the Crow varied. Christine and Jean-Marie changed their phone number and had themselves taken out of the directory. Monique and Albert alerted the gendarmes at Corcieux, their nearest headquarters. An investigation was started up, and the members of the family were advised to tape the Crow's obscenities in an effort to penetrate his disguise. Sometimes, when the Crow phoned, they would quickly call the person they suspected to see if the number was engaged. One couple even hired a private detective at the rate of £100 a day. That was a lot when wages were only £400 or £500 a month.

As life continued its daily course, the Villemins and Jacobs learnt to spy on each other. Relationships in and around the thronging family were wrapped about with the poisonous thread of mistrust. Backchat made the air unbreathable. And when the family met in Aumontzey for the ritual family lunches with Monique and Albert, news of the Crow was always at the centre of the conversation. Old family rivalries, small things, suddenly crystallised in their minds, and became encrusted with suspicion. Memories acquired a new resonance. But still the family stuck together.

But whatever hunches people had about the identity of the anonymous caller, no one ever came forward with convincing proof. All that remained were the letters and the voice, or voices: a distorted, amplified sound, sometimes deep and guttural – almost cavernous, sometimes high-pitched. In the background could be heard the buzz and burr of conversation, or the radio, or a record playing. As for the accent, it was unmistakably that of the Vosges. So thick you could cut it with a knife.

Nobody knows how often the so-called Crow was just another local eager to inject his own ha'p'orth of bile, or just to play practical jokes. When the family became suspicious, the Crow organised his practical jokes all on his own, summoning doctors or undertakers to the 'moribund' Albert.

What did the Crow of the Vologne want? The second letter to Monique and Albert seemed explicit enough:

Watch out, Villemins, I'm going to get you. If you want me to stop, I'll make a bargain: you must stop seeing the Chief. You must treat him like a bastard too, you and his brothers and sister must leave him out in the cold. If you don't do this, I'll carry out the threats I made to the Chief and his little family. Jacky and his little family have been left out long enough. It's the Chief's turn to be treated like a bastard. He can console himself with his money. It's up to you to choose: life or death.

The third letter was written in a more common joined-up style, although an intentionally disfigured one. It looked like the work of a semi-literate. The author seemed to be withdrawing the threats made in the second:

I see nothing has changed at your place. Always the same favourites, and the Chief still comes. You can show my letters to Jacky, 'cos I'm giving up. He's still out in the cold, so it's useless trying to defend him . . . Only your daughter and her old man have the right to come and dirty your plates on Sundays. It's all for the son-in-law. He's more important than your sons to you, especially you, old woman. Not a day goes by without Nonoche coming round and sticking his nose in everywhere. I don't want to hurt Mummy's toughy, or his stuck up little tart, or his bruv. You, old man, you've aged, you look pretty sick to me. Well, old man, I'm stopping. I've taken my revenge, 'cos I've got you worrying, perhaps you won't hang yourself but I don't care, 'cos I've got my revenge. I hate you so much I'll go and spit on your grave when you snuff it. Perhaps Jacky isn't any more respected, but I don't care, I've got my revenge. This is my last letter, you'll never hear from me again. You'll wonder who I was, but you'll never find me.

That was in May 1983. By now, the gendarmes at Corcieux were pressing ahead with their inquiries. Forty members or relations of the family had been interviewed. When Albert Villemin informed the investigators of this latest epistolary aggression, they decided to organise a family dictation test so as to identify the miscreant. Forty members and relations of the family were invited. The results of this test were never communicated. They did not need to be. The Crow's rasping voice had fallen silent.

4

The inhabitants of the Vologne could look back to the summer of 1984 and thank their local gods. They had got off lightly. On 11 July, a hurricane sent from the South of France blew roughshod over the Vosges, creating a corridor of destruction three miles wide. The winds reached 160 miles an hour. Two-pound hailstones thudded into the ground. Roofs were pulled off and buildings flattened. Whole forests were destroyed. Many others, including Epinal's, were severely damaged. In all, 100 villages were affected, and the damage extended over 470 square miles.

The Vologne missed it all. It lay a few miles to the east of the hurricane's passage. There had been no destruction, no emergency committees, only the effort to show solidarity and the knowledge that the whole region would suffer the economic consequences. That and the repeated conversations about family or friends who had been caught up in the Vosges' natural disaster.

On 16 October though, like most of the rest of France, the region was enjoying the glories of a short Indian summer – a brief respite before the winter harshness of its mountain climate. The violent rains of the previous few days that had swollen the rivers and streams had given way to a mild sunlight which bathed the evergreens and burnished the oaks. Here and there, bright red stains of geranium lit up the sober façades of the workers' terraces and the houses along the hillside. Flossy clouds processed across the pale blue sky. Autumn was the best season for the Vosges, lending variety to the monotonous swathes of forest, its gentle light softening the grimness of the villages. Now was the time to go mushrooming in the woods, a time to make jam and conserves with the autumn fruits. There were still a few days to go before bringing in the firewood.

Christine Villemin was on the day shift at the *Manufacture de Confection Vosgienne* textile mill in Lépanges. It was a run-down sort of place, with a crooked chimney and peeling paintwork: a survivor. Christine worked as a seamstress, putting shoulder pads and pocket flaps on shirts destined for the military. She worked from 8.30 a.m. until 4.50 p.m. for 4,000 francs a month. It was an average sort of job, but at least it was near home. Others had to go further afield. And then her son Grégory was nearby. When school ended at 4.30 p.m., twenty minutes before Christine was free to collect her darling boy, he was taken to the home of Christine Jacquot, a friend and former neighbour at Gaichamp. The council estate was only a few hundred yards away from Christine's factory. Its clean brown and white blocks stand out clinically from the hillside and surrounding houses. The municipal graft had not yet grown into its surroundings. At Gaichamp, Grégory could play with his friends. At Paremont, playmates were harder to come by. Often, he had to be dragged screaming and fighting from some all-important football match. He was tough, self-assured little child, there was no way you could push Grégory round. He was a chief, like his Dad. The leader of the class.

Moving up the hills had meant social isolation for Christine, too. On Paremont there were none of the easy contacts offered by the promiscuity of estate life. Such is the price of privacy. Christine and Jacquot became friends when they were living on the same landing. Jacquot had three children. One of them, Aurélien, was Grégory's schoolmate. Christine Jacquot had started looking after Grégory when he was a toddler. During her lunch hour, Christine Villemin would take Grégory round to Gaichamp at 1.00 p.m., making sure he had his fruit to eat after the end of school. Her namesake and herself were both the same age: twenty-four. A slim blonde always dressed in a sweater and tight-fitting jeans, Jacquot was a fair, blue-eyed complement to her friend's darker looks and slightly stockier build. She was Christine's closest friend in Lépanges.

These days, though, contact between the former neighbours was limited to their children's meetings. The Villemins were busy with life at Paremont: building their ideal home and solid future, and spoiling Grégory.

Clocking off on her way out of the factory, Christine ducked into the black Renault 5 she and Jean-Marie had bought second-hand to smooth her life as a working mother, and sped up the road to Gaichamp. The traffic was thinning out now. At most times of day, the D44 groans under the passing weight of heavy goods vehicles. The millowners could not have known that when they built their workers' houses there.

When Christine Villemin arrived, Grégory was playing football with his friends. It was the usual, passionate match, pursued with all the urgency of healthy, competitive children. Most days, Christine took advantage of the circumstances to have a chat with her friend, to make a few remarks about the behaviour of their offspring, or life with their respective husbands. This time, though, the exchange was a short one. 'Has he been good?' 'Yes, no trouble.' Jacquot smiled and offered her friend a coffee. Christine declined. She was in a hurry.

'I've got piles of ironing to do. It's incredible how dirty this kid gets!'

And with that she was half way into her car. 'Come on Titi,' she urged, 'let's go! I can't wait for ever!'

Of this brief, routine encounter, Jacquot later recalled that Christine seemed particularly on edge, and that she drove away at an unusually fast speed.

When Christine drove out of the Gaichamp car park, she turned left onto the D44, which runs through the lower part of Lépanges and then left again, up the Rue de Bellevue, past the cemetery that stands in the middle of the town. The dour, pink church was built to look down on the village, but now it lies below the farms and chalets that straggle up the hillside towards the woods.

The drive to Paremont was not much more than one kilometre. As usual, Grégory stood at the back, looking through the gap between the front seats. That way he could see where they were going, and put his arms round his mother's neck. He was a tender child.

'Five already!' said Bernard Colin, as he saw the Renault go past a hundred yards or so ahead of him.   Colin was a retired carpenter who lived over the road from the church. Every evening at around 5.00 p.m. he went out for a walk with Jimmy, his Dalmatian. Tonight he had just started and was talking to some neighbours, Adrienne Grandidier and Yvon Nardin, when he saw the black Renault 5. Its appearance was like a marker for the end of the working day. Besides, so few cars took the road up towards Paremont that you always noticed them, especially if they were driven by a stranger. Not that Colin noticed any but familiar faces that evening.

Colin's route usually took him along Rue de Bellevue and then up Rue des Champs, past the Villemins' chalet to the woods. He knew Grégory and his parents well. Whenever he saw Colin in his familiar beret with Jimmy at his side, the boy would come and exchange a few words with him and stroke his dog.

For Marcelle Claudon, 5.00 p.m. was time to bring her cows down for milking from their pastures above Paremont, just up the hill from Christine and Jean-Marie's house. The operation did not take long. Claudon usually drove up there in her Citroën Mehari jeep, rigged up a makeshift rope fence along the road to stop the livestock wandering, and then followed the animals down on foot to the farm, which was about a kilometre north of Paremont. If the cows were left too late, they would not give any milk. Cows, like young children, are creatures of routine and easily upset.

Christine says that she arrived home just after five. Frustrated at having had to abandon his friends at Gaichamp, Grégory was determined to enjoy the last minutes of daylight, and so she let him play with his bucket and spade on the pile of gravel that stood by the steps to the front door. It was a leftover from some of the work that Jean-Marie was always putting in to improve what, after his son and wife, was his greatest source of pride: his house. Only that summer Grégory had helped him build the second garage, aligning the bricks for cementing. The extension still had to be coated with roughcast, but it was good enough to shelter Christine's car.

'Here put this on . . . '

It was getting cold. Christine told Grégory to keep on his blue anorak while she went in to fetch him a striped woollen hat. Grégory had to dress up properly, he had just got over laryngitis.

Christine reports that Grégory asked permission to go and see Gilbert Meline, the farmer who lived just up the street. Meline kept bees for honey and had a son who was Grégory's nearest playmate. His farm, with all its outdoor activities, was an essential part of Grégory's imaginative geography.

Christine refused her son's request. She said she didn't want him to stay out too long. Then she went back inside to busy herself with the ironing, turning on the radio to accompany her domestic work: loud, because the hi-fi was in another room. Christine says she remembers tuning into a popular radio talk show, *Les Grosses Têtes*. 'Over to you, Nicole!' enthused the studio voice from Paris. Something light and funny to get her through the piles of clothes. What with the double glazing, it was impossible to hear what Grégory was doing outside.

Nor could Christine see Grégory: the shutters were closed. Jean-Marie had started taking this precaution in the days when the Crow had been prowling around their house, two years ago now. 'We worked hard to buy our oak dining-room suite,' he would say. 'We didn't want anyone to steal it.' There was no point in opening them for the half-hour or so of light that remained. Besides, the gendarmes had recently warned them about organised gangs prowling around looking for easy spoils. The house was exposed enough as it was, without inviting them to come in through the window.

From outside, the house on Paremont was expressionless, closed. An image of defensive domesticity.

Christine said she went out to get Grégory at about 5.30 p.m., twenty minutes or so after she had started ironing, just when the radio was advertising *La Vâche Grosjean*, a kind of processed cheese. It was time for his bath.

But according to his mother, Grégory was no longer on the gravel. He had gone. Perhaps he had run off to see Gilbert Meline? It would not have been the first time he had ignored her instructions and run off like that. Or maybe he was playing one of his pranks, hiding in some corner or cupboard, ready to jump out at her? Grégory loved to surprise his mother. He used to come up behind her in the kitchen and pinch her bottom, anything to catch her out. Christine says she made a quick tour of inspection in the rudimentary garden. But Grégory was not lurking around the house.

Gilbert Meline had not seen him either. Meline had been working around his home all afternoon and paying only distracted attention to what was going on around him. Christine remembered that he was busy with his tractor when she arrived with Grégory, and that he was sweeping gravel from his drive when she came out: but Meline had not seen her.

Perhaps, then, Grégory had run back to Gaichamp to finish that game of football. He had never done so before, but he was perfectly capable of covering the distance on his own.

Christine Villemin jumped back into her Renault 5 and set off back down the hill, her edginess making a sudden leap when she found herself held up by Marcelle Claudon's cows. A wheel got stuck. Claudon told her she was late, she had seen nothing.

At Gaichamp, Christine Jacquot was still outside when her friend drew to an abrupt halt in front of the building. She flung the car door open.

'Have you seen Titi? He's gone.'

Jacquot had not seen Grégory. Christine Villemin drove on, just remembering to ask Jacquot to phone if she did catch sight of Grégory, and to promise to do the same herself once the mystery had been sorted out. Then, says Christine Villemin, she drove on towards the town centre, where another of Grégory's friends lived. But no, Grégory was not there, either. She made a quick turn and headed back up towards Paremont.

Christine Villemin reported that she kept telling herself that this was not the first time. Only the previous Wednesday, Grégory had disappeared from his grandmother's home in Bruyères. Half an hour later, he had come back with a friend, perfectly nonchalant. They had been to the sweet shop together. There was no telling with young boys.

While Christine Villemin was ironing and listening to the *bons mots* of various French wits and showbiz personalities, her brother-in-law, Michel, was at home in Aumontzey, 12 kilometres from Lépanges. He was relaxing in front of the television before going off to work on the night-shift. It had been an ordinary day for him. He had spent some of the afternoon chatting with Bernard Laroche, a cousin from the other side of the village, and then he had taken a reading lesson. Michel's semi-literacy was a sensitive point. Perhaps that was what made him live next door to Monique and Albert – the need of parental reassurance. Aumontzey was the heart of the Villemin and Jacob family.

Michel's attachment to his parents could hardly have been more explicit.

No doubt, Michel did not hear the phone ringing at Albert and Monique's. However, he did not have to wait long. Albert and Monique were up the road, at the home of Monique's sister Suzanne. The caller was obviously impatient and cut out after three or four rings. Seconds later, the ringing took up next to Michel. He picked up the receiver.

'Hallo?'

'It's me! You recognise me?'

Michel did, and he did not. The voice continued:

'There's no answer next door. Tell them I've taken the chief's son and put him in the Vologne! His mother is already looking for him.'

Michel Villemin has always insisted: it was impossible to identify the voice. It had a rough, unstable sound. Muffled, distorted. A woman's voice, he thought, but it was so hard to say.

Michel remembered that his first reaction was to run next door. Lionel was playing in the garden. He told Lionel to go and fetch Monique from Suzanne's place. Then he brought his own two children inside. The Crow had not waited for them, but Albert and Monique would get the message all right. As soon as he saw his parents, Michel shouted the news:

'It's the Crow! He says he's thrown Grégory in the Vologne! Yes, the chief's son, he said! Yes, the Vologne!'

Michel ran back inside and dialled his work number. 'Hallo, yes, this is Michel Villemin. Tell them I might not be there for the shift tonight. There's trouble.'

The precaution was worth taking, even if the latest call was just another hoax: like Albert's false funeral, like Albert's hanging. This would be the first Grégory 'joke' – the worst bit of bad taste yet. They hadn't heard from the Crow for more than eighteen months, and now, out of the blue, this . . .

Immediately, Monique and Albert called the gendarmerie at Corcieux. Then the station at Bruyères. It was around 5.30 p.m., or so the duty officer remembered. He did not bother to note the call.

Monique and Albert now dialled the ex-directory number of Christine and Jean-Marie. No answer. Then they remembered: Jean-Marie was at Autocoussin. He was in the repair shop when his mother got through to him.

'Jean-Marie, there's been a call to Aumontzey. The Crow. He says he's taken Grégory.'

In the silence at the other end of the line, Jean-Marie clenched his anger. As if in some haywire martial arts routine, he struck out with his fist, hitting the factory wall.

'I'm coming right away. I know who did it, he won't get away with it.'

Jean-Marie had fractured his wrist. But his anger was enough to make him forget the pain. He dashed to his Renault 18 and set off for Lépanges.

By now, Christine Villemin was back outside the house, talking to the Melines. On the way, she had crossed paths with Marcelle Claudon's son, Christian, a local coach driver who had just clocked off for the evening. Running back into the house, she started hunting around again, in case Grégory had come back in her absence. Soon the phone was ringing. It was her mother, Gilberte Chatel.

'You'd better bring the little one inside. He wants to take him.'

'I can't, I've been looking for him for the last half hour. I don't know where he is.'

Silence. And now Christine could hear her mother sobbing.

The phone rang again. This time it was Monique. She told Christine it was the Crow who had taken Grégory.

Urged by the Melines, Christine decided to phone the gendarmes. She was still speaking when Jean-Marie burst in. He was livid. She knew where he was going. Christine tried, but it was impossible to stop him. Now he was dashing back out with his rifle. Christine grabbed the still-dangling phone. 'Hurry, please! My husband's just gone back out with his gun, I just know he's going to do something foolish.'

But when the gendarmes arrived they just started looking around the house, opening cupboards and doors – even the fridge. They had their orders. It was enough to make you frantic, that blind obsession with routine. How could Grégory be in a cupboard?

Jean-Marie Villemin was heading for Granges. On his way, he ran into Monique and Albert in their Simca. Michel was driving them to Lépanges. The two brothers flashed headlights and drew up on the roadside.

'So, it's the Crow is it? You recognised the voice?'

'Yes.'

That was all the confirmation the chief needed.

'I'll kill him. I'll kill him.'

'Just be careful Jean-Marie.'

It was too late. The white Renault was already hurtling on towards Granges. *He knew*. Grégory would be there. Granges was the Crow's nest. It had to be. Granges was where his brother Jacky lived with his wife Liliane and her parents Roger and Paulette Jacquel.

It took Jean-Marie seven minutes to reach Granges. But it was too late. Just as he was drawing up outside the Jacquels' house, the lights went out. There were two Renault 4 vans outside, the sort used by the gendarmes.

'Bastards, the police are here already.'

He waited, but nothing happened. It looked as if Jacky and his father-in-law had been warned. Perhaps they would free the boy anyway. Perhaps, after all, he had been wrong. Jean-Marie sat there, feeling a mixture of exasperation and the pain welling up from the broken wrist. There was no point waiting. Better get back to Lépanges. Maybe Grégory had already been found.

In the meantime, Gilberte Chatel had arrived at Lépanges. Minutes later, Jacquot was at the door.

'I was getting worried! Why didn't you call me back?'

Christine Villemin seemed beyond explanations. Her face was the explanation. Later, she would remember replying:

'If it's him who took the kid I'll never see the boy again. You can't imagine what he's made me live through all these years.'

People continued to pour in. Family, neighbours, police. Then

Jean-Marie: thank God! Michel, Monique, Albert. At a loss, all of them. Everyone was talking at once, throwing in their own ideas. The gendarmes tried to cool things down. All this family hysteria made them a little sceptical. What was needed was a thorough search.

No one quite remembers the order of events that night. They have been obscured by other memories of a more poignant variety. And it was all so unexpected.

Gilberte Chatel went out to search with Meline. The gendarmes had started looking round with their torches. Then, later, Michel, or was it Monique, mentioned that the anonymous caller had talked about the Vologne. Jean-Marie was furious. Why hadn't they said something earlier? He got back into his car and headed for the firemen's barracks.

It was a dark night. Christine stayed at home with her mother-in-law. She remembers an officer arriving at 8.00 p.m., two hours after the search had started. He was astonished to hear that the gendarmes hadn't got the dogs out. Christine gave him a pair of Grégory's pyjamas for the scent.

Outside, searchers had covered all the ditches and hollows and woods around the house. Others were on the slopes that led down to the Vologne. The mayor, André Claudel, was directing operations. He knew the river better than anyone. 'If the kid is there, we'll find him in Docelles by the run-off basin.' Docelles was more than three miles away. The child had been gone now three hours, and the river was swollen and fast.

Jean-Marie Villemin was in a frenzy of anxiety and impotent rage. Again, he dashed back to Paremont to get his rifle. The thought of Granges obsessed him. He could imagine them, gloating over it all. But he had already failed once. Instead of going back, he raced to catch up the firemen and other searchers in Docelles.

That was when the first reporter arrived, a photographer from the *Liberté de l'Est* in Epinal. Jean-Marie Villemin snarled: 'Already here, are you? You don't need to tell me who sent you.' For Jean-Marie, it was as if the Crow had not only announced the crime over the phone but also provided the means whereby it was to be recorded for posterity.

It would be.

From the banks of the Vologne, floodlights and torches wove flickering meshes over the black water. The air was alive with the shouts of searchers.

Then there was a silence. They had seen something near the footbridge. The light of a torch had picked out a small bundle bobbing against the current. It was floating amidst the branches and stones that clogged the overflow, held by the stone slab of the du Bellay dam. The thing was three quarters submerged. A plastic bag, you might have thought, chemical litter thrown into the river by some unthinking passerby.

A rope was carried out into the treacherous water, by a small chain of rescuers. One of them managed to reach the blue object. It was an anorak. As the rescuer lifted it up, those watching from the bank saw the green trousers and blue lace-up shoes that Grégory had put on that morning. They saw that Grégory's striped woollen bonnet had been pulled over his eyes. That his wrists and ankles had been loosely bound with rope and that his legs were crossed. About his neck they saw a length of string; the imitation of a noose perhaps, or the means of fastening a weight about him.

The child's body was carried out of the swollen waters by a fireman, a well-built man with prominent cheeks and generous whiskers. He was crying. Softly, as if this reverence could at least limit the damage, the boy was carried on to the bank. Under the torches and spotlights against the rushing of the waters, the scene was more like a nightmare than reality: something they might wake up from.

Like some prize catch, Grégory Villemin was carried to the firemen's barracks curled up in a big net. There he was laid out on a table. When the bonnet was peeled back from the face, the expression they saw was peaceful; almost that of a child in the middle of sweet dreams. Jean-Marie saw it, his second self, inanimate. He cried and could not stop. Then Albert took his grandchild in his arms. 'He's so soft,' he marvelled, in a daze. The body was limp.

To father and son it looked as if the child had been put to sleep with ether.

'It looks like a ritual murder,' said a gendarme.

Christine Villemin's last memory of that night was when a car drew up outside her house. There was a fireman at the door. He spoke with difficulty. 'Madame, the boy, was he wearing a red, white and blue bonnet?'

It was 9.30 p.m. Already, a crowd was gathering about the footbridge in Docelles. Word spread to the few cafés still open at this hour, late as it was for these small working communities: the Crow, assassin, child-murderer, death . . . Of course, the conversations were incredulous, peppered with all the expletives and oaths that could be summoned up for the unthinkable act. The inevitable, just and futile horror: the inadequacy of language to express it. Whatever form justice would take, no one could conceive of anything but immediate retribution: a shaft of lightning to burn out the thought of the crime, before it started to fester. The Vologne had its lynch-mob. The gendarmes would have to find their assassin very soon. An hour after Grégory was fished out of the Vologne, the news went out over local and national radio.

In Paremont, the family vigil had started. And the gendarmes had confiscated Jean-Marie Villemin's rifle. Outside, car doors slammed and voices rose and hushed in the night as witnesses were ferried to and from the chalet.

Christine and Jean-Marie Villemin spent what was left of that night in Aumontzey, watched over by their family. They would never sleep at Paremont again – only spend one or two nights of grief there in front of their son's coffin.

Outside the home they had come to think of as the symbol of their greatest happiness, Grégory's bucket and spade lay in the gravel where he had left them.

5

'D on't worry, Mummy, don't be frightened. I'm here, and if
the man comes I'll defend you.'

A courageous child, Grégory Villemin. Of course he had
heard of the Crow, had seen his mother despondent and fraught. Of
course, he had never been afraid.

Grégory Villemin was four years old when he died. He carried away
with him more than his share of personality, more than his share of
vitality. In a school photograph taken that September, it is his smile
that stands out. 'The little fellow had real character, and a quick
tongue. He was just like Jean-Marie as a kid.' Monique Villemin was
right: Grégory had the Villemin features, right down to the little toe
without any nail that his father and grandfather also had. This
resemblance had driven Jean-Marie mad with joy when he saw it. The
child was a confirmation, a chief in miniature who was always ready to
defend himself with his fists at school. And who hero-worshipped his
father.

Just for Grégory, Jean-Marie had bought a 125cc trial bike.
Together, they used to go scrambling in the woods behind Paremont.
The boy loved all forms of speed and movement. At seven months, he
was holding himself upright. At a year old, he was already running
around the house. His father had started showing him the elementary
blows of karate. Christine recorded every step with scrupulous pride
for the photograph album.

Grégory was a precocious child. So much so that his grandparents
sometimes wondered if he was not being force fed with grown-up
language and habits. As if Jean-Marie and Christine wanted to go too
fast.

But if precocious, Grégory was also tender and demonstrative

31

towards his parents. His room was like a place of worship. On the wall hung a huge framed photograph of the occupant: *le beau Grégory*. In tribute to his love of movement, hundreds of sports cars raced around the expensive wallpaper. A BMX bike rested against a cupboard full of toys.

Grégory was a sociable child. He loved to stay up late at his parents' parties. He had a passion for school. Later, Jean-Marie and Christine planned to send him to Epinal for a 'serious education'. It would give him a better chance in life than they had gained from the Lycée Jean Lurçat in Bruyères. Grégory's horizons would go beyond the valley.

But meanwhile there were skiing holidays to look forward to that winter, for the first time. He had started saving up. And perhaps, the summer afterwards, when he had learnt to swim, they would build a pool for him up on Paremont.

All that was cut short. Grégory was no longer a child now: he was an angel, forever in the first sharp flush of death.

6

The gendarmes set up their incident room in a prefabricated extension of the headquarters in Bruyères. All night long, in the forecourt, the black and white cars performed their high-speed arrivals and exits as Adjudant Lamirand and his men began their round of interviews. Lamirand was confident. 'We'll have got to the bottom of this affair in a few days from now. We have the Crow's letters.'

Just as importantly, the gendarmes also had the certainties of Jean-Marie Villemin: Roger Jacquel and his son-in-law Jacky Villemin were the Crows; or Crow and accomplice.

Jacquel was a militant for the Communist party. 'They give me the creeps, chiefs,' he would often say. Jean-Marie, the chief, had known him since 1974, when he was seventeen and Jacquel forty-five, and both were members of the CGT, France's big Communist-backed union. Jean-Marie remembered rumours of a fight that had broken out between Jacquel and a foreman at Autocoussin – a man called Demonges. That was in 1977, when Jean-Marie was doing his military service. When he returned from the army, Jacquel had gone on prolonged sick leave, because of lung cancer. And now, of course, Jean-Marie was a foreman.

Jean-Marie and Jacquel had already exchanged angry words in the past. The older man had lost his job at Autocoussin for repeated misconduct, and was convinced that Jean-Marie was behind it. His wife, Paulette, still worked at Autocoussin, and therefore had ample opportunity to observe Jean-Marie's behaviour in the factory. Besides, as a heavy smoker, Jacquel suffered from a throat problem which made his voice rough and uncertain – not so different from one of the many vocal styles of the Crow. Sick and unemployed, Jacquel would have every reason to say, as the Crow did once before hanging up: 'Anyway, I've got nothing left to lose.'

Most of all, Jacquel was the father-in-law of 'the bastard'. Everyone knew Jacky Villemin was conceived out of wedlock. Everyone knew Albert was not his true father. All right, Albert had recognised the boy and given him his name, but it was obvious that Jacky was an outsider in the family. No one knew it better than Jacquel. With his hatred of chiefs, he had every reason to avenge him: 'You must stop seeing the chief,' said the letter. 'Jacky and his little family have been left out long enough.' It was crystal clear. Killing Grégory was an ideal way to achieve his purpose and bring down a chief at the same time.

There was one more detail, an important one. In 1982, just after the Crow had started pestering Christine and himself, Jean-Marie had helped the gendarmes with their efforts to track him down: he made an anonymous call to Jacquel at two o'clock in the morning to see how he would react. In the days that followed, the Crow called twice, and each time he mentioned the calls to Jacquel.

And what of the bastard himself? No one can tell what it does to a child to discover that he is illegitimate, and that he will never know his true father. Albert and Monique had never told Jacky about the circumstances of his birth: that delicate task was assumed by an outsider when Jacky was already in his mid teens. The words opened a wound which festered for years. Perhaps it still smarted. And it was of no help when Jacky's brothers and sisters heard the venomous gossip that informed them of their older brother's origins. They too felt betrayed, soiled. Jacky was a scapegoat, a *mal-aimé*.

Jacky lived 'away from the family' with his wife Liliane and their twelve-year-old son Eric in a dour grey house on the Louise Seltz industrial estate in Granges – nothing like the chalet at Paremont. Jacky had bought up the place and made it habitable during a long period of unemployment. Now, at thirty-one, he worked at Ancel on what they called the Friday-Saturday-Sunday shift, earning as much as the others did in five days because of weekend rates. Jacky was always free on Tuesdays.

Recently, Jean-Marie and his half-brother had broken off relations with each other. There was only room for one of them at the family home. As Jean-Marie put it, 'over the last year and a half, Jacky has made himself marginal on purpose. It's because of his wife, Liliane. She's a real schemer, with a very strange character.'

Albert Villemin remembered the time Jacky and Liliane came round for dinner at Aumontzey. Liliane was edgy. She kept dropping her bag. Albert could not resist a little remark, one of those fatherly comments that unknowingly rub up old wounds. Liliane glared at him and ran out of the room, slamming the door behind her. Jacky knew where he stood: 'Don't bother coming round to our place,' he warned, 'or you'll get a bullet between the eyes.'

Jean-Marie Villemin now remembered that Jacky had always manifested a strong dislike of the irrepressible young Grégory. 'One day I'm going to throw your Titi into the Vologne,' he even said with that half-sarcastic way he had. It didn't sound like a joke now. More like a plot. Jacky had planned the killing with the complicity of his 'intellectual' wife Liliane. She was the Granges correspondent for the *Liberté de l'Est* newspaper at Epinal. She had arranged for that photographer to come and snap up the sadistic photo-opportunity of 16 October – Grégory being fished out of the river. Vengeance, the French say, is a dish to be eaten cold.

Jean-Marie Villemin was sure of what he said, impatient for results. But what about Christine, the last person to have seen her son? She remained silent, shrunk into herself. 'Surely, Madam, you must have seen something.' 'No . . . ' Nothing anyway that could filter through the studio hilarity of *Les Grosses Têtes* as it boomed from the radio. Just Bernard Colin and Gilbert Meline, neighbours busy with their routines. 'Unless, unless there was that green Renault 4 . . . I saw it on the way to Christine Jacquot's flat.'

The same car as Roger Jacquel.

That was enough. Roger and Paulette Jacquel were rushed into Bruyères gendarmerie, lumbering under the lights like bears awoken from a deep sleep, Paulette a big broad woman in a housecoat, cardigan and slippers, Roger in a frayed lumberjack shirt and jeans. Outside, the forensic squad began to give their green Renault 4 a thorough going-over. Inside, it was as if Roger and Paulette's guilt were all but proven. The gendarmes were in a hurry, and no one was expecting the case to be complicated.

This time it wasn't. It was a non-starter.

The Jacquels had alibis: they had been working when the abduction occurred. And those alibis proved as solid as a wall.

The Jacquels were free, as abruptly as they were 'guilty'. Free but stained, exposed to every suspicion, and to a hatred as intense as the communities of the Vologne were small.

They were not the last. Now it was Jacky's turn. He and Liliane were picked up from the Louise Seltz estate in Granges. The couple was brought into the station that same Tuesday night. They and their car experienced the same going over as the Jacquels. The questioning lasted two hours, during which other gendarmes were searching the suspect's house. Jacky, who was a lanky, nervous man, smoked cigarette after cigarette as he answered the questions. The expression on his face was one of timidity, extreme agitation. Jacky had something of the beaten animal about him: that, or the child who fears rejection.

Liliane, normally an attractive and mild-featured woman, was now fidgety, sharp and frowning with stress, brows wrinkling under the weight of accusation.

Jacky and Liliane protested: they knew, or half knew, that their lives depended on it.

'I spent all yesterday helping my neighbour repair the woodwork on his roof,' Jacky insisted. 'The gutters were coming away and I owed him the favour: he helped me out with my roof a while ago.'

Jacky had been seen by a good dozen neighbours, all through the day. And Liliane? 'I was at home, except when I went out to fetch a friend from the clinic. She'd just given birth. And at about 5.30 p.m. I went to the *Crédit Agricole* to put in a cheque for Eric, my son. Twelve years old.' Liliane too had been seen.

'Anyway, how could we be the Crow?'

'What do you mean?'

'Well, we've been getting calls too.'

It was just that Grégory's parents didn't know. The Crow called Jacky and Liliane regularly. For some strange reason, it was always around the full moon. 'Two or three times a day. He never wanted to speak to me – he always asked for Liliane.'

Perhaps the Crow was worried his 'protégé' would recognise him. Yet he was a skilled imitator.

'So,' he cajoled one day, 'have you bought your house?'

Liliane thought she knew that voice.

'Hey, cut it out Jean-Marie! I know it's you.'

There was silence, then:

'I'm going to hurt the chief. I'll go to the funeral, and it's you they'll accuse.'

The Crow was a master of prediction. And of menace:

'Once he slashed my tyres with a pickaxe. Another time I was followed.'

Jacky and Liliane knew they were on the list. And now they had no cover: they had testified.

'God knows what he'll do. He might kill us!'

That was a fear Jacky and Liliane would have to live with. Just as they would have to endure their association with infanticide.

So why did Jacky keep up the enigmatic, teasing tone to journalists? 'I can't tell you any more, the gendarmes forbade me to speak . . . Ah la la! If I told all I knew . . . The family has its share of secrets!'

All this publicity was a chance to put the family record straight. Jacky admitted he had broken with his brothers and sisters a year and a half earlier, but his version of events was very different from Jean-Marie's. Jacky had not become a marginal of his own accord. 'What they did to me was really dirty. I'm sure that when the Crow is unmasked and confesses there'll be a huge scandal in the family.' Jacky enjoyed dangling his knowledge in front of the microphones. No one else seemed to take him that seriously. But he was doing nothing to dispel the rumours about himself.

And then why did Michel, Jacqueline and Gilbert Villemin all claim they knew nothing of the reasons for Jacky's exclusion? It surely was more than family secretiveness. The bone of contention seemed to be between Jacky and Jean-Marie.

Jean-Marie and Christine were not easily convinced. Alibis could be invented. If Jacky had known all along that they suspected him, why had he never tried to explain himself? Neither he nor Liliane had ever mentioned the Crow's threats. Why? They had to be hiding something.

Judicial reality, however, was that the prime suspects had been cleared. Four down, at least seventy Villemins to go – or so some bright spark might have said, but the gendarmes were in no mood for jokes.

They were beginning to discover the extent, and the cloudiness, of the Villemin-Jacob family, which had spread out from Herpelmont, a few kilometres away, some fifty years ago. With its alliances and families-in-law, the extended clan had at least two hundred members. Five of them, together with several cousins, worked at Autocoussin, but none – or so he insisted – under the authority of Jean-Marie. Hearsay even endowed Monique and Albert with eighteen or twenty offspring, generously allowing each of them an earlier marriage just as fruitful as the present one. It was true of course that Monique came from a family of twelve children.

As their hearings and interrogations continued, the gendarmes discovered that almost every member of the family had at one time or another played at being the Crow: some to take advantage of the cover to settle a personal score, others, like Jean-Marie himself, to try to winkle out the true culprit. Unwittingly, the Villemins and their circle had been working for their enemy, promoting the contagion and mutual suspicion that the Crow thrives upon. Like a mortal parasite.

What was needed was material evidence.

The gendarmes did not have to wait long for their first outside testimony. Soon after Grégory's body was fished out of the cold, swirling Vologne, a young woman arrived: Josyane Guyot. At about 5.30 p.m. she had been walking back to her home in Docelles after taking her daughter to catechism classes. Home was a big house over the other side of the river.

'When I was crossing the footbridge, I caught a glimpse of a big blue bin liner that had caught against the rocks, just where they found the child. I didn't really give it much attention, it just looked like something unusual, that's all. Who could imagine it'd be a kid? But now I think about it, I'm sure it was the little boy. It was the same long shape.'

Bin liners were an unusual sight on the Vologne, especially full ones. Of course, like any other watercourse, the river had its fair share of negligently-thrown rubbish, bio-degradable or not. But the bin liner Josyane Guyot thought she had seen was not found further downstream by the gendarmes.

The conclusion was obvious. Grégory had been thrown into the water a little way upstream. It had taken his killer less than half an hour to cover the 5 kilometres between Paremont and Docelles, bind him, throw him in the water and then phone the Villemins in Aumontzey. It had been a masterly operation – quick, precise, meticulously planned. For if Guyot's testimony was accurate, the boy had been killed during the Vologne rush hour, when the factories were emptying or changing shifts. Either the murder had been meticulously planned, or the killer had been miraculously lucky.

The next morning, the gendarmes traced the drowning to a spot 700 metres upstream, where a mud track forked off from the road leading into Docelles from Lépanges. At its end, a small bridge led to the railway on the other bank and, beyond them, a farm.

Few people ever went down the track, no one but anglers or lovers hoping to end their Sunday walks with a peaceful bit of trysting. From the road, it was 40 metres down to the river bank. There, bushes and poplars would have sheltered the murderer from any passersby. The killer must have known that that particular stretch of the river was one of the few places with deep trenches of water. Perhaps he had been talking to the locals.

Nearby, 600 metres from where Grégory was found, the gendarmes found two footprints: boots – a man's judging by their size, and high heels. They had sunk deep into the mud. Marks had been left by tyre treads too. A couple, in a car.

Wednesday morning brought a grey, cloudy sky. A flat dullness hung over Lépanges, Epinal and Bruyères.

In France, schoolchildren work on Saturdays and Wednesday is a midweek holiday. Grégory, who loved school, had always found that strange. 'They should make up their minds,' he used to say. 'Is it school or is it holiday?' Now, along the Vologne, many mothers were refusing to let their children out to play. Grégory always spent Wednesday in Bruyères, where his maternal grandmother Gilberte Chatel lived alone in her fourth-floor council flat. It was the highlight of her week. They used to go shopping together and talk 'like grown-ups', and Grégory would play with the other children. But this Wednesday, routine, like the life of Grégory's family, had become a vacuum.

At 9.00 a.m., two gendarmes were outside the house at Paremont waiting for Jean-Marie and Christine to come back from Aumontzey. They had come to take a look at Christine Villemin's high heels and Renault 5 – a routine check. While they were waiting, they observed Grégory's bucket and spade, and made sure there were no signs of a scuffle, no flattened grass in the nearby meadow. And they saw the postman drop a letter in the box. When Jean-Marie and Christine arrived a little while later, the gendarmes picked up the missive with a pair of pincers. The envelope bore the Lépanges postmark and had been stamped the day before. It was addressed to Monsieur Jean-Marie Villemin, Lépanges. In stick writing. Inside, there was a short text in the same, malformed block capitals, with the same shaky grammar. Considerate souls that they were, the gendarmes refused to let Christine Villemin look at the Crow's latest text. She had suffered enough as it was. Only Jean-Marie saw the letter that had been addressed to him.

I HOPE YOU DIE OF SORROW, CHIEF. NOT ALL YOUR MONEY CAN'T GIVE YOU BACK YOUR SON. THIS IS MY REVENGE, POOR FOOL.

There was no question of revealing the missive to the press either. The valley already had enough budding vigilantes without stirring up their passions with this proof of premeditation.

If child murderers are not as rare as all that, few are as calculating as this one appeared to be. When the investigators spoke to the postmaster at the Lépanges office, they began to get an idea of the murderer's prowess. The head clerk was adamant: the letter could only have been posted during the half hour between 4.45 p.m. and 5.12 p.m. or 5.13 p.m. It had not been among the envelopes collected at the first of these two times, but he had noticed it when he emptied his box again at the second. He remembered being struck by the funny writing and the fact that it was addressed to an inhabitant of Lépanges. People in a town this small never bothered writing to each other; it was easier to use the telephone or go round to his house. People wrote to mail order firms or to the social security and employment offices: but the rest was between neighbours.

Whoever the Crow was, he must have known what he was doing: for the letter had been posted before Grégory's death. Whoever slipped it into the box knew they would not fail. The words left no room for Grégory's survival: 'Not all your money can bring you back your son.' The assassin had taken a ferocious pleasure in keeping his victims informed. His motive was written large: vengeance. He had to be a familiar.

As of Wednesday afternoon, two men would be responsible for tracking down the mind that conceived such revenge: Etienne Sesmat, captain of the Epinal gendarmerie, and Jean-Michel Lambert, the examining magistrate at the *Palais de Justice*.

Sesmat was a typical product of the Saint Cyr military training school which prepares officer-cadets both for the army and for the gendarmerie. Tall, with a thin, sharp-featured face, his short blond hair and blue eyes gave him an intent, austere appearance. Sesmat came across as a dry kind of person, and his reedy voice and clipped diction did nothing to soften the effect. But rigour and the discipline instilled by military training should not be mistaken for aloofness. Sesmat was a man of the heart, too. As a thirty-year-old father, he would surely be as eager as any to satisfy Jean-Marie and Christine Villemin's desire for understanding and justice. Sesmat would not drag his heels.

As head of the gendarmes' investigation, he would be reporting to Commandant Chaillan, director of the research team at Nancy, and Colonel Tanguy, departmental chief of the Vosges gendarmerie.

Like Sesmat, Jean-Michel Lambert was a young man, and he looked it. A short, bespectacled figure with smooth dark hair growing long about his round face, Lambert might have been a student or executive just out of professional school. His features showed no signs of suffering or wear – just as, during the investigation, his politeness and urbanity would never fail, or reveal his thoughts.

The examining judge, or *juge d'instruction*, has a key role in an investigation. He is responsible for gathering information and directing the activities of the gendarmes or police. He has the power to arrest and charge suspects. He works with the public prosecutor, who represents society. The prosecutor gives his opinion on whether a suspect should be arrested or his case sent before a Chamber of Accusation. But the *juge d'instruction* is empowered to override his colleague's recommendations. Of course, this should rarely happen, since the two men are supposed to be in agreement. Up to now, Jean-Michel Lambert was lucky to have enjoyed smooth working relations with his public prosecutor, Jean-Jacques Lecomte.

Le petit juge, as he would soon come to be known, was a hard worker. When the death of Grégory Villemin landed on his desk at Epinal, courtesy of the deputy public prosecutor, M. Violette, the dossier was marked 'No.180'. That year, Lambert had already had to deal with 179 other cases, many of which were still unfinished: cases of petty delinquence that he had dutifully dispatched along with the occasional murder or *crime passionnel* since he came to the town in 1980 at the age of twenty-eight. This was his first posting after graduating from magistrates' school in Bordeaux.

When Lambert arrived in Epinal, the President of the Nancy judiciary told him it would be an easy posting. 'If you like walking, you'll be happy in the Vosges. And then you'll see that it's good from the work point of view. This is a quiet *département* where nothing happens.' Certainly Lambert had begun to appreciate the scenery and walks afforded by the hills, but he had had more than enough to keep him busy. Still, he was young and on top of things.

That evening, at the forensic institute of Nancy, an autopsy was carried out on the body of Grégory Villemin by Professor De Ren of the Nancy Institute of Forensic Medicine and his assistant Doctor Pagel. Lambert and Sesmat were both present. According to De Ren, Grégory had been alive when he was thrown into the river. He had died of immersion syncope. It was the sudden cold that had killed him, not drowning. That was why there was only a small quantity of water in his lungs. De Ren also found some apple in the stomach, but it was impossible to say when the food had been swallowed.

The loose knots seemed to have been tied about Grégory's wrists and ankles 'as if in play', remarked De Ren, and they looked like the work of an employee from one of the region's many mills. Likewise, Grégory's woollen hat had been pulled down over his face 'without violence'. There were no marks on the body to denote the effects of violence or torture. This abduction had been a gentle affair. The lack of scratches on the boy's face suggested that the body had not travelled far down the Vologne; it would otherwise have scraped past the trees and branches caught in the swollen waters.

Grégory's body showed no traces of adrenalin. On his lips, there were some bluish-purple remains of cyanosis, the discolouring that occurs because of a lack of oxygen, but there was none under the fingernails. The boy had not struggled: he had not been afraid.

'It's a woman's crime,' concluded the professor.

'It's as if the child had just gone along with it all,' commented Etienne Sesmat in astonishment. 'As if he got into the water of his own accord.'

Beyond that the autopsy did not go. 'There's no point in chopping the poor little body up any more. We know who did it.' With these words, unopposed by Judge Lambert, Etienne Sesmat put an end to the painful examination of France's new infant martyr.

It only remained for the rope binding Grégory's limbs to be sent off for laboratory analysis, and for the child to be made ready for his coffin.

7

'I really don't understand. I thought Grégory must have been beaten or put to sleep. He'd never have followed a stranger. He was a lovely little boy, but he was very strong for his age. He used to fight like a devil when you tried to catch him or take him home. Neither I nor his mother could get a hold of him when he had decided to resist . . . The assassin couldn't even have attracted him with a sweet, Grégory would never have fallen for it . . . He wasn't wild, but he was very wide awake, very much a smart little man. He wouldn't let himself be played with like a baby. No, it's inconceivable, he would at least have shouted or warned his mother.'

Christine Jacquot was not the only one to be surprised when she heard the conclusions drawn by the autopsy. Gilberte Chatel, Christine's mother, shared the same astonishment:

'Grégory might just have followed another child, but not an adult. The assassin or his accomplices must have known him, or else they pulled down his bonnet by surprise and he thought it was a joke.'

The only certainty at this stage was that the crime had been committed by a member of the family, or a close friend or relation. Who else could have known Christine's movements so intimately, or have managed to whisk away the tough little four-year-old with such efficiency? How otherwise could he have known about the small cross-country road that started just below Christine and Jean-Marie's villa and, skirting the centre of Lépanges, led down to the road for Docelles?

On 18 October, Noël Grandjean, a local policeman, made a discovery that cast a new light on the abduction. In Docelles he found a plastipak syringe and a phial of insulin lying by the banks of the Barba, a stream that runs past Docelles church from the south and joins the

Vologne near the spot where Grégory was found. The substance can induce a state of coma if taken by non-diabetics. Perhaps that was why Grégory had not struggled, and looked so much at peace.

The Vologne was buzzing with curiosity. In shops and bars, locals kept an attentive ear cocked for radio and television broadcasts. The sale of local newspapers had doubled. The news stands were empty by lunchtime. 'An atrocious revenge with seventy suspects' titled one national daily. In the Vologne they knew: the Crow was among them. And he was still active. A colleague of Jean-Marie's had just been threatened by him: 'If you go on seeing that shit I'll burn your house down.' The same incendiary obsession as with Albert Villemin.

Curiosity, and indignation. 'There are 1,150 people here', said one man. 'Give us the assassin and we'll take it in turns to stick our knives into him.' Grégory's fate had injected a new bitterness into the French debate over capital punishment. The death penalty had been abolished less than three years before. It was one of the new Socialist government's most controversial measures. Robert Badinter, the Minister of Justice, had become the scapegoat for the families of murder victims all over France. His name was mud for the righteously aggrieved. As a letter written the day after the crime to the local paper, *La Liberté de l'Est*, put it: 'They are going to try and defend this kind of monster, and they call it justice. But I shall never believe that such a person really feels regret. France, you are losing your honour and your dignity. I am ashamed to be a citizen of such a country.' Humanitarian considerations are wasted on a child killer.

By now, nearly all the major papers and radio stations had reporters in Lépanges or the outlying towns: Bruyères, Brouvelieures, Granges-sur-Vologne, Epinal. Editors had caught a whiff of *La France profonde*. Numbers would vary from day to day, swelling into the fifties and sixties at the prospect of major developments, falling during quiet patches. But for months on end, journalists would become an intimate part of the affair, befriending the protagonists, collecting statements and testimonies and acting as intermediaries. It was as if local gossip has suddenly found itself equipped with an enormous PA system. Communications were speeded, rumours intensified and thickened.

First among them was the wealth that caused the Crow to envy Christine and Jean-Marie with such bitterness. Had Jean-Marie won the national lottery? How else could he have paid for the 'luxurious villa', the two cars and the couple's holidays in Italy? If indeed they had won the lottery, went the local gossip, then no one would have been curious, but 'Believe me,' people said, 'it's something to do with money'.

Jean-Marie's answer went out on one of France's most popular national radio stations, RTL. The holidays? It just so happened that Rimini was cheaper than its French equivalent that year. Besides, he and Christine had not been alone: they went with Albert, Monique and Jacqueline. 'Everything I have I worked to get, with my wife. We never won the lottery. But there are good-for-nothings who envy others, and there are madmen stalking this earth.'

The remark could easily have been directed at Jacky or Michel. Blunt and proud as he was, the chief would not be making many new friends in the Vologne that winter.

At the *Palais de Justice*, just behind Epinal cathedral, Jean-Jacques Lecomte had given official confirmation of the murder note found at Paremont, and presented the journalists with their first official progress report. So far, the footprints were the determining element. 'I have my ideas about the couple,' he pronounced, 'but they are only hypotheses. We think we have found the woman. As for the man, we expect to be able to find him among three likely suspects.'

And, with the promise of forthcoming revelations, Lecomte added his penny's worth of mystery to the plot:

'There seem to be a number of skeletons in cupboards. Jealousy over social, professional and financial success is not the only hypothesis we're working on.' In the excited atmosphere of the investigation, it was hard to believe that Lecomte's image was gratuitous. Whose were the skeletons, and whose were the cupboards?

It did not take long to find them. The Villemin history had its share of dark spots. In 1935, Léon Villemin, Albert's brother, was killed by the Vologne after a heated altercation about fishing. Léon breathed his last just by the dam where Grégory was found, fifty years later. Pure coincidence, apparently.

But that was nothing on Gaston Villemin, Albert's father. In the late 1920s, Gaston married Jeanne Hollard, a simple-minded creature with a tendency to drink. The couple had several children, but not in happiness. Jeanne had become a loose woman, and her infidelity soon turned into a war with her crushed husband. One evening, Jeanne must have got unusually drunk. The confrontation with Gaston was even more bitter than usual. Emilien, the oldest of their children, saw it all. Perhaps he tried to intervene, or break up the fight. Whatever he did, it was too late; his parents were in a blind haze of rage. They turned on him and beat him, causing him to fall and smash his head against the stove. Emilien was killed. He was eight years old.

Jeanne Villemin was sentenced to three years of prison, but Gaston remained free. However, rumour continued to hint at his guilt.

When the war came Gaston was enlisted and the children were sent to stay with their aunt and uncle at Clos Fays, several kilometres from Herpelmont. Like most French soldiers, Gaston soon found himself a prisoner of war. That gave him ample time to meditate on his life in the Vosges. When he was released, he discovered that Jeanne had been having an affair with a German soldier. Collaborators were not appreciated in France after the Liberation. Feeling himself doubly betrayed, and sinking under the weight of the social ignominy it brought down on his head, Gaston had more than he could bear. He was tortured by remorse and now socially ruined. Gaston hanged himself in the trees above Herpelmont. Or, as some local memories had it, in his barn.

And that was not all. Rumour also spoke of Jeanne giving birth to a daughter in prison. Yvette was the child's name: she had since left the area for the Val de Marne, near Paris, they said.

It did not take much imagination to fit the death of Albert's father with the Crow's gallows theme. Just like Monique with her illegitimate child, Jeanne Villemin could be the prototype of the loose and slatternly woman behind the insults directed at Christine or Liliane. Jeanne was the whore they all resembled: the archetype who haunted the Crow's imagination, and Grégory's death the sacrifice exacted to pay for Emilien's.

All very neat.

And what of the aunt who had brought up the orphaned Albert?

Thérèse Villemin still lived in her run-down house in Clos Fays, a few kilometres from Lépanges. She had lost her husband five years earlier, in 1979, and the shock had made her thirty-year-old son Michel mentally unstable. After working in a butcher's shop and then in a mill, he had gone to rest in a sanatorium. But Michel continued to make regular visits to Fays, and he knew all about the Villemins, and about Albert's debt to his parents. He could observe Jean-Marie's prosperity and compare it to the hardship endured by his mother.

In Bruyères, Etienne Sesmat was also conducting a press briefing. 'Every avenue has to be explored,' he told reporters. 'What about the mother?' shouted one journalist. The reply was forthright, and indignant: 'You can't be serious.' There are limits. And the letter posted on 16 October? 'No such thing.' So had Lecomte been lying when he mentioned it a few hours before?

'Ah, I see.' Sesmat was taken aback. 'Well, in that case . . . We wanted to keep the letter secret so as to provoke the murderer to send another one.'

It was the first sign that all was not perfect in the coordination between Epinal and Bruyères, between the *magistrature* and the gendarmes. Perhaps this case was too urgent for them to be in step on every little thing . . . Too much personal investment, perhaps.

In fact, Sesmat appeared to be vying with Lecomte to capture the attention of the journalists. Six hours after his afternoon press conference, he was back outside the gendarmerie, looking into a thicket of microphones:

'It's an extraordinary affair,' he announced, 'as I'm sure you're all aware. But it is probably even more extraordinary than you think. You will be horrified when you discover the ending. We are in a jungle and there is a wolf howling there, and as long as it goes on howling, we shall follow it and in the end we shall flush it out.'

As he continued, the wolf turned into an armed pack:

'They have ammunition, but we have more than they do!'

On Friday, state prosecutor Lecomte's next broadside strengthened the impression:

'Everybody in the family is suspect, I repeat, everybody! Anything is possible in this affair, even the incredible.'

There were now eighty men looking for Grégory's murderer. Not to mention the packs of journalists. Many of them spent their time following up clues or ideas floated by the gendarmes, or working on their own hunches.

One of these ideas was that the Crow had spent weeks observing the Villemin's chalet with binoculars. How else could he have known as much as he did about the young couple's existence?

'I see you've had your decoration redone,' he would remark, or 'You've got a new sofa,' or 'You spent the whole day working on your wall.'

The idea was confirmed by Gilberte Chatel who recalled an evening spent at Paremont in the company of Jean-Marie's parents. When Albert Villemin went outside to make sure no one was prowling around the house, the Crow chirped back over the phone: 'I saw it all.'

The chief's house was in an exposed position. Possible observation posts were found all around Paremont. Branches had been cut so that the observer could see without being seen. From Prey, the village facing Lépanges, there was a perfect view. Tyre treads were found in the mud. A number of witnesses claimed to have seen a man equipped with binoculars in the days leading up to the murder. A local postman who had been out hunting on the afternoon of 16 October also confirmed this lead. At around two o'clock, he had seen a couple dressed in dark clothes. The man, wearing a Bordeaux-colour pull-over, had a case dangling from his arm. At five o'clock, the postman saw the same couple on the road between Lépanges and Deycimont, which goes to Docelles. The gendarmes issued an appeal, but there was no answer.

Another hunch was more far-fetched. Might not Jacky's natural father have sought to avenge his son out of the conviction that 'the bastard' had been slighted by his adoptive family? Forget Roger Jacquel. Never mind that thirty-two years had elapsed since Jacky's birth, the main thing was to take every possibility into account. Sure enough, the police sought out Jacky's natural father and subjected him to a series of vague, but carefully-weighted questions: for the sake of thoroughness and, for the journalists who followed him, in the hope of a major scoop. He was a woodcutter in a small mountain town in the

Haut Rhin *département*, far away from the Vologne. Yes, he remembered Monique Jacob, along with other female companions from the days of his military service. He had not seen any of them since. Yes, he had heard of the little boy murdered in the Vologne. But when he latched onto the gendarme's insinuations, he roared with indignation: and the gendarmes, with profuse apologies, got back into their cars and drove back to Bruyères.

As for the fact of Jacky's existence, and his part in it, it was left to the journalists to inform the startled woodcutter. Jacky Villemin's begetter had had to wait thirty-two years to find out that Monique had conceived by him. It was a little late in the day to be taking his responsibilities. He did not try to get in touch with his natural son. None of which can have soothed 'the bastard's' wounds.

Thursday was a busy day for Christine and Jean-Marie Villemin. In the morning, Jean-Marie had to answer the undertaker's questions about Grégory's coffin: the child's height, the colour of the lining, pine or oak? They had to plead with the judge prosecutor to have the lid left off for them. Then, in the afternoon, it was the drive to Epinal to confirm what, somewhere, they were still hoping was only a bad dream. It was time to collect Grégory from the morgue.

The journalists were there before them. 'How do you feel? Who did it, Jean-Marie?' And the photographers, always ready to negotiate a price, insisting that they be let into the morgue too.

With the other members of their family, Jean-Marie and Christine cleaved a slow passage through the crowd. It would soon become second nature. Inside the funeral parlour, Grégory lay on the catafalque. He seemed to be dreaming, absent but not suffering. Christine hugged her son's chest, collapsing onto her knees. For nearly an hour, she knelt there wailing, racked by sobs, caressing the infant and burying her head in his shroud. And, as if taken in by the serenity of her son's expression and the careful preparation that had been carried out on the body, she set up a kind of incantation:

'My darling, my darling! Come back my love! Come back! You can't abandon us! Come back! Why did they do that to you? Why did they pick on you? They had no right! Come back my darling!'

She had to be pulled away.

The coffin was loaded into a van and driven back to Lépanges. In Grégory's room, Jean-Marie and his family had cleared away or dismantled the furniture, making a space where they had set out trestles and a shroud.

Everyone was there. They would all be there, on and off, during the next two nights, taking turns in the vigil before Saturday's funeral.

Then the gendarmes came. One by one, the members of the family were asked to go out to the kitchen to take a dictation. They had to write scraps of nonsense, and passages from the Crow's letters. First with the right hand, and then with the left. Then they had to speak into a microphone for the voice analysts.

Altogether, during those early days, the gendarmes gave dictations to more than 140 suspects and recorded the voices of them all. One of them, at least, had to be the Crow.

8

In Henri Clouzot's film, *Le Corbeau*, the funeral of the Crow's first victim is a key scene. In spite of warnings to keep away, the main suspect has decided to brave the suspicion of the townsfolk and to attend. The emotion and the tension build with every slow step taken by the funeral cortège. By the time the crowd of mourners has reached the cemetery, the desire for revenge is at boiling point. The last rites cause it to spill over. Recriminations burst out, threats are made. The suspect panics and starts running. She is pursued through the streets to her home. Stones come shattering through her windows.

Perhaps Commander Chaillan had been mugging up on film history. After all, the film was based on a true story. The day before Grégory was to be buried at Lépanges, he declared on a local radio station:

'We shall be at the funeral, for we think that the Crow will be there too. We are going to film the ceremony. We believe the Crow will drop his guard.'

Grégory's funeral was to be held at two o'clock on Saturday 20 October, four days after his death. Obviously, the police were trying to tighten the mental thumbscrews on the murderer. Surely, they thought, he must already be undergoing extreme moral torture. Only devils are without a conscience. Monique Villemin, who had a long experience of the subject, was not of the same opinion. 'I'm sure he'll be there,' she said, 'laughing at us.'

It was a mild, grey afternoon when the coffin was brought down to the church. Christine and Jean-Marie walked painfully to the front row. Around them, the Villemins and Jacobs, Gilberte Chatel, relatives from both sides of the family, and sympathisers from work or the neighbourhood. The women were in flower-pattern dresses, the men in dark suits – navy blue or black, and manifestly too big or ill-fitting. Exceptional wear. Jaws were tense, fists clenched with the effort to hold in emotion.

In the aisle, under a white shroud, stood the coffin. In front of it they had placed a huge photograph of Grégory, set against white cloth, as if the joyous and bright eyes of the portrait would force the assassin to break down under the weight of their silent, innocent reproach. Mothers held up their children so they could see 'the poor little boy'.

Six hundred people had come to bid Grégory farewell. There had never been so many Villemins and Jacobs together. Among them, Chaillan had planted his four plain-clothes policemen. In fact, several of them were merely hiding their gendarmes' blue trousers underneath their coats. But they were still less conspicuous than another variety of observer, the journalists. Two hundred observers with cameras and notebooks.

The stage was set. Now, every one of those present was waiting, watching the others. Would the Crow give himself away?

Four absences were noticed: Jacky and Liliane Villemin, and Liliane's parents, Roger and Paulette Jacquel. In fact, the gendarmes had advised them not to come. 'It would be better that way,' admitted Jean-Marie. Better to avoid any occasion for recriminations, and to avoid stirring up bad memories after what had happened since the sixteenth.

It was a subdued service. The priest plugged in the microphone and the choristers, elderly women from the village, sang tremulously into it. As if to counter the strategy of the police, the homily avoided any strong appeal to the emotions. The priest just spoke, fleetingly, of 'the death of an angel'. Christine with her tear-swollen face seemed to be sleeping on Jean-Marie's shoulder. She was half there, half submerged in fatigue.

'Rest in the peace of the Lord, Grégory, you who were taken too early from the parents who cherished you. May God welcome you in his mansion.'

There was a long pause, tense with restrained sobbing. Then it was over.

'Take the side exits please, to avoid congestion.'

As this piece of practical advice from the priest closed the ceremony, the Villemins and Jacobs formed a cortège behind Abbé Grivel. Coming out of the church, the procession filed past rows of photographers: the echoes of church were swamped by the clicking of cameras.

Grégory's plot was at the far end of the cemetery, amid new-looking slabs bearing the names Claudel, Jacquot and Villemin. Here, the view carries over the concrete panelling surrounding the graveyard to the hills. As if the town is a mere accident.

Behind the light oak coffin decorated with a white crucifix, Jean-Marie was almost carrying his wife. Christine sobbed into her husband's shoulder. To her right, her mother, blurred and ruffled with shock, and, behind them, Monique and Albert, both sobbing. As they approached Grégory's resting place, those outside the family hung back. They were diffident, respectful of feelings they could share only from a distance.

So far, nothing had happened to break the cloud of tense, restrained grief that hung over the mourners. Then, as the priest performed the last rites over the coffin, and the bearers prepared to lower it into the earth, Christine seemed to come to, as if she were racked by a sudden sense of urgency. Grégory was leaving her.

'Grégory, darling, come back!' she screamed. 'No! No! Stay, my Titi, don't let them do it!'

And then she fainted. There was a flurry of shutters. The gendarmes looked sharply around.

By now, the slab had already been lain over the coffin. Mourners piled thick wreaths of white roses and lilies on Grégory's resting place For the mother, the child had died a second time.

Now Monique fainted. She had been struck down by the nervous tension of the last four days. There was a new round of clicking cameras. While a journalist called an ambulance, the eleven-year-old Lionel warned off the encroaching photographers.

'Leave us to mourn in peace!'

Other members of the family were beginning to seize stones. André Claudel, the mayor, rushed towards them. The Villemins could just be persuaded not to throw their ammunition. Grégory's funeral had narrowly escaped the indignity of a scuffle. And the air remained thick with the undirected desire for revenge. Bernard Laroche, Jean-Marie's cousin, muttered what everyone else was feeling: 'The bastard who did that deserves to be killed.'

By 3.15 p.m., the crowd was beginning to disperse. Monique was driven off to hospital to be given an injection of sedative. Christine and Jean-Marie took the road back to Paremont with forty other members of the family. The Villemins and the Jacobs would continue their watch over the memory of Grégory.

Soon, the cemetery was empty. As for the mayor, he had a wedding at 3.30 p.m.

The gendarmes went back to the station to scrutinise their new film, and to reflect that in Lépanges, life did not work quite like cinema. The set piece had been a failure. But perhaps Chaillan should have been grateful. In the film, the suspect hounded by the funeral crowd is innocent.

9

The third weekend of October was an emotional time in the Vologne that year. After the interment of Grégory in Lépanges on Saturday, it was the turn of Bruyères to take the limelight. By a strange twist, the mute agony and distrust that had pervaded Lépanges for Grégory's funeral was followed by a mixture of exoticism and celebration. Dozens of short Asiatic men in their fifties and sixties paraded proudly through the streets, their chests laden with medals. In addition to its horde of journalists, it seemed that the Vologne was now being invaded by an army of Japanese or Mongolians, all of them dressed like mid-West Americans.

In fact, the marchers were Japanese-Americans, veterans from Hawaii. They had been interned when the United States entered the war after Pearl Harbour and their one opportunity to prove themselves as good Americans was to join the *samurai* squads recruited for suicide missions as the conflict neared its end. They had come to the rescue of a Texan battalion surrounded by the Germans on Banzai hill. These elderly marchers had flown in from Honolulu. They were veterans from the army which, at great cost of life, had liberated the area from the desperate German rearguard that dug into the Vosges foothills in 1944. After the battle of Biffontaine, one of the hardest-fought in American military history, they had marched down the streets of Bruyères on 20 October. The locals thought they had been invaded by another of the Axis powers. 'The Mongol hordes have come.'

Ever since the end of the Second World War, Bruyères, an obscure town of 4,000 inhabitants, has been twinned with the 800,000 souls of Honolulu. Besides the usual military street names, the town boasts a Rue de Honolulu and a Rue de la 443ème unité de combat. Now the survivors of that cannon-fodder regiment were there to celebrate the fortieth anniversary of their victory.

It was hard to imagine any of the Vosgiens having the opportunity of exploring their American counterparts' hometown. And even harder to believe that the events in Bruyères and Lépanges partook of the same reality. Of course, the *samurai* veterans thought the TV cameras were for them, and produced bulletproof smiles specially for the occasion.

That same morning six cars were parked in the garden of Monique and Albert's home in Aumontzey, one of them with the tricolour symbol on its number plate. Commandant Chaillan was holding a family get-together. He had taken the cassettes of the Crow and would be questioning each member of the family about the meaning of his calls. Only Jacky and Liliane were absent, their exclusion like a lingering wound.

The rest of the family stood or sat around the dining-room table in a daze, still in a state of shock: a grim parody of the traditional Sunday get-together when the women donned aprons and made cakes and the men talked work and plans.

They stared out from a murk of confusion and pain, faces half hiding doubts and fears. Behind them, a home-made embroidery in the Monarch of the Glen style – more echoes of rural nobility. At the front to the right, Christine Villemin, sitting slightly apart, looking into nowhere. Sympathies and antagonisms are under a hoar frost. But they are there, as to some extent they are in all families, ready to flame up at the slightest injustice.

The gendarmes had done their homework. They had made up a Villemin family tree: against the names of the hundred or so potential suspects they had crossed off those with alibis, and left blank boxes against those that could not be checked. But the Villemins seemed unwilling to supply further information. 'We've told you all we know,' insisted Monique, domestic as ever in a mauve apron. 'Of course we'd tell you if we knew anything.' It was hard to discount the sincerity of a woman who had fainted with sorrow at her grandson's funeral, but the sheer size and complexity of the family was enough to sow doubt. Besides, the gendarmes found the family's response to questioning discouragingly obtuse. As one investigator complained, when you told them that they had no alibi to back up their statements, 'they just went on repeating the same phrases, without reacting to our questions'.

'The Villemin family presents a united front against the police' proclaimed one daily. The weekly *Paris Match* spoke of 'this clan which has nourished in its breast irrepressible quarrels in a whirlpool of jealousy, sometimes bloody brawls and suicides'. To no avail, Monique and Albert insisted that they were a united family. 'There's no clan here.' Or, as Albert said: 'We were happy once. We will never be happy again.' The words were simple, and from the heart. But hadn't the Crow said in one of his calls: 'Monique, I've got her in a corner.' And then there had been Jacky's declarations. Not to mention the talk of a second bastard.

Jean-Marie and Christine had never kept their suspicion of Jacky a secret from Monique, but she just replied: 'No, he might be the Crow, but I really can't see him going that far. Not Jacky.' It seemed now as if she had been keeping something from them. As if she knew something they didn't. The gendarmes had the same impression. Trying to probe the murk of the family background, they played Monique Villemin a tape of the Crow's. 'I can take revenge,' it said. 'I know Monique can't talk, and that there's no danger.' Grégory's grandmother started, but then insisted that she had no idea what the Crow was referring to. The family was a swamp.

At 2.00 p.m. the next day, the gendarmes received the visit of a young blonde from Aumontzey. Marie-Ange Laroche entered the station anonymously, in spite of the throngs of journalists and onlookers. The wife of Jean-Marie's cousin from Aumontzey, Bernard Laroche, Marie-Ange thought she could contribute something to the inquest by telling the police what she knew about the family. She wanted to speak to the gendarmes directly: best to avoid getting involved in the Villemin tangle.

The hours ticked by. A little later in the afternoon, Judge Lambert arrived from Epinal and was soon followed by Jean-Jacques Lecomte. With the hearing still in progress, Lecomte came out to field the customary questions. 'This person came of her own accord,' he said, 'to give evidence and is now under custody.' Her testimony was, like the case itself, 'astonishing'.

Marie-Ange Laroche managed to leave the gendarmerie without being identified. She was crying, and hiding her face with her coat. 'Leave me alone,' she shouted to the journalists. And, in spite of an incident when he threatened the over-curious cameramen, her husband Bernard would also pass unnoticed when he came to pick her up in his khaki-green Peugeot 305. Unnoticed, but remembered by Chaillan and his men. It was rare for those close to the Villemins to volunteer information as Marie-Ange had done.

Attention had switched to the two couples who arrived with an escort of gendarmes just as the Laroches were leaving. The gendarmes were carrying a pair of boots, some rope and some cassettes.

These new suspects were the brothers Daniel and Claude Hollard, and their wives. They had just been taken from their homes in Laveline-du-Houx. Searches had been carried out and had yielded booty the gendarmes were now carrying back to the station.

As their name revealed Daniel and Claude Hollard were related to the Villemins through Jeanne, the ill-fated wife of Gaston Villemin. Of course, that was all a long time ago, but it was unfortunate: and more recent relations did not look too good either. Daniel and his wife had quarrelled violently with Monique and Albert when they were neighbours. Now they hardly ever saw each other.

Was that enough to make the Hollards child murderers, driven by some ancestral law of revenge? For the moment, no one was bothered with that kind of question.

The new quartet of key witnesses was kept late into the night. After a few hours, they were joined by a tall, wiry young man with a moustache. Outside, a crowd of fifty or more journalists and locals had formed. Exasperated by the repeated failures of the investigation, the more hot-headed among them had started muttering grimly about taking the affair into their own hands. The lynch-mob mentality.

It was 1.30 a.m. when the gendarmes made their appearance. But instead of another cliffhanging announcement, they merely joked and disappeared in their cars. Commandant Chaillan finally came out with the familiar words:

'No, it's not them. The witnesses are being released, but we're not giving up! We're going back to the beginning!'

And as his driver whisked him off into the night, the Hollards edged timidly onto the gendarmerie steps, shielding their eyes against the flashes of the waiting photographers for whom a false suspect was better than a blank in the next day's article.

'Speak, speak, or else you must be guilty,' said a journalist.

But the Hollards were mute, sworn to secrecy by their questioners and condemned to suspicion by the mere fact of their presence. The Hollards had been cleared, but not their name:

'For our kids,' said Claude, 'it's horrible that we were treated as if we were guilty. Why us? Our consciences are clear. We know the police have to do their job to find the bastard who did it, but really!' And his wife Chantal added, with a quaver of indignation in her voice: 'Me too, I've been getting anonymous phone calls.'

One day, she remembered they picked up the phone and heard a woman's voice. 'It's Jacqueline Villemin', it said. 'Papa's dead. He's hanged himself.' The couple dashed to Aumontzey to buy a funeral wreath and then headed straight for Monique and Albert's house. They had barely got their breath back when the front door opened to reveal Albert. The hanged father had just finished dinner.

Like Jacky and Liliane Villemin and Roger and Paulette Jacquel, the Hollards were lucky enough to have good alibis for 16 October. Claude, the older brother, who was in his mid forties, had been picking mushrooms with his father and wife, and they had had the good sense not to be too discreet about it: there were abundant witnesses. Daniel and his wife had also been busy with autumnal harvesting. Fortunately, they had been accompanied in their apple gathering session by Daniel Michel, a colleague from the *Filatures de la Vologne* in Laveline-devant-Bruyères who went by another animal name, 'the Weasel'. He was the tall, thin man with the moustache. Since Michel had come to testify on behalf of his friends, and since on the fateful day he had himself been seen by the grocer when he went to pick up some wine at 5.15 p.m., just after he left the Hollards, the gendarmes had decided to call it a night. They had no intention of adding weasels to crows and they had not yet reached the state where suspicion knocks down every alibi in a kind of police domino effect. A gendarme has to keep his sanity, after all, and the *Petit Grégory* affair, as it was now beginning to be called, was exactly the kind of phenomenon to make you lose it.

The next day, the photograph of the mystery witness in the local paper created something of a stir. Jean-Marie and Christine Villemin eventually managed to identify her when they saw Marie-Ange in the street and recognised her coat. They couldn't understand. Why hadn't she told them first, and what had the Hollards got to do with it all? Anything now made them suspicious. In fact, the gendarmes had become interested in the Hollards all on their own. Marie-Ange had merely repeated the family gossip about Jacky.

Having failed with their latest hunch, the gendarmes now issued the photofit of a possible suspect. It was based on the testimony of an employee at the Post Office. The so-called man was in his forties, about five foot ten inches tall with dark brown eyes and hair, and heavily built. The photofit showed him with glasses on his chubby, and surprisingly genial face. In fact, the face was androgynous, and bore a striking resemblance to Claude Hollard's wife.

On the day of the crime, this enigmatic personality had been sighted wearing a burgundy-coloured sweater with boots. Like the man with the binoculars.

But the photofit was a flop. Only Lionel Villemin manifested any great interest, drawing and re-drawing the image released by the gendarmes, as if to give this hypothetical criminal a reality in his own mind, or to participate in the search for the killer of the nephew who could have been his younger brother. In his seriousness, Lionel was like the younger children who had started turning up at the gendarmerie. Their parents had warned them about the Crow. Now they came and opined with great earnestness to the investigators: 'If you ask me the Crow should be strangled,' or: 'But what if perhaps Grégory went into the Vologne to play with the Crow.' Those who had known Grégory at school were learning, slowly, to understand the meaning of his absence. When Christine Jacquot asked Aurélien where his friend was, he replied: 'Under the flowers'. Grégory's schoolmates were among the most regular visitors to his grave.

Finding the inquest in a cul-de-sac, Etienne Sesmat decided to try the direct approach:

'It is possible, or rather likely, that this abominable act was committed by several criminals or accomplices. I cannot believe that there is not at least one of them who does not feel the need to ease his conscience by unloading what he has on his mind.'

At Saint Cyr, you acquired a strong sense of honour. But Grégory's murderer probably had not been trained at Saint Cyr. Yet perhaps Sesmat was right. If the murderer could not be cornered by evidence, perhaps he could be made to bend to psychological pressure. On 26 October, an anonymous caller announced: 'I know who did it . . . I know why.' After a tense pause, he hung up. The gendarmes would never know if the caller had lost his nerve or if it was just a hoax.

That Wednesday, Christine and Jean-Marie had their first real meeting with Jean-Michel Lambert in Epinal. In the first few days, Lambert had let the gendarmes do most of the interviewing. Now he had his own questions to ask, especially to Christine. And on her own.

'Is Grégory really Jean-Marie's child?'

This came as a surprise. 'Of course.'

'Have you had any lovers?'

Christine said no, she wasn't the type.

'What about rejected advances, anything, think back as far as you can.'

There was not much, but Christine Villemin was a conscientious interviewee.

'It was seven years ago, when Jacqueline Villemin got married to Bernard Noël, Nonoche. At the party, I was sitting next to Bernard Laroche, that's Jean-Marie's cousin. He started trying to play footsie. I pretended not to notice, but he kept on. When I got up to avoid him he wanted to dance with me, and when I sat down again he started up again. In the end, I had to change seats with another guest.'

After the party, Christine explained it all to Jean-Marie. He was less surprised than she expected: his brother Michel had already told him about Laroche trying the same thing one night with his wife, Ginette. They would just have to avoid seeing Laroche as much as they could.

And that was as far as Christine Villemin could provide Lambert with any concrete information about Laroche's sex life, marital or extramarital. Nor, when she left the *Palais de Justice* at ten o'clock, could she fathom the purpose of Lambert's questions. Bernard Laroche's sexual tendencies?

It was precisely because they wanted to understand the investigation better, that Jean-Marie and Christine Villemin decided to become *partie civile*: in other words, to become a party to the process of prosecution. Under French law, the *partie civile* has direct access to the information gathered by the investigators. It is therefore well-placed to try to influence the course of the investigation and, if it comes to that, to answer any insinuations or calumnies made against it. By now, Jean-Marie Villemin was more or less convinced that Jacky and his father-in-law were innocent. But he had other hunches. Above all, he had a burning desire to know – more so, apparently, than Monique and Albert, who declined their son's invitation to join him. 'I have faith in the gendarmes, but I need to know what's in those files,' he announced on Wednesday 24 October. 'I can't take any more.' There was only one solution: 'We demand that vengeance be done.'

The parents' choice of barrister was perfectly in keeping with the emotions revealed by Jean-Marie's demand. Maître Henri-René Garaud was France's leading advocate of the death penalty, and a counsellor of the Legitimate Defence organisation. *Légitime Défense* upholds the idea that violence is an understandable reaction to crime. It defends victims who have defended themselves. Garaud's best known case involved a garage mechanic called Legras. After several thieves had plundered his car, Legras resorted to booby-trapping his new radio. Needless to say, it exploded in someone's face. Garaud obtained acquittal for his client.

Of course Jean-Marie and Christine Villemin were ignorant of the notoriety attaching to their Parisian counsel. Legal matters had never been their speciality before and they had contacted Garaud on the advice of one of their many 'friends' from the press. But, unwittingly, they were helping to make their plight symbolic. Not only was their barrister controversial, he was also an adept communicator and would become one of the most prominent actors in the affair. Consciously or unconsciously, sympathy with Jean-Marie and Christine would be coloured by their association with the law and order lobby.

Maître Garaud was no closet fascist, however. Far from it. An avuncular, mustachioed sixty-year-old with white hair, courteous manners and a warm smile underlined by the richness of his southern accent, he was a pastmaster at arousing sympathy for his clients. He was also well versed in the art of combining media and legal matters. It is a skill which many of the more renowned French barristers possess.

Garaud lost no time staking out his emotional and legal position: 'It's not my way to bother with niceties,' he declared. 'I am here to defend a father and a mother. I think that a crime such as this one, whose atrocity has aroused the anger of the whole of France, must not go unpunished. My presence is not dictated by the desire for vengeance, but by the desire for justice.' Garaud already had an eye to covering his client's gust of vindictiveness.

But justice looked far away. Nothing seemed certain any more, not even Grégory's drowning. Had the body really been thrown into the water by the bridge? Given the turbulence of the water and its load of fallen branches, it seemed incredible that the boy's face had not been scratched. Perhaps Josyane Guyot really had seen a dustbin liner. Adjudant Lamirand was keen to carry out some experiments on the water.

So, to shore up their crumbling scenario, the gendarmes set about testing the Vologne with a wooden mannequin of the same dimensions and weight as the murdered child. A blue plastic covering gave the lifeless puppet a grotesque resemblance to Grégory. Four locations were tested. The object was thrown from the bank or dangled from the bridge, its course downstream accompanied by a policeman in waders. The mannequin was constantly taking the plunge, never coming up in the right place; rather like the investigation itself. It was true, the water level had changed in the nine days since Grégory's death.

The Vologne is not a simple river. Entering Docelles, it splits into two and is enriched by several tributary streams. There were a lot of possibilities.

Eventually, the gendarmes had to conclude that the child had been thrown into the Vologne from the other bank, near the firemen's barracks or possibly further up, on the last stretch of the Barba, a tributary that flowed down to Docelles from the south-east. Repeated tests from these two points always ended with the mannequin coming to a halt where Grégory Villemin had also ended his journey. Either way, it seemed that the boy had been thrown into the water no more than fifty or a hundred metres upstream of his resting place. This was inconvenient: the shoe and tyre prints were found hundreds of yards further upstream.

All this was hard to believe. Either nature was playing tricks with the gendarmes, or the murderer had been extraordinarily lucky. Dozens of windows overlooked the probable spot, and there was a café just by the bank. The place had its small band of *habitués*, mainly retired men from Docelles who would while away the days playing cards and drinking beer or the local mix of red wine and lemonade. From inside they could see everything that happened on the river. Besides, as the regulars told Lamirand, they were always on the lookout for mates who might buy them a drink. And then, the bar being primitively equipped and the intake of drink regular, they made regular trips under the footbridge. 'I never close before seven-thirty,' said the owner, 'and there are always customers coming in and out.'

They had seen nothing. Had the boy been drowned much later, hours after the phone call announcing his death to Michel? Or had the crime been committed much further upstream?

'It is totally inconceivable,' reasoned Captain Sesmat, 'that what took place on 16 October in full daylight and over a considerable area should not have been seen by more people.' To which Lamirand retorted, with a touch of humour: 'People here sleep like battery hens.' Much as they worked, in fact.

On Friday 26 October, the gendarmes renewed their efforts with a second photofit. The first one had become obsolete when a man turned up in Bruyères to lay claim to his portrait. Yes, he told the gendarmes, he had been at the post office on several occasions, but that was a week earlier and he had strong alibis to back him up. On the evening of 16 October he had been twenty miles away from Lépanges, in Rambervilliers.

Possible suspect mark two was a good deal more virile than his predecessor. A well-built but fit man in his thirties, this hirsute character had a thick mop of dark hair swept sideways across his brow, a downward-curving moustache and heavy, meat-cleaver sideburns of an auburn colour. As befits a child murderer, he glared sideways from under emphatic eyebrows. This was much more like a killer.

The new portrait had been composed on the basis of a statement made by a hotelier in Docelles. At 4.35 p.m. on 16 October, Michel Cornillie had seen the man come into the bar of the Hôtel de la Poste. The newcomer ordered a beer and downed it in haste, tapping nervously on his cigarette packet as he did so. Five minutes later he left. After a lapse of twenty minutes or quarter of an hour, the same customer was back for another beer, which this time he sat down for, drumming his fingers on the table. There was no one else in the bar at the time, but the solitary drinker just turned his back and drank. He made it clear he did not want to talk. This time, he had already prepared the five francs and fifty centimes needed to pay for his drink. Such unsocial behaviour came as a surprise to Michel Cornillie:

'He made no attempt to start up a conversation, and yet we're a chatty lot in this trade! He didn't even ask for a newspaper, he just kept looking outside and checking the time. It was the first time I'd seen him, and I couldn't help noticing his anxiety. It was obvious that he wasn't there because he was thirsty.'

The man with the sideburns left the bar at 5.15 p.m. He was not seen again. L'Hôtel de la Poste was only a few yards from the Vologne, just by the footbridge where they found Grégory. It would be a strange form of poetic justice if the Crow were to be arrested because of the deposition of a man whose nickname, Corneille, was French for rook. But never mind wordgames, this was certainly one of the strongest pieces of evidence so far.

The presence of the stranger in Docelles or 'the man with side-burns' as he soon came to be called was confirmed by other witnesses. Of course, this whiskery person could simply have been waiting for a bus; the stop was just outside. But not many people get that nervous about taking public transport. Given the coincidence of his presence with the time in which Grégory was abducted and killed, it looked more than likely that he had been a party to the crime. He could have made the phone call to Albert or posted the letter in Lépanges, acting in coordination with the man and woman whose footprints had been found on the river bank.

The investigators could feel pleased but certainly not proud of themselves: Cornillie had made his statement to the local gendarmes on 17 October. They had simply 'forgotten' to pass it on to Commandant Chaillan. 'I told them it probably wasn't important,' said the innkeeper with a shrug, 'and they must have believed me.' Michel Cornillie was an understanding sort of man. It was true that when the information had first been volunteered, the gendarmes were ninety per cent sure they had found their man – Jacky Villemin. Put it down to the inexperience of the investigation's heady youth.

After days of rumour and counter-rumour, the arrival of Henri Garaud on Saturday 27 October brought a reminder of the emotional reality of the affair: the bereaved parents. Garaud's first action was to have them take him to Lépanges to see Grégory's room. Jean-Marie and Christine had set it out just as it used to be for their son. When he came out, Garaud's eyes were moist. He had found a heartfelt basis for his conviction. To the constant pressure of the media Garaud added the voice of outraged justice: 'I have just been to see two heartbroken parents,' he declared. 'Suffering can be seen, not told. To lose a child is itself beyond understanding: to do so in conditions such as these is to be plunged into the world of Greek tragedy. Their son can never be restored to them, but they can find the killer. If he is not found, the consequences for our society will be grave in the extreme.' The murder of Little Grégory had become a fully-fledged national issue. And, with his reference to Greek tragedy, Garaud had added a new dimension to public perception of the case.

Garaud also lost no time in criticising the gendarmes for their failure to make progress and their organisational weaknesses. He called for Judge Lambert to hand the case over to the Judiciary Police, the plain-clothes investigators based in Nançy. But the gendarmes put up a brave front. 'We'll get him sooner or later!' they insisted, 'Tomorrow, in ten days, in six months, it doesn't matter!' With the intensity of national interest in the case, they would have to move quickly.

Their best hope seemed to lie in the results to be provided by the graphological analyses of the dictation scripts from the days after the murder. In Wiesbaden, West Germany, specialised police units of the *Bundes Kriminel Amt* were analysing the notepaper used for the letter of

16 October. They were particularly interested in the pressure from the writer's hand, as well as in the specks of dust on the page: above all though, there was a chance they would be able to read the barely perceptible imprint that had been left in the paper, no doubt from a signature written on the sheet above it. They were also pinning their hopes on the work of Professor Ceccaldi in Paris. He was busy examining the saliva on the stamp that carried the murder note to Paremont so as to determine the blood group of the sender. It was all getting highly technical.

As Jean-Jacques Lecomte said: 'The fact that we have reached such a scientific meticulousness totally contradicts any allegations that have been made about the negligence that has characterised this investigation.'

10

Two weeks had gone by. Two weeks of faltering progress and abrupt setbacks. Two weeks in which the man, men, woman or women who had murdered Grégory Villemin seemed to have been slipping further away from the gendarmes' grasp. The local joke summed up what everyone was beginning to think, inhabitants and journalists alike: 'Here, no one gets away with anything, except criminals.'

The remark had a history, one that went back well beyond the events of 16 October and the harassment of the Crow. The shame and fear that journalists spoke of, that most confessed, had their roots in memory. The shadow of the Crow was darkened by the obscurity of past mysteries: unsolved murders, brutal violence. Grégory's assassin, 'The monster' as he was commonly called, fitted into the local demonology. You could imagine him observing the villages from the inviolate safety of some hillside refuge. It was unwise to visit unannounced, or when night had fallen. Hunting is a popular sport in the Vosges; most households had their guns within easy reach.

'Here, there is a big crime every year, and they never find out who did it.' There are no comparative statistics for violence in and around the Vologne. Facts, though, are more powerful. Everyone knew about the murder that took place near Brouvelieures in September 1983.

Pierre Petitnicolas was a retired schoolteacher from Epinal who came to the valley every year to spend a few months in his country home. Petitnicolas was sixty-three, and something of a personality: 'The poet' they called him, in recognition of his published descriptions of the beauties of the Vosges. Hardly the sort of person to inspire hatred or envy.

His was an isolated house. Just before eleven o'clock, on the night of

7 September, a gang of three or four men parked their car a hundred metres away and stole through the forest to the back of the building. They smashed a window, opened the door and turned out the lights. Petitnicolas was out of bed the moment he heard the noise, but the men overpowered him. Another bound his wife. During the next two hours, Petitnicolas was beaten, then flayed, in order to extort the combination of his safe. His wife was beaten to silence her screams.

She remembered the thieves saying 'That'll do' when they left the house after midnight. Petitnicolas was unconscious, and lying in a swelling pool of blood. It was one o'clock when neighbours heard Mme Petitnicolas screaming. She was half naked, and had run out into the cold to get help. Petitnicolas was dead with multiple fractures, haematomas and skin wounds.

It was 'a terrible tragedy, but sadly none too unusual'. So said the *Liberté de l'Est* in Epinal. The comment was not gratuitous. Three weeks earlier, the same newspaper reported the death of sixty-year-old Marie-Juliette Demangeon in Hérigoutte, near Laveline-du-Houx. No one had heard when the thieves smashed her kitchen window, nor when they beat her, leaving her with a haematoma on the right side of her skull, with strangulation marks about her neck and burn marks on her insteps.

In spite of such methods, the gang left empty-handed. This time police caught two of the youths. They were both under eighteen, cousins of the Villemins, people said. In the same breath they added: 'But don't say I told you so.' You never knew who would find out. And then, didn't people say that the gang was helped by a woodcutter from Herpelmont who had been seen around the house that summer? He was still at liberty.

The villages in the Vologne are surrounded by forest; anyone can hide there, or use their special knowledge of local geography to make them a base for special operations and quick escapes.

The gendarmes often spoke of roaming gypsies. It is a convenient notion. Gypsies, as the image of Epinal would have it, are by nature rootless and inclined to violence and theft. But the gypsies were rarely seen these days. Everyone agreed that the gangs who haunted this corner of the Vosges were of local origin. They came from the woods. The phenomenon was decades old.

Fays is a village only a few kilometres away from Lépanges. It too nestles against the trees. Antoinette Balland, another retired sixty-year-old, lived there with her handicapped son Roger. One February morning, their milkman heard groans coming from behind the closed shutters. When he managed to get into the house, he found Antoinette lying in her blood. She too had been flayed. It took two months for her to die of her wounds. Roger was already dead. He had been beaten with a rod, then with stones. Finally, he was shot through the temple at close range: twice.

It was the thirtieth such attack in recent memory, and Roger Balland's the seventh death.

The pattern kept repeating itself: violent aggression, successful or attempted thefts of large but not extravagant sums of money, preferably pensioners' nest eggs. Like the eighty-year-old Erneste Pelgrand, who lived in Deycimont. The killers who beat her to death for her modest savings were never found. There had been at least six such incidents in 1975, two in 1976. Tendon seemed to be the major centre for brutal crime. The village is near the source of the Vologne, just near Gérardmer. Its post office is hardly the most lucrative in France, but it was nevertheless held up twice in as many years. Everyone said the gangs were local. And then there were the unexplained deaths. A local resident was found dead on the road: 'A drunken driver,' said the police. 'Clubbed to death,' said hearsay. Another man was discovered lifeless in his bed: 'A natural death,' insisted the police. 'Beaten beyond endurance,' went public opinion. Another mysteriously breathed his last by the petrol pumps of the local garage.

The catalogue could be made to yield connections. In Faucom-pièrre, near Lépanges and Laveline-du-Houx, another, yet another elderly woman was beaten to death with yet another club. Hélène Terry, a well-liked sixty-year-old who ran a café near the town hall, was a distant relative of the Villemin family. After the crime, and the usual declaration about gypsies, the gendarmes arrested the next best thing: a tramp. The man had been living with a lady friend two kilometres away, near Docelles. He was arrested and spent twenty years protesting his innocence behind bars. No one knew who the real killer was. In 1980, the gendarmes found a busted safe in the woods near Fays. The money, 200,000 francs from a hold-up in Bruyères, had gone. This was just next to Herpelmont, where Gaston Villemin killed himself.

If you believed in those things, you would have to say the area had a special magnetism. Or you might say that the combination of unemployment, boredom and harsh living conditions – not to mention the marked inclination to alcohol – were conducive to brutal crime, just as they say it is the flat, monotonous countryside of the Beauce that gives this area west of Paris its high suicide rate. People could, and did, say lots of things to explain the disturbing sequence of violent acts, and as long as the crimes remained unsolved, then rumour and fact would merge into each other like fog onto the hills.

Death by, or near to the water: that too was unduly common, and unduly unpunished. Nineteen-year-old Marguerite Schuler was killed and left in the pond by the La Croix-aux-Mines sawmill. In 1978, a seventeen-year-old student, Eveline Pivat, was found dead in the woods of Cheniménil, 150 metres from the Vologne. It was two weeks since she had last been seen on the platform of the local railway station. Eveline had been in the year above Christine Villemin at the Jean Lurçat secondary school in Bruyères.

The worst year was 1983. That was when the police fished Ginette Agenauer's body from the Vologne, three kilometres from Lépanges. She was thirty-five. She had been shot through the head; had shot herself, the gendarmes said. The conclusion did not seem logical. Three weeks later, the pistol was found when an unsuspecting walker stepped on it by the river bank. It was 300 yards downstream from where the body was found.

Three other deaths marked 1983. That of Brigitte Saudot came just before Christmas. Saudot was a likeable, if reserved young woman, a model employee with what they call an irreproachable private life. It was her workmates who started the search when she failed to turn up one morning. The missing colleague was found at her home in Golbey, near Epinal. She was lying by her bed with her throat cut. A blunt instrument had been used. As Professor De Ren from Nancy confirmed, there had been no sexual violence.

Saudot was immediately linked with two other victims killed that autumn. Emmannuelle Lauber disappeared from Epinal on 8 October. Her body was found floating in the Moselle four days later, in

Golbey. She had been in the water for three of them. She was naked. So was Marie-Christine Amet on 7 October, when they picked her out of the Moselle canal. She had gone missing on 24 September after a night at the Epinal fair. Professor De Ren recorded that Marie-Christine Amet had been strangled and Emmannuelle Lauber's body showed traces of sexual intercourse.

It was Jean-Michel Lambert who led the investigation with the men of the Nancy judiciary police. When news of Grégory Villemin's death broke a year later, the murders in Epinal were still unsolved. The gendarmes were convinced the judge had let the guilty men get away. They said Lambert was too scrupulous about detaining suspects.

The little Grégory affair came loaded with a dense background. As one investigating weekly pointed out, it even had its predecessors. In 1949, round about the same time as Gaston Villemin hanged himself, Claude Delaville was found floating down the Taintroué river, two hundred yards from his parents' home near Saint-Dié. He was six. His killer was never caught.

Perhaps, amidst all the murk of untraced criminals, some small patch of history was repeating itself: or working out a variation from a common stock of crime: like an exotic plant sprouting suddenly from a rich, dark humus.

11

As the investigation neared its third week, the second photofit began to yield a few results: in all, some fifteen witnesses contacted either the gendarmes or Michel Cornillie himself. The affable hotelier had achieved fleeting fame as the man who had seen the murderer, or murderer's accomplice. One typed letter arrived from Macon informing him of a crime committed by a man known to the police for his cruelty, a crime paid for by a 'fat, wealthy woman in the Lyon-Marseille area'. Unless he was stopped, warned the correspondent, he would start again. Also from the South of France, a woman warned by phone of a former legionnaire who was 'violent or at least strange', and had spent several weeks in Lépanges at the end of September. He was, she claimed, a close cousin of the Villemin family. The informer said she did not dare contact the gendarmes.

From Dieppe, a woman warned that the murderer was about to cross the Channel. And, closer to home, a barber put the investigators on the trail of a customer who came in to have his whiskers shaved off; surely, the sign of a bad conscience. But, on reflection, hardly the sort of rash behaviour one would expect from as cool an operator as the Crow.

The fact was that scores of men in the region wore moustaches. But this consideration did not prevent the popular national television network, TF1, from showing the photofit to its viewers with the very unequivocal appeal: 'If you see this man, tell the police. He has killed a child.' The last week of October 1984 was an uncomfortable one for a good number of hirsute males all over France.

In the Villemin family, the tension was beginning to take its toll. Albert was a nervous wreck, sensing menace in the slightest noise, be it the telephone or just a bird moving in the hedge. Michel had begun to lose weight. Jean-Marie was growing fat with the effect of tranquillisers. And Jacky continued to lick wounds that it seemed would never close: 'I'll never be at peace again. I don't know what people think, but I know that they are all watching me.'

It was at this moment that *Agence France Presse* sent out a dispatch confirming that 'the couple' had been identified. The news came as a surprise to everyone. It was, according to Lecomte, 'perfectly unfounded', and to Lambert 'totally aberrant', while the gendarmes condemned the release as 'false and abusive'. Lecomte threatened to stop communicating with the press. But the AFP did not retract. So where did the information come from? The journalist responsible merely shrugged and gave an enigmatic smile.

The next day, on Tuesday 30 October, Commandant Chaillan and his men held a 'summit meeting' in Nancy, in the presence of their expert on handwriting, Madame Jacquin-Keller, and a newly commissioned graphologist from Paris, Madame Berrichon-Seyden. Although the dictations conducted two or more days after Grégory's death had not been conclusively analysed, the gendarmes were in a hurry to get on, and were hoping that the two women could give them valuable confirmation of their working hypotheses.

Jacquin-Keller, who was recognised analyst for the Appeal Court of nearby Colmar, was an expert in the formal analysis of writing. She studied the pressure of the hand, the quality of the pen strokes and the formation of the letters. Berrichon-Seyden, a graphologist from Paris, specialised in the use of handwriting for psychological analysis. As she was at pains to point out, 'The expert should not be concerned with the writer's personality, nor should he or she be aware of the circumstances that have brought him to analyse the writing he has before him.'

Neither of the two women could claim ignorance of the Grégory affair: unless of course they had not seen a newspaper, watched television or listened to the radio for two weeks, and had come to Nancy blindfolded. Did they know whose writing they were looking at?

Whatever the role of the two experts in Nancy, the gendarmes suddenly seemed to be moving ahead with surprising rapidity. They had started conducting interviews with the Villemins, Jacobs and their entourage in Aumontzey. They had also been holding further dictation sessions.

Rumours began to circulate about a couple being held for questioning. The woman had apparently given herself away in the dictation with her 'M' and 'L', which closely resembled those on the envelope posted at Lépanges on 16 October. Presumably, she had written the letters. The man and the woman were from Aumontzey. After the unfortunate effects of the previous, well-publicised question and answer sessions, though, people were being more cautious, and that included the impulsive Jean-Marie Villemin: 'You have to be careful, you know. For the moment, the couple are just helping the gendarmes with their inquiry. You can't say anything until you're sure. If you give a name, it'll be just like it was with the Hollards.'

On the afternoon of Wednesday 31 October, Etienne Sesmat gave a tip-off to the journalists waiting outside the Bruyères gendarmerie. Divers were busy in the Vologne at Docelles, searching the area where Grégory was thought to have been thrown into the water. The dozen or so reporters who hared down to the river found two frogmen throwing the mannequin around in a desultory fashion while another took notes and two more paddled around and occasionally dived, like ducks looking for titbits. The additional clue they were apparently looking for was never found, nor even named. That day, the real action was elsewhere.

Just before 5.00 p.m., *Agence France Press* sent out another dispatch: 'The twenty-six-year-old who was questioned at his home in Aumontzey this Wednesday has been taken into custody in Epinal and charged with murder by Judge Lambert. His name is Bernard Laroche, a relative of the Villemin family employed at the Ancel mill in Granges-sur-Vologne.'

Bernard Laroche: Michel's friend, someone the whole family knew. He had been at the funeral.

While the divers had been exploring the depths of the Vologne, gendarmes had been heading in the direction of Aumontzey, where Bernard Laroche would be taking his afternoon nap after the night-shift. They cordoned off the road leading to his chalet at the top of the town, then conducted their searches. At Laroche's home they found an old telescope, and then looked further down the road at the house inhabited by his aunt Louisette. The investigators also rummaged through the houses of friends and neighbours in Aumontzey.

Bernard Laroche had been identified as the probable author of two anonymous phone calls: more damningly, the gendarmes were sure that it was his writing on the murder note. Berrichon-Seyden and Jacquin-Keller had confirmed. Moreover, initial studies had revealed that the traces of initials found at the bottom of the murder note were BL: B for Bernard, L for Laroche.

As the gendarmes continued their questioning, others had gone to Profilage in Gérardmer to pick up Marie-Ange. When she entered the house, neighbours heard her wailing: 'My son, my son'. Then the gendarmes closed the shutters. A short while later, the two suspects were driven off to prison for individual interviews.

Elsewhere, other investigators were trying a reconstruction of the events of 16 October, dividing their work into segments of time: from 4.50 p.m., when Christine left Jacquot, to 5.03 p.m., when she last saw Grégory: then to 5.20 p.m., when Michel Villemin answered the Crow's phone call.

It was all very novel. This was the first time Laroche's name had got beyond the front door of Bruyères gendarmerie. Jean-Marie Villemin was amazed: 'It's not possible, not him,' he exclaimed. 'He's the last person I'd have thought of! My childhood friend! He was rather quiet, but we got on well. He used to come round to our place a lot, before.' He had also been round once or twice to enquire about the state of the investigation. Christine Villemin was silent, but Jacky shared his half-brother's scepticism: 'Bernard? Do that? It's absurd! What did he have against us?' Besides, the crime had been too successful, too smooth an operation for someone like Bernard. 'Not only did he kill Jean-Marie's son, but he also made all the suspicion fall on me. Bernard couldn't have done something like that.' Liliane agreed: 'Bernard was always kind and sociable with us. He never took any notice of the family quarrel.'

There were practical points too. Like the fact that Michel Villemin, who knew Laroche so well, had failed to recognise him over the phone on 16 October. Michel was adamant that the caller was not Laroche. The Villemins, in Liliane's words, were 'knocked out' by the news.

And mystified. No one had ever had any quarrel with Bernard Laroche.

And yet, Bernard and Marie-Ange Laroche been on the list of suspects ever since Marie-Ange's ill-advised visit to the gendarmerie on 22 October. An informer who informs wrongly inevitably becomes suspect. Especially since Marie-Ange had already admitted that she didn't like the Villemins much.

Now, after the summit meeting at Nancy, Chaillan felt he could move ahead. Expert opinion was on his side. And Laroche's alibis for the afternoon of 16 October looked weak. In an earlier interview, Laroche had told the gendarmes he had arranged to go and buy some cheap wine in Bruyères with a friend from work, Pierre Zonca. But Zonca had not been at home to meet him. And no one had seen Laroche during the crucial hours.

The gendarmes also knew that Bernard Laroche's mother-in-law, Jeannine Bolle, was a diabetic: which could explain the syringe and insulin found in Docelles.

So much for the evidence. The gendarmes had fished up some more far-reaching motives, much more than the rejected advances Christine Villemin had mentioned.

Bernard Laroche was born in March 1953, from the marriage of Marcel Laroche and Thérèse Jacob, Monique's sister. He had never known his mother: Thérèse died in the Epinal maternity ward where she gave him life. And since Marcel could not bring up his son alone, he entrusted him to his mother-in-law, Adeline Jacob. Adeline also took care of Monique's older children, and Laroche grew up with Michel Villemin, getting to know Jean-Marie, Jacky and the rest of the family. Bernard was like a son to Monique; a brother to her children.

But children fight. In the Villemin family, Jean-Marie was always picking on his older but weaker sibling, Michel. Naturally, as Michel's milk brother, Laroche defended him. On one occasion during the summer, Jean-Marie threw Michel into an inflatable swimming-pool with only one hand, and Bernard exclaimed: '*Il est balèze, Jean-Marie!*' The term had stuck.

Baléze, which means tough, was the word used to describe Jean-Marie in the Crow's letters.

Like the Crow, Laroche was in a fine position to know about the

Villemins. From his home in Aumontzey you could see over to Albert and Monique's place (and even better with a telescope). And from his continuing friendship with Michel Villemin, Laroche could garner all the information he needed about events at Paremont.

Laroche had good reason to be critical of the family. Rumour had it that the Villemins had blackmailed his father, Marcel, over some half-veiled robbery, or even murder, that they had committed together. When Marcel died, a few years before, Laroche had discovered the compromising evidence. The beginning of the Crow's activities had coincided more or less with the hospitalisation of Marcel Laroche, in November 1981. That was when the harassment of the Villemins had really started.

As Laroche had himself told a journalist, two days before he was visited by the gendarmes: 'Oh, the Villemins! They haven't always been perfect. There's a lot you could say about them.' This 'lot' being in part their attitude to Monique's mentally handicapped sister, Louisette, and her daughter, Chantal. The Villemins wanted to lock them away in some asylum instead of taking proper care of them.

Louisette needed care. In addition to her mental handicap, she suffered from the consequences of incest: she had conceived Chantal with her own father, Léon Jacob. Chantal was also mentally handi-capped. But Monique 'did not want to know.' Now the two women, mother and sister, lived together in the house that Bernard had been left in his father's will. And Bernard visited them frequently.

The other side to Laroche the semi-orphan and champion of the weak was his rivalry with Jean-Marie.

Laroche could not bear to be outpaced by the success of his false brother. Where the latter had built a spacious chalet on the heights of Lépanges, his cousin had followed suit with a home on the Bois du Creux, above Aumontzey, built on a plot of land inherited from his father. Jean-Marie had become foreman at Autocoussin: so, a little bit later did Bernard at Ancel-Seit. Where Jean-Marie had a Renault 18 and a Renault 5, Laroche had a Peugeot 305 and a clapped out Citroën Ami. Jean-Marie had bought a hi-fi, so had Bernard Laroche. So far, so good. But the older man was said to having financial problems maintaining his lifestyle. Laroche was feeling the strain.

Laroche even had a son the same age as Grégory: Sébastien.

Laroche called his son Titi, the name used by Christine for Grégory – as if Sébastien were supposed to match the elder boy in every way. Only a few days separated their dates of birth. The only difference was that Sébastien was a boy of fragile health. As a seven-month-old baby he had undergone surgery to right a deformation of the cranium. He suffered from hydrocephalus, or water on the brain, and his head was swollen from the fluid that had been unable to escape. There was still a valve in his skull. Sébastien had none of the impish dynamism of Grégory, and then his pallor, flat blond hair and large watery eyes made him appear especially weak and mentally ineffectual. Sébastien ran, fell and bumped around like most other children his age, but many considered him mentally retarded. His memory and elocution were under-developed for his age.

Sexual jealousy could be added to paternal jealousy. A small, portly woman with fleshy jowls and metal-rimmed glasses that hid the charm of her blue eyes, Marie-Ange could not be compared to her rival at Paremont. Bernard Laroche, unlucky in love, unlucky as a father and frustrated as a lover. It was a convincing combination. Just as he should covet Jean-Marie's wife, so Laroche should wish to destroy the evidence that he had failed; the evidence being Grégory, the lively, precocious child who was like a constant reproach to a man whose conscience was already burdened with the knowledge that he had killed his own mother.

Such strong motives ran deep. They were not apparant from the outside. Bernard Laroche was a placid, undemonstrative character, slow to show anger or indignation. You could see it in his doggy eyes. A burly, good-natured man with pouchy cheeks and a big, thick moustache that Grégory, like other kids, loved to play with. A hard worker, a lover of food and a well-liked friend of the Villemins. 'When he and Marie-Ange saw Grégory these last few months,' recalled Jean-Marie, 'they always gave him a kiss.'

If either or both of the Laroches were guilty, then their monstrosity knew no bounds. They had acted with ice-cold meditation to kill a child they had seen and played with only weeks before. They even continued to frequent Albert and Monique at Aumontzey to find out about the progress of the investigation. It would have to have been the act of a schizophrenic.

Of course, the gendarmes knew Bernard and Marie-Ange Laroche had their partisans.

The most vocal among them were the Bolles, Marie-Ange's family, who lived in the exotically-named Rue de Maroc in Laveline-devant-Bruyères. Names, of course, are deceptive. The reality of Rue de Maroc was that of a drab workers' town springing out of the fields with all the harmony of a power station.

The Bolle family was even more extensive than the Villemins. Lucien and Jeannine, the parents of ten children, even offered a slight parallel with Albert and Monique: the man short, wiry and discreet, the woman more demonstrative and apparently dominant. Jeannine Bolle was a small, stocky woman, her aged face reflecting the hardships undergone by her body: Jeannine had been in childbirth twenty-three times, and her sense of family was commensurate. 'It's impossible, horrible, they're innocent!' she cried. She was seconded by Lucien as he swore on the crucifix that hung in the kitchen. Bernard and Marie-Ange were a model couple: kind, considerate and well-liked by those who knew them. Of their eight daughters, Marie-Ange was their favourite. And the Bolle family was nothing if not united. Turbulent, aggressive even, but united.

Of course, they had all known that the gendarmes were interested in the couple. A group had been round to their house to look for recordings, they said, and for some records: among them, the Charlots' song, '*Chef, encore un petit coup!*' It was one of the Crow's favourites. Not to mention the repeated visits to the house at Bois du Creux, above Aumontzey. But Marie-Ange had told them not to worry, saying that it was the same for everyone in Aumontzey. The Bolles had been satisfied with their daughter's reassuring words. Just as they were sure of their innocence. 'I'm sure they're innocent, otherwise you can't trust anyone.'

In Aumontzey, everyone admired Bernard's daily devotion to his aunt Louisette and her daughter Chantal. He was seen as a solid, hard-working type, always busy in the forest when he wasn't at the Ancel factory in Granges-sur-Vologne, where he and his workmates transformed raw cloth for the fashion houses of Paris. Like many of the rural proletariat of the region, Laroche continued the traditional activity of woodcutting to top up his salary. Where would this benign workaholic have found the time to play the Crow? 'Bernard is the hard-working, family-loving type,' said a friend. 'He's not the sort to write anonymous letters, let alone kill a kid, I'd stake my life on it.'

His workmates were equally enthusiastic. Laroche was a 'good mate, always ready to give you a hand. The kind of man who never raised his voice. Shy, and not very talkative, but a great worker.' With qualifications as a metal worker and draughtsman, Laroche worked on the mill's complicated spinning machines. He was considered one of Ancel's best technicians, and also played a part in the CGT trade union which was closely involved with the running of the factory. As a man of responsibility, Laroche had even run in the last local elections: but was too timid, and too little-known to win many votes.

'I'm an honest bloke,' protested Laroche. 'I was even at the funeral. How can you imagine it was me?' It was a candid denial.

Two and a half hours later, *Agence France Presse* sent out a new dispatch cancelling its predecessor and stating that the said Laroche had simply been detained for questioning. Apparently, the AFP had fallen victim to intoxication, the measured leaking whereby the gendarmes tried to prepare public opinion for their next moves. The obverse of the coin – journalistic interference in judicial activity – was already well known.

After their disappointments with Jacky Villemin, Roger Jacquel and the Hollards, the investigators surely couldn't have got it wrong once again. They were more competent than that. The earlier suspects had every reason to hope so. The arrest of Laroche had been a surprise, but at least it meant they could breathe again.

And yet Bernard and Marie-Ange were released after twenty-four hours of custody. They had been interrogated separately and confronted with surprise witnesses, and they had denied everything. Neither of them had written anonymous letters or made threatening phone calls. Marie-Ange insisted that she had been at work, in Gérardmer, on the afternoon of 16 October. She had come home on the coach at 9.30 p.m. At Aumontzey, she had been seen by her younger sister, Muriel, who was babysitting with Sébastien. Marie-Ange had surprised the gendarmes with her tenacity. And her alibis held fast.

As for Bernard, he had remained his usual calm self. Patiently, he had repeated his statement: 'I have an alibi, I was at Aunt Louisette's place; Muriel, my sister in law, saw me. She was watching TV when I came in.' Naturally, the gendarmes had gone to find the key alibi in Laveline-devant-Bruyères, where she lived with her parents. Muriel Bolle was a boyish fifteen-year-old with flaming red hair, and very attached to her brother-in-law. Muriel had confirmed. That night she had taken the school bus to Louisette's place as usual, to mind Sébastien. And Bernard was there. He was watching television eating ravioli.

All that week the gendarmes had been preparing public opinion for Laroche's arrest. Now they had no choice but to hang fire. French law provides for two twenty-four-hour spells of detention before charges are brought to bear, and no doubt Judge Lambert wanted to keep the second session in reserve. So, at three o'clock on Thursday afternoon, two police cars roared out of the forecourt at Epinal. But, like the rumours of charges, they were empty. The car containing Marie-Ange left a few minutes later, from the back exit. The procedure was repeated two hours later. Back to Aumontzey.

Not that the gendarmes were giving up. There had to be another way of getting at the Laroches. The couple were, as Lambert declared, 'more than ever at the centre of our investigations.'

12

Bernard and Marie-Ange Laroche had been relaxed, as one gendarme put it. But freedom was not all sweetness and light. Marie-Ange was now out of work. Just before her arrest, she had received a registered letter from Gérardmer in which the *Société Vosgienne de Profilage* duly informed her that she had had to be replaced because of repeated absences. It was all because she had taken two days to attend Grégory's funeral and to watch over the body with the parents. The company's motives were of course 'purely practical': nothing to do with the affair.

Marie-Ange had seen it all: she had been held in custody for having co-operated in Grégory's death and was now unemployed for having mourned it.

At Profilage, Marie-Ange earned 4,200 francs a month, like Christine Villemin: the minimum wage. She spent her day at the soldering table, hitting the pedal an average of 500 times an hour to keep up with the rhythm. And so it had been for twelve years, since she was sixteen. Marie-Ange had soon forgotten her modest dream of working in a department store. The opportunity had come and gone.

Now there would be no more morning shifts, no more coaches to catch at 4.15 a.m. Now, because jobs were hard to find, there would be nothing. No one had lifted a finger to protest against the management decision.

As for Bernard, he was still the number one suspect, and everyone knew it. He made no attempt to hide the fact. When interviewed by the radio, his declaration was resigned, and strangely askew: 'I have nothing to feel guilty about. I think the experts must have made a mistake. So has everyone else. But I have to admit that the gendarmes still have their eyes on me.' Laroche sounded neither angered not traumatised. He spoke slowly, calmly, as if he were absent from the events he had just experienced. Absent, or resigned. For some, Laroche's resignation stemmed from centuries of servility as peasant and, now, industrial labourer. Others would find more sinister motives. Where was the just anger of the wronged man?

Laroche claimed he had never been envious of the Villemins: on the contrary, he appreciated them as good neighbours. And Marie-Ange added, with a touch of aggression in her voice: 'I really can't see why we should have been jealous of the Villemins or of Jean-Marie.' The idea was like an insult to her.

By now, though, French television seemed to have invented all sorts of reasons. The lightning arrest and release of Laroche had whipped up public curiosity into a fresh new froth. A visiting crew had presented the Villemins as a kind of Vosgien mafia, with the flashy and suspiciously wealthy Jean-Marie embroiled in decades of murky family dealings. The press spoke of '*Omertà* in the Vosges'. For Albert Villemin, it was all deeply wounding. 'Sometimes, when I think of all the venom people have spat out on us, I can't help wondering if my poor little Grégory isn't better off where he is.'

Once again, Jean-Marie found himself repeating his list of dec-laimers. He and Christine lived quietly: 'Outings are just in the family.' They never went to the cinema, restaurant or café – except once, in Epinal, three days before Grégory was killed. Where was the glamour? And as for all this clan business: 'If there really was a clan or a secret, we wouldn't have needed the police and everything would already have been sorted out.' The speech was worth learning off by heart.

The anger of Jean-Marie's outburst soon gave way to sorrow. There was a catch in his throat as he remembered his escapades with Grégory. Taking the Honda bike, the two of them would go scram-bling in the forests up behind Paremont. Grégory was already a fearless rider, and the relationship with his father was one of equals in adventure. 'If we fell,' remembered Jean-Marie, 'he used to say: we won't tell Mum, will we? And now they've gone and destroyed it all. We'll never finish the house now. The money we saved'll go to buy a beautiful tombstone for Grégory.' Paremont, 'the house of happiness', was up for sale. Their life was going into boxes.

Jean-Marie did not have the stomach for hatred on All Saints' Day. He and Christine spent 1 November remembering their dead, standing in Lepanges cemetery in the wintry air. They heard the news of the Laroches' release when they got back home. There was no anger, but no room for reconciliation either. 'We know he didn't do it, but we'll never see him again. This thing'll always come between us. We just don't have it in us. I don't suppose they do either.'

Laroche's release was no surprise, but it brought back the ever-present fear. Jacqueline Villemin was even thinking of leaving the Vosges. 'The Crow is lying in wait for us. You'll see, he'll pick off the Villemin family one by one and they'll never find him.'

An ashen lull seemed to have come over the affair. Judge Lambert was considering going to his parents' home in the Loire valley to get away from the heavy air of the Vologne. Time to think about his next step. Time to let a bit of scar tissue form among the Laroches, Bolles and Villemins. Jean-Marie and Christine had the same idea. In Aumont-zey, the atmosphere had become unbearable with all the talk of Laroche. On Friday, Jean-Marie had a heated row with Michel. Jean-Marie was trying to imagine how Laroche could have been the Crow. It was Michel who saw most of Laroche. He and his big mouth could have been responsible for giving Laroche all the information he used in his calls. It made no difference that Laroche was no longer the Crow. Michel still talked too much, and the two brothers' prickly relationship was enough to do the rest.

Jean-Marie felt he couldn't trust his family, and that was final. So he and Christine told Sesmat they were going to stay with Christine's sister Danielle in Nitting for the weekend.

The gendarmes continued their probing. Marie-Ange Laroche's alibis looked pretty secure, but there was plenty of room for doubt where Bernard was concerned. It was true that Zonca had confirmed the meeting he and Laroche had arranged for the late afternoon of 16 October, but Zonca had been very vague. And no one had seen Laroche outside Zonca's place, or on his way there.

As for other witnesses, Louisette and Chantal Jacob were disqualified by their mental handicaps. Judge Lambert had tried talking to them but was defeated by their poor articulation and heavy Vosgien accents. The gendarmes knew that Muriel adored her brother-in-law: you couldn't expect her to condemn him just like that. However, poring over her deposition from 1 November, they noticed an interesting contradiction. In Laroche's version, Muriel had been sitting in front of the television when he returned to Louisette's place. In Muriel's version, the roles had been reversed: now Laroche was watching TV, and eating ravioli, and she was the one coming home.

Was this a kind of dyslexia of the memory? If so, then Muriel had serious problems. Three of her schoolmates had told the gendarmes that she had not been on the school bus that evening, and the driver shared their conviction. With her flamboyant mane of ginger hair, Muriel was the kind of person you noticed. Besides, two other classmates had seen her going up to a car parked outside the school. It was a khaki-green vehicle. A Peugeot 305? Yes, that was it. The man at the wheel also answered to the description of Bernard Laroche. It seemed, too, that Muriel had given herself away. When the gendarmes asked her to describe the coach driver, she had pictured a young man with a beard and a moustache: Monsieur Chassel. Unfortunately, the driver on duty that evening was Monsieur Galmiche. And he looked as different from Chassel as innocence does from guilt.

At 9.30 a.m. on Friday, 2 November, the gendarmes drove to Laveline to take Muriel Bolle back to their headquarters for questioning. She was left in an interview room with Adjudant Lamirand and two constables.

'So tell us what happened on the afternoon of 16 October.'

Muriel was nervous.

'Well, like I said, I took the school bus. As usual. I got off at the *Crédit Agricole* stop in Aumontzey and I went to Louisette's place. Bernard was there.'

And so it went on. The same answers. Now it was one in the afternoon. The gendarmes decided to get out the big stick. It was obviously no good trying to sweet-talk people like this: they did not understand such language.

'Muriel, you weren't on that school bus . . . You wouldn't want to lie, now, would you? Do you know what it means, complicity in a murder?'

The self-assurance of a fifteen-year-old confronted with four uniformed representatives of the law is a fragile thing.

'Well . . . Well . . . '

'Where were you Muriel?'

'I was . . . '

'With Bernard Laroche?'

' . . . Yes.'

Muriel had cracked. Suddenly, Muriel Bolle was confessing, talking in tongues. The gendarmes typed.

'No, I didn't take the school bus as I told you last time. I lied. Bernard came to fetch me outside school in Bruyères, at about five. "Get in, Bouboule," he said.'

Her brother-in-law called her Bouboule because of her chunky, round features.

'Then what happened?'

'We drove on.'

'To Lépanges?'

'Yes. We passed by that factory – Cipa, and then we went through Champ-le-Duc. Then we took the steep road to Lépanges and stopped. I could see two houses. One roof was higher than the other.'

'And the boy?'

'I didn't recognise him – he was wearing a hat. Bernard got out and told me to keep an eye on Bibiche – that's Sébastien . . . He said "It's Popov and Sébastien". Bernard was very nice with him.'

'And then they got in the car?'

'Yes.'

'And then?'

'We drove off.'

'Down?'

'Down the hill, near a bridge. We stopped and then drove on. It was very fast. Then we stopped.'

'You got out?'

'No.'

'But Bernard did, didn't he? He got out with the boy and he came back alone, didn't he Muriel?'

' . . . Yes, that's it. I didn't see where they went. Bernard came back alone. I thought he'd taken him to someone – someone to look after him. I was playing with Sébastien in the back . . . '

'Is that all, Muriel?'

'Yes.'

'All right.'

This was manna for the gendarmes. They had been expecting something like it, but nothing as precise and complete. As soon as the confession started, they phoned Captain Sesmat. Sesmat came immediately and had Muriel repeat her statement.

'You realise what you're saying, don't you?'

'Yes.'

Sesmat felt satisfied; Muriel's attitude was impressive. Now he got on the phone to Lambert. However, the judge could not come to Bruyères immediately. He would hear whatever Muriel had to say on Monday morning.

With that, the gendarmes set up a bed for their precious ward. Let her sleep on what she had said before asking her to confirm it in the morning. Then they would take her back to Laveline. As for her own role in the murder, there was no question of bringing any charges. At the time, Muriel can't have known what was going on; when she did, she must have been petrified at the consequences of saying what she knew, and anxious to protect her brother-in-law. That was natural enough. As Louisette said: 'She's a nice girl Muriel, she gets on well with Bernard.' In such a predicament, you could hardly expect an adolescent not to panic. Muriel had needed time to come out with the truth.

The next morning, Muriel had the obligatory medical check-up after her twenty-five hours of custody. When the gendarmes drove her back to Rue de Maroc, Bernard and Marie-Ange were there with the rest of the family. They said nothing. Laroche just looked at them with his big, soulful eyes. A little surprised. But everyone knew where Muriel had been. Her father had even come to the gendarmerie to see what was going on. He had been given a friendly, if not informative reception by the duty officer; 'It's not as if we're torturing her, is it!' And that was it. The family had no reason to suspect anything.

'Leave her in peace for a while.' As they gave their parting advice to the Bolles, the gendarmes knew that the end was in sight. They would soon have their child murderer. And, with a bit of luck, Muriel would not get into too much trouble with her family: Marie-Ange and Bernard would leave her alone. After all, Muriel was hardly the first key witness in the case. And Laroche was already expecting trouble, with or without his sister-in-law. When Marie-Ange had gone to Ancel to tell him his Muriel was being held in Bruyères for questioning, he hadn't registered even the mildest surprise. There was obviously nothing to worry about, she concluded. The gendarmes' insistence was just something to be endured. Why complicate things with hatred or simply hostility. After all, as Bernard had said on 2 November, the day after he was released: 'The gendarmes were perfectly decent with me. They even wished me a good weekend.'

That weekend was now coming to a close. On Sunday, Bernard Laroche came out onto his porch to speak to the journalists who were waiting there with their tape recorders and cameras. A weary, disabused smile playing about his face, Laroche rehearsed his blunt argument: 'The experts are mistaken.' And the resigned acknowledgement: 'Yes, I know they'll be back to get me.' And then he retired to watch television. It had been an ordinary Sunday: a family lunch followed by a walk in the woods. Laroche seemed the only person not to sense the tension.

He was not the only one to anticipate his arrest. Word had spread all around the valley. Jacky Villemin knew, but he wasn't giving anything anyway. As usual, he enjoyed tantalising the journalists who came to talk to him in Granges at 10.30 a.m. His face rough with unshaven stubble, he seemed more relaxed than before: he and Liliane were relieved at the prospect of regaining their full innocence. 'At last we'll be able to breathe. I know who did it, why and how. You'll see.'

On Monday morning, in Bruyères, a Parisian journalist was buying his newspapers when the seller volunteered the information: 'They're going to arrest him at work today. Seven gendarmes will go and take him.' The local version of the bush telegraph was working at peak capacity. More intoxication, perhaps.

In Bruyères, there was no sign of activity at the gendarmerie. That morning, Jean-Marie and Christine Villemin paid a visit to Etienne Sesmat after their short break in Nitting. Sesmat said nothing, just handed them a pair of bibles that had been donated by an elderly sympathiser. The accompanying inscription said: 'Those receiving this bible will find their problems are solved the very same day.'

It was quiet, too, in Aumontzey, where Bernard Laroche's house was locked and the shutters drawn. The same calm reigned at Albert and Monique's home, a few minutes away, and in Laveline Bernard's family-in-law had gone off to work, as usual.

At 9.00 a.m. that same morning, Jean-Jacques Lecomte appeared before the journalists gathered outside the *Palais de Justice* in Epinal. Would he be 'concluding'? 'I don't know, I don't know. But stay around, you never can tell.' Lecomte was on edge. He mopped his brow. Something of the same nervousness had taken over Judge Lambert, who was puffing on a cigarillo. The two men were waiting for Muriel to come and repeat her declaration.

The young redhead arrived a quarter of an hour later, escorted by the gendarmes. She seemed calm. Would she deliver?

Muriel did deliver. Exactly what she told the gendarmes on Friday.

'You understand what this means, don't you Muriel?'

The girl did not flinch for one moment. Muriel was no genius, but, thought Lambert, she is no fool. She knew what she was doing. When Lambert and Muriel left the magistrates' offices, the judge had an arrest warrant in his pocket.

At 11.00 a.m., Lambert and Muriel were in the back of a police car, followed by a convoy of squad cars. The red-headed adolescent was re-enacting her journey. They started at the Lycée Jean Lurçat where Bernard Laroche had come to pick her up. From there, they drove to Paremont, stopping by the pile of gravel where Grégory had been playing. Then, on to the post office in Lépanges, where the Crow had posted his murder note. Finally, Muriel 'guided' the gendarmes to Docelles, where the Barba flows into the Vologne, behind the firemen's barracks. In fact, she could not remember the route exactly, it had all happened so quickly: but she knew this was the right place.

'Is that it, Muriel?'

'Yes.'

And so on.

Throughout this exercise, Muriel seemed almost detached as she indicated the route to Lambert. Her statements exactly confirmed the route imagined by the investigators. It all fitted, was almost too good to be true. 'If she retracts,' sighed Lambert, 'then the whole thing will be ruined.'

Meanwhile, Marie-Ange had gone to Ancel again to warn her husband that her kid sister was back with the gendarmes. Laroche just shrugged. Laroche thought they were mistaken, but what could he do about it?

The squad cars arrived in Granges just before 12.30 p.m., followed by journalists and TV crews. They drew up outside the ugly mill built by Prosper Ancel in the mid nineteenth century. They were expected. Bernard Laroche was in his blue boiler suit when the gendarmes came to take him in. He stopped his work, and wiped the oil from his hands with a cloth. He knew, and his colleagues knew too. The silence in the workshop was as thick as rumour. Tentatively, almost with embarrass-ment, colleagues walked up to shake Laroche's hand and reassure him that they would never doubt his innocence. They did not know if they would ever see him again.

Outside, there were the seven men in uniform and the squad cars. Captain Sesmat slipped on the handcuffs and one of the gendarmes told Laroche: 'I was sure it was you because the first time I saw you you said "The bastard who did that deserves to be hanged."'

Laroche went quietly, surrounded by camera crews. He was frown-ing. He understood that the gendarmes were doing their duty, just as he would. Besides, what else could he do? As a candidate in the last local elections, Laroche was a believer in civil obedience.

Laroche was driven to Epinal's gendarmerie for further question-ing before they took him on to the magistrate's office. There Marie-Ange was answering Judge Lambert's final questions about her own knowledge of the affair. For Bernard Laroche's wife, it was merely a question of clearing up a few formalities.

It was 3.45 p.m. when suspect number one was bundled out of the police vehicle outside the *Palais de Justice*. There were 400 people there to see the 'assassin', the 'swine' who had slaughtered an innocent and made a mockery of a decent community. They had had ample time to assemble: the radios had all spoken of Laroche's arrest in their lunchtime bulletins. The thrusting of the microphones and popping of cameras made Laroche blink: he was exposed to the vengeful eyes of the public, deprived of the customary coat or sweater to hide his face, but he was too stunned or too fatalistic to want to. Published the next day, the photos of his slurred, heavy-lidded face and raised fist gave a perfect image of the child murderer.

'I'm innocent!' Laroche still had it in him to protest, but his voice was clouded with sobbing as he was led indoors to be charged with infanticide. 'I'm innocent!'

The words that followed cannot easily be rendered in English. '*On ne m'a pas mis dans le coup.*' This can mean either 'I wasn't told about it,' or 'I had nothing to do with it.' But the first is the more obvious meaning, and it left a lot of questions. If Laroche had not been told, then who should have told him? A gang, perhaps, the other killers? Was Laroche ignorant of the whole abduction and killing, or just the killing? The words suggested the thought that Bernard Laroche had participated without knowing what the end result would be. That might explain the statement 'I think the experts were mistaken.' In other words, Laroche had meant 'They were nearly right.'

But who can tell what a man is thinking when he is about to be imprisoned for infanticide?

As the doors of the *Palais* closed, two gendarmes took up guard to ward off the press – and to hold back the lynch-mob. And yet, while some of them had shouted at the assassin, others had been surprised to find that the child murderer and telephone terrorist was such a bearish, harmless-looking creature. Well, of course, that was how he had taken everyone in? As one national daily asked of the 'innocent' Marie-Ange: 'Did she have the slightest idea that she was living with a monster'.

Or, as a local paper put it, the operation was 'a victory for youth'. Sesmat and Lambert could blush with pleasure.

Now, with the monster behind bars, the Vologne could get back to normal life, and nothing is more normal than watching TV. That night the national networks opened their news bulletin with a special report. It showed the images of Bernard Laroche being arrested. Next came the American presidential election.

13

With its roots in Catholicism, French law is much attached to confessions. However, unless he underwent a sudden change of heart and mind, Bernard Laroche looked unlikely to oblige. The monster of Aumontzey continued to protest his innocence and Jean-Michel Lambert was left to speculation. 'The motive was probably jealousy,' he concluded, 'but that's only a deduction, since Laroche continues to deny his guilt.' Not that the judge was worried. 'I've got enough in the dossier to have a clear conscience.'

The gendarmes had their suspect, and that was the best possible answer they could give their detractors. But it would not be easy to conclude. 'This bloke held out for three years in the company of people he was torturing by phone. And then he endured another three weeks after the murder, without ever giving himself away. He'll never confess.' So ran local opinion.

People felt a mixture of relief and surprise, or just plain amazement. In Aumontzey, Laroche's neighbours and friends were staggered. 'You see,' said one woman, 'Bernard was something of an idol here.' He was a gentle, timid man, Bernard, and a respected employee. 'A calm man,' said the director of Ancel, 'who was on good terms with everybody.' Jacky Villemin had every reason to be relieved but 'If it is Bernard,' he said 'then all I can say is that you can be spotless on the outside and black on the inside.' The same old story. And yet when Jacky heard Laroche's voice over the radio on 1 November he was sure it was the Crow's.

Albert was at a loss. 'I just don't know what to say,' he stammered. 'For twenty years I went cutting wood with his father Marcel.' The frail fifty-year-old felt an abyss opening between the present and the certainties of his past existence. 'I thought of him as a brother. I'll never be able to trust anyone again. He even bought some flowers for Grégory's tomb.' Typically, Monique Villemin's disbelief was tempered by more practical considerations: 'He belonged to our family as a kid. But we're relieved. Now we know, at last.' Monique trusted the investigators. Like the mayor of Aumontzey, for whom Bernard was the last person he would have considered, she just wanted to get things over with. Especially since the indignation of Bernard's family-in-law might break out into violence. Lucien Bolle was already threatening to chase off journalists with his gun. The Bolle family had been grievously betrayed, and their vengeance, like their rage, threatened to be blind. Everyone knew that the family in Rue de Maroc was, well, rather wild. The salt of the earth, of course, but the stone-throwing, gun-toting variety. They were people you had to shout at to make yourself heard. You could see it in their thick, heavy-jowled features. Reason had a limited place in their existences.

Marie-Ange Laroche alternated between anger and stupefaction. She remembered her visit to Bernard on the day of his arrest, when the news of Muriel's presence at the *Palais de Justice* left him as calm as ever. Surely, then, he had nothing on his conscience? 'I won't say anything to my sister Muriel until I know what happened. Bernard couldn't hurt a fly. He's always been unlucky. The Crow has to make a sign. Anonymously, of course, as he usually does. He has to do it to prove Bernard is innocent.' The appeal was so naïve it would have been comic in any other situation.

When Jean-Marie Villemin heard the news of Laroche's arrest over the radio, he put his hands on his head and kept repeating 'Why, why did he do it?' But now he had jumped from disbelief to absolute certainty. Jean-Marie had never been one to sit on fences. Doubt was poison to him, and Muriel's statement had forced him to renounce his previous opinion. 'I don't rule out more surprises in the affair,' he admitted, but he had found the keystone of his conviction: Bernard Laroche's 'bad luck'. As Jean-Marie saw things, Laroche had destroyed everything out of envy for his cousin's success and happiness: 'It was like night and day, my boy and his. And then we made a better couple than him and Marie-Ange. All of a sudden, it just exploded, and he's the only one who can explain it.' To Jean-Marie, Laroche's sympathy with the losers in the family now looked like the effect of his own past. It was a kind of alliance, born of bitterness not generosity. In Laroche's mind, Louisette and Chantal were the comforting proof of the Villemins and the Jacobs' corruption. Laroche had manipulated things. 'He's the one who used Muriel as a false alibi,' he insisted. It was because of Michel that Bernard knew every detail of our daily life, the ones the Crow used to frighten us . . . We'll never forget, nor forgive. They've got to bring back capital punishment. The killer of our little one has to be condemned to death.'

In Lépanges cemetery, a plaque had been removed from Grégory's tomb. 'To our dear cousin,' it said, 'From the Laroches.'

Jean-Marie was not the only one calling for the death penalty. The day after Laroche was arrested a petition was started calling for its reintroduction – although, as Henri Garaud pointed out, even if capital punishment were brought back, Laroche could not be condemned since his crime had been committed under a different regime. Nevertheless, Jean-Marie Villemin needed to imagine an absolute punishment to symbolise the justice for which he thirsted. 'If I'd known earlier, I'd have gone to get him myself,' he said. He had already tried with his own brother. But Jacky was forgotten now.

Bernard Laroche was taken to Charles III prison in Nancy. A dour brick building from the nineteenth century. There, he was greeted by cries of 'Assassin' and 'The killer in the Vologne. Kill him!' Prisoners have a strict code of ethics, and child murders are far beyond its pale. Those in Epinal had threatened to lynch 'the monster of the Vologne' if ever he was locked up within their walls. Nancy would be safer, if only because it was further away. Laroche would be protected from the hatred welling up in the Vologne.

It was Bernard Laroche's employer, Ancel, who set about finding him some form of legal protection. Their choice fell upon an associate of the Communist trade union, the *Confédération Générale du Travail*, of which Laroche was an exemplary member. Paul Prompt was a Parisian barrister and specialist in labour law. He also happened to be a friend of the director of Ancel's holding company. Prompt was renowned for his sharp-tongued vehemence and it was no secret that his social and political opinions were in total conflict with those of Henri Garaud, barrister to the *partie civile*. The case was acquiring a political subtext – political and personal too: Henri Garaud had recently represented the *partie civile* in proceedings against Prompt's son-in-law. The young man had been prosecuted for his role in violent demonstrations. And Garaud had pushed for maximum penalties.

Never one to shirk a good fight, Prompt was eager to accept the case. It would make a change from all that labour law. Besides, his wife was a *Vosgienne*, so the work would be bringing him close to her roots.

Prompt's first move was to appoint a local associate to deal with the case on a daily basis. His chosen partner, Gérard Welzer, was another young man like Lambert and Sesmat (or Laroche, or Jean-Marie Villemin), an ambitious twenty-nine-year-old whose social and professional ambitions were mirrored in the white Porsche he drove around Epinal, and whose success had made him France's youngest practising barrister. But Welzer had to swallow hard. Not every potential client would approve of him defending a child murderer. However, after a first visit to Laroche in Nancy on 6 November, he declared, 'I went expecting to find some kind of primitive character but instead I found a man just like you and me, a man protesting his innocence with striking and surprising sincerity.' Laroche was convinced that his truth would soon come to light. He was 'withdrawn, but at peace with himself'. Welzer had been roused by his new cause.

The young barrister would soon feel his position strengthened. It started with a point of procedure.

Jean-Michel Lambert had a reputation for being extremely scrupulous about bringing charges. Although Muriel's statement was sufficiently strong as a basis for arraigning Laroche, the girl was nevertheless a minor and her mother Jeannine needed to sign her statement for it to be fully valid. For a minor is not bound by oath: they can say anything, and it is easier to make them say what you want to hear. Lambert reasoned that if the girl had confirmed her interview on Monday, after spending the weekend with her family, then she wouldn't retract now.

On Tuesday evening Muriel arrived in Epinal with Jeannine Bolle. This time they had come under their own steam. Lambert read back to her the statement she made to him the day before. But this time, he found himself up against a wall of emotional refusal. 'I broke down. The gendarmes told me Bernard had admitted he'd come to fetch me at school. But I never went with him to Docelles, where they found Grégory . . . I was on the school bus at quarter past five . . . My brother-in-law is innocent. He was watching the TV at Louisette's place with Sébastien. It's the gendarmes who forced me to change my statement. They threatened me with borstal if I didn't tell them what they wanted.'

Muriel had retracted.

Was it the pressure from her family, or the simple presence of her mother? Had Marie-Ange threatened her? The Bolles' neighbours had their opinion. Muriel had spent the night of 5 November crying under the apple tree in her parents' unkempt garden. That at least was what a carpenter living next door told the gendarmes. The idea certainly fitted with the Bolles' reputation. They were excitable people. By way of illustration, on 6 November, one of Muriel's brothers threatened a journalist from the *Parisien Libéré* with a gun while another urged him to shoot. Muriel just managed to stop them.

Now Muriel was as dogged in her denial as she had seemed calm during the reconstruction of the events of 16 October. It was as if the fifteen-year-old had chosen obstinacy as the only way of dealing with the conflicting pressures around her. On one side, the Bolles, on the other the gendarmes: two forms of violence. She sounded like the slow-witted pupil who gives an answer she doesn't understand just to avoid the teacher's anger.

Muriel was impenetrable, an enigma. No one knew how much they could believe, or how aware she was of what she was saying. Muriel was an awkward, boyish young woman at an awkward age. At school, she was one of the best pupils in her class, but then the level was low in the CES, specialised education centre. Teachers described her as 'an alert child, but aggressive towards her classmates. A difficult character, left to her own devices by her overgrown family.'

The next day, under a fine drizzle, Muriel gave a 'press conference', one of the many informal sessions that the participants in the affair conducted outside their homes: Jacky, Jean-Marie, Laroche, and now her, the latest media star of the Vologne. She was pale, her face puffy and marked with lack of sleep, her appearance made all the more mournful by her black sweater and trousers. Marie-Ange was in attendance, too, along with Muriel's other brothers and sisters. Each question was repeated a dozen times with false spontaneity as the journalists secured their sound bite. 'Muriel, were you threatened? Muriel, were you threatened? Muriel, were you threatened?' etc. Muriel looked awkward, not sure whether to snigger or cry. 'The gendarmes told me Bernard had admitted that he'd come to fetch me at school, that I had to talk . . . ' Then came the same version of the facts: the school bus, the ravioli, the television, Sébastien. 'One of the gendarmes started shouting and I got afraid. No, Bernard didn't do it! They have to give us Bernard back!' Muriel had become the spokesperson for the entire Bolle family. And she had her prompters. 'Don't forget to tell them the gendarmes accused you of sleeping with Bernard!' whispered one sister. Muriel was silent, she flushed. Then out came a torrent of protestations. 'I'm a minor . . . only fifteen . . . ' (She had been mugging up on legal procedure.) 'They just put the words in my mouth . . . Grégory, I don't even know him!' And now Marie-Ange joined in, unable to hold back any longer: 'Bernard's not guilty, because we love each other. It's not him, because I adore him.' It was the logic of the heart: the head was becoming a no go area.

The two sisters were using whatever came to hand to push back the *fait accompli* of Laroche's arrest. Not all of it was useful. As Monique Villemin would later confirm, Muriel had babysat for Jean-Marie and Christine. She did know Grégory. Was the adolescent deliberately lying, or just blindly rejecting a reality she found unbearable?

In fact, Lambert had been half expecting a denial from the young woman all along. He remained convinced that Muriel had told him the truth; his 'intimate conviction', which in French law is considered adequate grounds for an examining judge to bring charges, remained intact. 'There's enough in the dossier for me not to give much attention to Muriel's declarations.' The testimonies of Muriel's schoolmates were there to back him up. They were adamant that she had not been on the coach on 16 October. 'I'd have noticed her red hair if she was,' said one. And two others mentioned the car that had picked her up. 'We always remember because we feel frightened when cars stop outside the school.' The coach driver, too, was categorical. It was said the gendarmes had recorded a phone call from Laroche to Muriel in which he demanded that she be his alibi. One magazine published an article quoting Laroche as asking the Villemins, 'I don't have a double personality, do I?'

'If anyone's been putting any pressure on Muriel,' insisted Lambert, 'it's the family, not the gendarmes.' Muriel had been fully aware of the implications of her testimony against Bernard Laroche; he had taken all the necessary precautions. 'I told her that if she was lying it wouldn't count against her.' Muriel had had the whole weekend to think about it, but had not gone back on her statement until Laroche was arrested: 'You have to remember, at fifteen years of age, one is very easily influenced.'

If Muriel did accompany Laroche on his infanticidal drive with Grégory, she can hardly have been ignorant of its significance. She would have spent nearly three weeks with a tortured conscience. Muriel was not the kind of girl who hides such feelings. One of her teachers at Bruyères commented that 'She seemed careworn to me at the time: I tried to talk with her but she was evasive.' With Laroche in prison, Muriel's distress was manifest. Twice, she had tried to throw herself in front of a train. Her mother and sister had just managed to prevent her.

And Muriel was humiliated, too. Jeannine Bolle took the gendarmes' insinuations about her relations with Laroche as an insult to her motherhood. 'Shame on them! I'm going to take her for a medical inspection, then we'll see.' Muriel had become an object in a tug-of-war.

The investigators were hoping she would come out with the truth on 9 November, when she would be brought face to face with Bernard Laroche in Epinal. It was a slim hope, and one that Jean-Marie Lambert took care not to over-indulge. He knew Muriel would be coached for the occasion. He knew too that Laroche's lawyers would be doing their utmost to weaken the case against their client. Before the meeting, Prompt spoke out against the proceedings so far – or rather, against Garaud: 'This case has been manipulated by the party to the prosecution. As for me, I'm no detective or recruiter of witnesses.' Things were warming up.

Epinal still bristled with the aggression that had surrounded Laroche's arrest. So did the Vologne, so much so that Abbé Herriot of Saint-Dié, the local diocese, had made a statement appealing for calm.

'When will the hasty judgements cease, the rash words that hurt, the suspicion that undermines confidence, destroys people and threatens to poison our social relationships for many years. It is time to call a halt.'

Epinal had become the national hot spot for the law and order lobby. Bernard Manovelli, a lawyer and failed candidate from the recent local elections in Marseille, had come up north for the occasion to campaign for the reintroduction of the death penalty. He was outside the magistrates' court, handing out tracts. Jean-Marie Villemin was there too, wearing dark glasses to avoid photographers and looking like some kind of masked avenger as he cruised around the *Palais de Justice* in his car. He had come to see if Laroche would crack, but he was also on the lookout for tell-tale signs from anxious accomplices.

Marie-Ange was there of course, hoping desperately that she would be able to see her husband and still overwhelmed with anger – and fear: the death threats had started. 'It's Muriel who did it all,' she asserted bitterly. 'Bernard and I have been married ten years. If he'd killed the little one I would have known about it. I swear I never noticed anything out of the ordinary.' It sounded as if she were still trying to ward off doubt.

Muriel was the first to arrive. She hurried in, chaperoned by Jeannine: Muriel was not to be exposed, but she was to be certified. Mme Bolle had kept her word. 'I personally took her to a gynaecologist in Gérardmer to have her examined. She's a hundred per cent virgin, is Muriel. And we have a certificate to prove it, which I've given to the barristers.' Jeannine Bolle took things too much to heart.

A few minutes later, Bernard Laroche was whisked past the waiting crowd. He had ridden from Nancy in a covered van. He had been given a close shave and looked ready for a Sunday outing in grey jacket and grey flannel trousers. As soon as she saw her husband, Marie-Ange rushed forward to embrace him; but the gendarmes pushed her away. She spent the next six hours in a state of nervous tension outside the big waiting-room where the meeting was being held: Lambert's office was too small.

But was it worth it? Apart from the fact that Garaud and Prompt almost came to blows, the result of the confrontation was thoroughly predictable. Muriel stuck to her position and Laroche reiterated his version of events. 'I was supposed to meet Zonca at 4.30 p.m. I waited at home and then went to look for him in Granges. It was 5.00 p.m. I nearly crashed into a Volkswagen Golf GTI. Zonca wasn't there. Then I went back to Louisette's. It was 5.15 p.m. She heated up a tin of ravioli and Chantal arrived from Saint-Dié. She works in a centre for the handicapped. Then Muriel came from the school coach. I left for Bruyères with Sébastien to go and get the wine. I arrived at Champion at about quarter to six. At about six, I went to the betting counter to pick up some *tiercé* winnings: 160 francs.

Prompt and Welzer requested that Laroche's alibis be summoned to Epinal. First among them was Pierre Zonca. Zonca was notorious among his friends for missing meetings. He confirmed Laroche's claims: yes, they were supposed to meet at 4.30 p.m., and yes, he had been delayed. In fact, the fine weather had encouraged him to go and help a friend pack some animal fodder in his silos: 'I remembered that Bernard often took his siesta at that time, so I didn't want to take the risk of waking him up with a phone call.'

Zonca agreed with Laroche. Perhaps he had a bad memory. Three days earlier, he had told the gendarmes that he and Laroche had made no firm arrangement to go to Champion on 16 October. 'If we had,' he said, 'I'd never have gone to do the ensilage with my friend.'

Laroche's account was also confirmed by the check-out girls at the Champion supermarket, although they couldn't give an exact time, and his cheque was traced. Finally, Julia Collomb, whose *Hôtel de la Renaissance* doubled up as a betting counter (and now a journalists' centre of operations), finally brought herself to remember someone coming late for their winnings. Whether or not it was Laroche, she was less sure.

Laroche's alibis had all come up trumps. Or rather, none of them had failed. Only the owner of the blue Golf had failed to respond to the gendarmes' appeal for testimony.

At the end of the evening, Prompt and Welzer came out to make a joint declaration: 'The events are of such gravity that we will be issuing a written statement. The only handwriting analysis to have been consulted points to someone other than our client.'

So far so good. Except for one minor detail. Discounting Muriel, none of Laroche's alibis could clear him for the crucial time between

5.00 p.m. and 5.30 p.m. As for the handwriting analysis, Welzer and Prompt were referring to Antoine Argoud, the former Colonel and now expert attached to the court of Nancy. He it was who had analysed the 140-plus dictation scripts gathered on and after 18 October. Argoud had strong grounds for believing that the Crow and 'X' were one. But no one was talking about 'X', because, 'X', alias Roger Jacquel, had been cleared weeks ago.

Since then, of course, further dictations had been given and further analyses made by Mesdames Jacquin-Keller and Berrichon-Seyden. But their reports had not been officially incorporated into the investigators' dossier, and could not therefore be used. Nor had the opinions of a gendarme and expert called Klein. Klein had very definitely designated Laroche, but he was not the investigation's official graphologist, only an adviser. Moreover, although the two women had communicated their preliminary conclusions to the gendarmes, and to Chaillan in particular, and Chaillan had assured Lambert that they had designated Laroche, what they said about suspect number one was much less black and white. For Berrichon-Seyden, 'It could be him. It's only a personal opinion and therefore rather insubstantial if not backed up by some other elements of the investigation.' Jacquin-Keller was also reserved. 'The work is slow and painstaking. I would prefer to give up and am returning all the exhibits to you.'

This was hardly the tone of unshakeable conviction. Worse, Jacquin-Keller would later complain of harassment by the gendarmes. They had been pressing her to yield a conclusion that her professional conscience was not ready to hatch.

Everything rested on Muriel. Muriel, and an intimate conviction.

Now the gendarmes had to strengthen their case against Laroche. They were in possession of a handwritten technical report made by Laroche on 15 October, and were awaiting the results of the analysis by a forensic laboratory in Wiesbaden of the note of 16 October. It was expected to confirm the imprint of Laroche's initials on the claim note. If it did, then it would be impossible to deny his connection with the Crow.

Meanwhile, there was plenty for the excitable bystander to get his teeth into. As Bernard Laroche was driven off into the night, a cohort of militants from the capital punishment lobby ran after the police van with raised fists shouting 'Death to Laroche'. They left Jean-Michel Lambert to consider Welzer and Prompt's appeal for the release of their client and to pore over the anonymous help letters that were trickling into his office. One of the writers had been looking over the funeral photos and advised the judge to arrest 'the man with the harsh face and pointed nose – obviously a cruel type.' It was Jean-Marie Villemin.

14

In the Vosges, opinion remained as divided as the tension was strong. 'If they free him, they'll be getting their guns out in the Vologne.' Thus ran the general feeling: a showdown was in the offing. Maybe word had got around about Jean-Marie's visit to Sain-Dié the day after the confrontation. For 2,990 francs, he had bought himself a riot gun to replace the rifle confiscated by the gendarmes.

The revenge faction was increasingly active. The petition circulated by the Marseille lawyer, Bernard Manovelli, had been a success. Henri Garaud found himself in the difficult position of having to cool the ardour of the more excitable elements in *Légitime Défense*. It was becoming increasingly appropriate that this right-wing figure should have opposite him a lawyer working for the Communist CGT, Prompt, and another who had close sympathies with the Socialist party, Welzer. The Little Grégory affair was becoming a touchstone for defining your personality. In France, there were *les gens de gauche* and *les gens de droite*. On the right, Jean-Marie, the acquisitive, outspoken individualist; on the left, Laroche, the union man, family man, victim of the gendarmes. The election of the country's first Socialist government in decades had aggravated this political self-consciousness; and the abolition of capital punishment had made violent crime one of its touchstones. Jean-Marie Le Pen, leader of the extreme right-wing National Front party, would take ample advantage of the issue at a rally in Epinal on 15 November: the deadline for Lambert's decision on Laroche's appeal.

Nationally, too, the Little Grégory affair had become a symbol for law and order campaigners. One future presidential candidate, Raymond Barre, had already linked Laroche's arrest and his own support for capital punishment during a television interview. And while the mayor of Epinal, Philippe Séguin, attacked the 'half-baked sociology' used by certain media in their treatment of the case, a mixed group of politicians from the Vosges formally urged the government to ensure that the perpetrator of Grégory's death be punished with 'the severest sentence possible', and without the smallest chance of parole.

All of which made many people forget that Bernard Laroche was, until proven guilty, innocent. Perhaps the French word for bringing charges, *inculpation*, had something to do with it. It contains too clear an echo of the word for guilt: *culpabilité*. Bernard Laroche had been *inculpé*, or struck with guilt. Besides, if the judge could justify arresting him, he had to be guilty.

The arrest had done anything but ease the pressure. Anonymous letter-writing flourished. Some correspondents claimed to know the identity of the Crow, others threatened to kill the examining judge: 'I'll slit your belly,' promised one. And on Monday 12 November, the gendarmes found their task being complicated further by the arrival of a letter claiming the murder: they had to check, even if most of the details it contained could have been lifted from the newspapers. At the *Palais de Justice*, Lambert had 232 written statements to examine. His concentration had to contend with the constant comings and goings of the case (interviews, meetings, reconstructions), not to mention the scores of files from other cases in progress. Serenity was a difficult art.

On 15 November, the judge formally refused to release Bernard Laroche. Naturally, Welzer and Prompt appealed. Lambert gave three main reasons for his decision. First and foremost, the investigators were still searching for Laroche's probable accomplices: the gang theory had not been abandoned. If Laroche were at liberty, he would be able to obstruct their efforts. Secondly, and predictably, the judge emphasised the risk of bloodshed. And thirdly, Lambert and the gendarmes were still waiting for those vital laboratory reports.

The investigators had thirty days before the Nancy Court of Criminal Appeal deliberated on the wisdom of releasing or retaining the prime suspect. Already Laroche's barristers had pointed out that the statements by Muriel's classmates and the coach driver were dubious because they had been taken two weeks after the crime. And then there was the suspect 'X', Argoud's deduction, whom the gendarmes had dismissed from the outset: the defence would certainly take advantage of him, if only to cast doubt on the later reports. As for Muriel, she now seemed unmovable. If you confronted her with her contradictions, she would say, 'I have a bad memory,' or if you reminded her of her classmates' statements, 'They can say what they like.' The girl was sheltered from any uncomfortable contact with her schoolfriends: Muriel had not gone back to her Centre for Specialised Education in Bruyères since 5 November.

The void of proof was filled by opinion in search of a motive. Jacky Villemin was, as usual, a voluble source. Bernard, he said, was not a violent type: 'He was even a bit of a softie. He was a great friend of Jean-Marie's, and liked Grégory a lot too.' If the two men saw each other less frequently since their marriages, he thought, 'It was because of their work, and because of their wives.' Christine, it was true, might have had a few flirtations before marriage, 'but she surely wouldn't have chosen Bernard.' 'Nanar', as they called him, was the slow, shy type, certainly not the sort to attract Christine Villemin, and certainly no great success with women. Everyone in Aumontzey knew that.

Perhaps, though, Laroche had acted because of a woman. Jean-Marie didn't exclude the possibility: 'It's no coincidence that the Crow was always going on about the chief and his stuck-up little woman. Marie-Ange couldn't bear Christine.' It was true that Christine came from a another milieu, that her aspirations were not those of the Villemin family *en bloc*. Christine stood out, and so did her mother. They looked more refined, more elegant than the Villemins, Jacobs or Bolles. It was the clothes they wore, their hair, something about their faces. One of those indefinable but unmistakable differences. In such a situation, common sense tells you to be discreet if you want to stay on good terms with your family-in-law. Christine, like her husband, was not always that prudent. As the slighted and less-fortunate cousin, Laroche could have felt stung by her pretentious ways. Or Marie-Ange by what she took to be her callousness. No doubt the Laroches had found out from Michel and Ginette what Christine said when she heard Sébastien would be starting school that autumn: 'Why don't they send him to a special place? He'd be much happier there.' It was the kind of remark that always sounded venomous at second hand. Even as condescension it was bad enough. The effect could be judged by Marie-Ange's vehemence in defence of her 'mentally handicapped' son:

'Titi is not mentally deficient. He was operated on three years ago and they put a valve in his head. You simply have to be a bit careful with him, that's all. My child is normal. Bernard is mad about his son, he's not ashamed.'

As if to substantiate the idea of a female demiurge behind the crime, rumours began going round on 16 November that a woman 'very closely related to the Villemin family is about to be charged'. The woman from outside the post office? The one whose high heels had left their imprint on the banks of the Vologne?

At 3.10 p.m. on 22 November, Christine Villemin arrived in Epinal for an interview with Judge Lambert. There, she found herself confronted with four workmates. They had all seen her on 16 October – outside or near the post office. According to the account that emerged from their individual testimonies, Christine Villemin had turned right on her way out of the factory, towards Bruyères, and Lépanges post office. Jacquot's flat was to the left. Christine Villemin's car had been seen empty outside the post office with the driver's door open. After posting a letter, said the witnesses, Christine Villemin made a half-turn and headed back into Lépanges.

Christine's answer was straightforward: 'Yes, I did drive past the post office on that day, but later. I was half mad with panic, and looking for Grégory.' Christine Villemin pointed out that her colleagues had been mistaken about her clothes. They all remembered her wearing a beige jacket. In fact, she said, the weather was so mild she only had on dungarees and a blouse: the jacket was from the day before. That day, she had posted two envelopes: a cheque to a children's clothing company, *Vert Baudet*, and an entry form for a competition (the hope of the miraculous windfall).

Christine called her workmates 'the brats'. 'Let me tell you,' she said, 'the brats sit near me all day and yet they never even speak to me. How can you expect them to remember my movements?'

When the four employees from MCV had left, Lambert turned to Christine Villemin: 'Madame,' he said. 'You are lying.'

The law of numerical superiority.

But why would Christine Villemin lie?

Of course, no charges had been made, or even threatened, but such was the atmosphere that the mere fact of Christine's interview made her look faintly suspicious. If she was not guilty of the crime, then she had at least confused the investigators. Perhaps worse. It did not take much for the gossip and backbiting of the last months to congeal into murmurs of accusation. Christine's response was her first statement to the press since 16 October. People had never considered her as anything but the grieving mother, walled up in her agony, hiding behind her supportive husband: a dreamy, self-effacing woman who read Harlequin romances and looked after her man. The sort you would expect with Jean-Marie. But Christine Villemin had a voice. 'I get the feeling that people suspect me. They're mistaken. What would I have gained? I have no kid. I have nothing.' There was a note of sarcasm, too: 'They'll have people believing that I set the whole thing up with Michel and Laroche.'

And then, to conclude, as if thinking out loud: 'I mustn't crack before Laroche confesses.'

It was only a matter of time, surely.

Christine's statement was a mistake. As *partie civile*, she was not supposed to comment on the conduct of the case. It was not a good thing to be lacking in legal etiquette.

Jean-Marie's patience was wearing thin. The whole thing was a diversion, an attempt to cloud the investigation. 'We know it's Laroche,' he insisted. There was no irrefutable material proof, but it was all coming together in his mind. 'Laroche is what we call a "dog" – the shy, silent type who is attracted to women.' You could see it in his relations with Ginette and Christine – and with Muriel too. It was a woman who had pushed him into it. Jean-Marie had been thinking back to their conversations on the phone. Laroche always left it to him to do the talking. Well, Jean-Marie knew Bernard was timid. Now, though, he realised that those harmless-sounding calls when Bernard blustered and mumbled, leaving him to make the conversation, could easily have been information-gathering exercises.

As for the murder itself, and the special knots, 'Everyone knows that Laroche was an expert on them at work'. And Jean-Marie had found a reason for Sébastien's presence in the car on 16 October as well; the boy was being used as bait.

All of which meant one thing: 'If they let Bernard Laroche out, he's a dead man.'

Jean-Marie had good reason to be obsessed with the idea of a woman accomplice. On many of the Crow's calls, the voice seemed to change from male to female, as if there were two people on the line. '*Cherchez la femme,*' as Jacky had said in one of his enigmatic moods. *Cherchez* above all Muriel. On 30 November, Judge Lambert spoke to Lucien and Jeannine Bolle about events during the crucial weeks before and after their daughter's confessions. What kind of pressure had there really been in the family? But Lambert could expect only one answer: none. The family comes before the law.

Henri Garaud could bang his fist down on the table and warn that, 'If the law can't deal with Laroche, then I will: the assassin of little Grégory shall not go unpunished.' But that did not stop one of Muriel's schoolmates being mistaken. The evening she 'had not seen' Muriel proved to be a week later than she thought: the fact could be verified by reference to family events – the day her father went in to hospital.

Now that Muriel had withdrawn her statement, it did not take much to make the case against Laroche look weak – assuming of course that you really believed in Muriel's retraction. Little things, like the fact that none of Muriel's schoolmates had heard Laroche call her Bouboule, or that Michel Cornillie did not recognise Bernard Laroche as the suspicious character in his bar. Either way, you had to take a leap of faith.

At Ancel, there had never been any doubt. Seventy-four of Laroche's ninety co-workers had signed a petition demanding his release. They were about to present it formally to Judge Lambert. The company had continued paying Laroche's wages to Marie-Ange during her husband's absence. She deserved a little good fortune after being sacked from her own job – and all for attending Grégory's funeral.

Marie-Ange had gone through other upheavals, too. The house at Aumontzey was empty: she and Sébastien were now living with the Bolles in Laveline, under the same roof as Muriel. Just as Christine and Jean-Marie had now settled, temporarily but indefinitely, in Bruyères, in the three-room council flat of Gilberte Chatel. They had

114

given away or sold Grégory's toys. 'Our family was like a car. Now there's a wheel missing. It doesn't work any more without Grégory.'

Jean-Marie was swollen with the tranquillisers he had been taking since his son's death. It was the first sign that the Crow had begun to achieve his aims: the chief was degenerating, his martial arts' muscles growing slack.

In Epinal, the graphological report that had just arrived on Lambert's desk said Laroche could have written the letter of 16 October. Berrichon-Seyden was not categorical, but Laroche's writing was the only one which presented no incompatibilities with that of the Crow.

It was headway, of a sort.

The next real test of the investigation's solidity would be the hearing at the Criminal Appeal Court of Nancy, in December, prior to the court's decision concerning the liberation of Bernard Laroche, a week later.

The session lasted six and a half hours. As seemed to be the custom, Assistant Public Prosecutor Renauld gave three reasons for keeping the prime suspect in jail: Muriel's testimony against him, and the fact that this had been echoed by her sister Isabelle. Isabelle said Muriel had told her about seeing Laroche throwing a blue bag into the Vologne. Finally, as ever, there was the need to maintain law and order: everyone knew what might happen if Laroche was released. Laroche was the 'likely culprit' and Renauld would make him the 'certain culprit'.

But if the magistrates were sympathetic to the content of Lambert's dossier, they were highly critical of the form. The gendarmes had been given too much freedom; whereas French law stipulates that the examining judge should appoint all the experts consulted, the handwriting and voice analysts used on the Grégory case had all been chosen by the gendarmerie. As Laroche's barristers pointed out, Berrichon-Seyden had been present at the 'summit meeting' of 30 October before she had been officially hired and sworn in – a breach of regulations – and the voice analysis had been conducted without proper measures to guarantee anonymity. Renauld joined with them in condemning the lack of serenity of the investigation, which had led the graphologist Jacquin-Keller to write to Lambert on 5 November: 'I'm sick of being harassed. I prefer to give up.' The gendarmes knew where they wanted to go, and they had been in too much of a hurry to get there. When they asked Berrichon-Seyden to sketch a psychological portrait of the killer, Laroche's was the only script they gave her to work on. This was called begging the question.

This excessive zeal in guiding the experts was paralleled by a certain sloppiness of method. Why, asked Welzer and Prompt, had the gendarmes not conducted searches at the homes of all the main suspects? Or checked all their tyres against the cast taken from the imprint found by the Vologne? Laroche's Peugeot, they knew, definitely did not use the same type. They added that Muriel had never mentioned either the posting of the letter in Lépanges or the phone call to Michel in her initial statement. How did the gendarmes account for those? They still hadn't come up with any accomplices.

The motion that appeared to be bringing Laroche back up was a see-saw one that sank the Villemins deeper into suspicion. On 12 December, Lambert was out and about with his watch timing the trip supposedly taken by Bernard Laroche: but also the movements Christine claimed to have made after leaving the factory. And a neighbour of Christine Jacquot's at Gaichamp, Marie-Christine Balland, now came forward to assert that at about 5.00 p.m. on 16 October she had seen a black Renault 5 heading for Docelles – the opposite direction to Christine's house. How many black Renault 5s could there have been outside Gaichamp at that time? Balland had hesitated for weeks before coming forward with this evidence. As soon as she did, Lambert was round to Gaichamp to try the view from her windows.

It was all too much for the exasperated parents. Grégory was being forgotten and the investigation was meandering down culs-de-sac. They would have been spared all this if the gendarmes had done their job properly at the beginning. The next day, with Garaud's encouragement, Jean-Marie and Christine Villemin sent a telegram to the French president, François Mitterrand: 'We are the parents of Grégory. We are asking you to put an end to the calumny that is torturing us. We are sick of having people cast doubt on our words. We authorise you to give us the truth drug that is practised in America.'

This blunt statement of weariness was also good, heart-rending publicity. But the truth drug, as Henri Garaud knew, is illegal in

France. For all it mattered, he and his clients could just as well have been bluffing.

Perhaps their appeal was answered by the decision delivered by the court at Nancy on 14 December. Its president, Jean Alteroche, stated that Bernard Laroche would not be released. Although his guilt had not been convincingly demonstrated, there nevertheless remained 'serious, precise and agreeing presumptions'.

The magistrates of Nancy had produced a daunting set of arguments for keeping Bernard Laroche in jail:

Muriel's 'extremely serious and impressively detailed' declarations to the gendarmes could not be dismissed because of her retraction. Her interview had been conducted in proper conditions, the best proof of which was that the girl had repeated her statement to Judge Lambert on Monday morning, two days later. The fact that Muriel met Marie-Ange Laroche on the morning of 6 November made it easy 'to imagine the pressure that might have been put on her' to make her retrait.

Similarly, the magistrates held that the vagueness of one schoolgirl's memory about when she saw Muriel with Bernard Laroche 'was not enough to invalidate the statements made by the three others'. In contrast, they pointed to the disturbingly vague and fluctuating nature of Zonca's three statements about his supposed rendezvous with Laroche. Significantly, Zonca had been passive at the confrontation of 9 November, merely confirming the details mentioned by Laroche, but never adding any of his own.

Muriel had been equally unconvincing. The magistrates noted that she had added extra details in her statement during the confrontation of 9 November, and that it was unclear whether Bernard Laroche had left for Zonca's place before or after Muriel arrived. Moreover, if Laroche really had been seen outside the Lycée Jean Lurçat, as witnesses said, and then, as he claimed, he had gone to Louisette's house just after 5.40 p.m., he still would have had the thirty-seven or forty minutes needed to kill Grégory.

All of which, added to the ever present security risk, made a lot of reasons for extending Laroche's stay at Nancy. The horizon of his monotonous, pointless existence remained as distant as ever.

It was now Laroche's turn to demand the truth drug. In self-imposed solitary confinement since his arrest, he had not seen his wife and son for forty days. Lambert had not granted them a visiting permit. Any communication had been through the intermediary of Welzer. Perhaps Lambert was hoping to weaken Laroche's defences.

Laroche's impassiveness and calm had impressed the other inmates, softening their hostility, but now he broke down and sobbed. He had been expecting to get out. Like his accusers, he looked to the drug as an almost magical way out of the nightmare.

Although gnawed by anxiety, Marie-Ange was learning patience in adversity: 'I am confident,' she declared. 'Bernard must know that the whole family send their love and that, above all, Sébastien misses him.'

Marie-Ange had constantly to shrug off insinuations about her life with Bernard, about Bernard's 'dog-like' need of women. 'Our couple works very well. My husband gives me everything I want. Last Christmas he even bought me a video recorder.' Such was the language of love.

For Jean-Marie the decision merely proved what he already knew. But Jean-Marie had been developing his ideas. If Laroche was guilty, he could not have been alone, and Jean-Marie knew who had been with him: his brother Michel, and Michel's wife Ginette.

Jean-Marie and Michel had already clashed during family discussions of the murder during the short stay at Aumontzey. And one evening, when Michel was not there, the rest of the family had all agreed that the child's voice heard on one of the Crow tapes belonged to Daniel, Michel and Ginette's son. The discovery had thrown Monique into a panic: 'Please, you mustn't tell the gendarmes!'

For Monique Villemin, as for Jeannine Bolle, it was family before justice: the discovery was hushed up, and Jean-Marie felt cheated. What about Grégory? He felt something of the petulant anger of the child who suddenly discovers that his parents' affection is governed by a pragmatic concern for fairness or family unity, and not individual merit.

He and Christine had had no choice but to leave Aumontzey.

Now, away from Monique and his brothers and sisters, Jean-Marie gave free reign to his suspicion. 'Even when we were kids, Michel and I got on badly. As for Ginette, she was always jealous because I was more successful than her husband. As the years went by it became a kind of obsession for her. I think they chose Grégory as their target as soon as he was born. I was thinking of them when I complained to the police in 1982. I want the law to find out exactly what there was between them and Laroche. I'm sure he killed the kid, but he could have been manipulated. Somewhere there is a woman who may not have been with him on 16 October, but who knows exactly what happened.

Michel and Laroche both claimed they had spent the early afternoon of 16 October reading a catalogue together at Michel's place in Aumontzey. But two men don't just sit and indulge in speculative consumption: they talk, they make plans. And Michel Villemin and Bernard Laroche could just as well have mentioned the intolerable arrogance and prosperity of the chief.

Jean-Marie's hunch was that the murder had been sparked off by an event a few days earlier. On Sunday the fourteenth, 'the family' had come over to look at his and Christine's new leather suite. A right procession through the house. Everyone had been curious to know how they were going to pay for it, what with the payments they were already making to reimburse the extension loan. Jean-Marie knew people would be envious. 'Just to be sure, we even locked the living-room door.'

But Jean-Marie's obsession with the alliance of losers motivated by fierce sibling rivalry and spite fell on deaf ears. Anyway, Michel and Ginette had alibis. There was nothing you could hang on them.

Michel and Ginette, wisely, and unlike everyone else, made no comment.

Christine had seen Judge Lambert three times that week. Always those stupid, nagging details. She was beginning to despair of the affair coming to an end. 'There are times when I feel like joining my son. But that would bring too much happiness to Marie-Ange and Laroche's lawyers. Then they'll be able to say whatever they want. But they should know that I'll go on fighting to the bitter end.'

But even fighting was difficult. Their efforts to discover the truth only exposed them to suspicion or attracted the attention of the gendarmes. 'We feel aggressed, criticised by everybody. All those people would just love to see me crying all day long.' Christine knew that her parents-in-law disapproved of her behaviour – all those declarations, her sarcasm. They found it unseemly.

More to the point, they could do nothing to speed up the investigation. On 19 December, the magistrates at Nancy cancelled the gendarmes' voice and handwriting reports. New dictation sessions would have to be held, new tests carried out: Lambert would have to choose new experts.

New experts, more waiting.

Christmas was cheerless that year. In Gilberte Chatel's cold little council flat in Bruyères, Christine, her mother and Jean-Marie sat glumly around their buttercream log and *de rigueur* champagne. Printed on a souvenir plate, Grégory's photo grinned michievously down on them from the pink walls. Two and a half months already. The trio struggled with their memories, sunk in a gloomy lassitude. Since she had stopped seeing Grégory on Wednesdays and Saturdays, Gilberte Chatel had fallen ill.

It was a cruel time. Christine remembered the ritual of buying the tree, how they kept it until the end of February, when all the needles had fallen off. Last Christmas, Grégory had helped her decorate it. 'He handed me the garlands. For Christmas Eve I had on white trousers and a black and white checked shirt. He said "You're beautiful." He stayed up with us all night. It must have been 3.00 a.m. when we went to bed.'

Christine sat dreaming of a new life. 'We want another baby. It would be really wonderful to have another child like Titi. When all this is over, we'll go away. We'll buy a clothes shop in the south.' Sun and glamour: the good life, miles away from the Vosges.

Jean-Marie remembered past happiness on Paremont: the space of the house and its light airy feel in summer. 'We were really happy there.' Grégory's murder had twisted the dagger in their hearts, and the house was empty. He had just finished packing their possessions into cardboard boxes: children's clothes, toys. But life had to go on, banal as the phrase was and however pointless it now seemed: soon, Jean-Marie would return to Autocoussin. If Christine had another child, though, she would give up work for ever 'so she can be with him all the time'.

In Laveline, Marie-Ange continued to struggle with her anxiety for the future, the days when Bernard's pay would stop coming in. In the same house, Muriel had not been back to school since the beginning of November. The two sisters never said a word to each other.

In early January, Président Mitterrand replied to Christine and Jean-Marie Villemin's letter. It was a balm, even if the president did point out that the affair was not within his competence, and that the truth drug would no doubt be refused by the Minister of Justice, Robert Badinter. But it was a reply, and it meant that they had not been forgotten. Jean-Marie and Christine felt less alone. And even Judge Lambert seemed to be taking a better view of Christine. 'He has at last stopped doubting my word,' she said. 'He even told me he didn't really need to see me any more. Of course it won't bring my little boy back to me, but I can breathe more freely.' The cheque she claimed to have posted on 15 October had been traced – an order for some clothes to the value of 163 francs, addressed to *Vert Baudet* in Tourcoing. Christine's version of events was at least partly confirmed.

But the investigators had got no further with identifying their culprit. Doctor Koehler from the Wiesbaden laboratory had written to say that the letter of 16 October had been rendered unusable by all the previous tests that had been carried out on it: these included the scattering of a primitive magnetic powder to show up any finger prints on the paper. As a result of the gendarmes' heavy-handed zeal, the original now looked like a grimy photocopy. Nor was there any hope of identifying the murderer's blood group from the saliva on the stamp: Professor Ceccaldi in Paris informed Lambert that his 'exhibit' was also barren of revelation. At best, the stamp-licker belonged to the twenty per cent of the population whose blood group cannot be discovered using saliva tests.

So Lambert proceeded to organise the new graphological tests: properly. His choice fell on two Parisian experts, Françoise de Ricci and Alain Bucquet. This time, the experts would conduct the dictation sessions themselves, not the gendarmes. Everything would proceed with the necessary serenity. The big day would be 24 January.

Marie-Ange Laroche was the first of eight candidates to take the test. She was followed by Jean-Marie, Christine, Jacky, Roger Jacquel and several other relatives of the Villemin family, Michel and his wife Ginette and Gilbert Villemin's wife, Marie-Christine – and of course, Bernard Laroche. Lambert and the experts visited him in his cell in Nancy. Like all the other participants, Laroche was asked to copy down the letter of 16 October, including the address on the envelope: first with his left hand and then with his right. The usual routine.

De Ricci and Bucquet promised to deliver their conclusions in a month's time.

And the legal wrangling continued. On the same day, Bernard Laroche filed a suit against the gendarmes for 'forgery and usage of forgeries': the attack bore on the 'invented testimony' the gendarmes had used to make Muriel confess and on the fact that her twenty-five hours of custody had not been officially cleared: the legal limit for continuous detention being twenty-four hours. The investigators had committed another serious procedural irregularity in their haste to extort a confession from the young girl. None of which prevented Judge Lambert from refusing Welzer and Prompt's second request for the liberation of their client on 5 January. But at the same time, as if to soften the blow, he gave Marie-Ange official permission to visit her husband.

Lambert's position nevertheless seemed to be growing weaker by the day: the driver of the coach who claimed not to have seen Muriel on 16 October now said he had simply not noticed her. Why this sudden caution? Fear of condemning a potentially innocent man on the strength of what was merely a hazy memory?

Perhaps some sense could be made of it all on 29 January, when Muriel was to confront the gendarmes.

Judge Lambert started the day with a long discussion with Adjudant Lamirand, Captain Sesmat and Commandant Chaillan. Under what circumstances had they coaxed, or extorted Muriel's confession?

But the big event was for the afternoon.

The normally quiet square outside the *Palais de Justice* was filling up with journalists and simple spectators. Ultra-powerful zooms were trained on the windows of Lambert's office.

Muriel arrived at 2.00 p.m., with her mother. Muriel was dressed in black. She was pale and swollen with sedatives – like all the other victims of the affair. And she was tense. There was a lot to play for. She

16 October 1984: Grégory Villemin's body is carried out of the River Vologne, and one of the most sensational investigations in French criminal history is begun.

Christine Villemin, Grégory's young mother – the 'humble seamstress' of the Vosges. Did this woman kill her own son in cold blood?

An example of the work of 'the Crow' – the mysterious figure, almost certainly the murderer of Little Grégory, whose letters full of threats and accusations poisoned the atmosphere in the neighbourhood in which the Villemin family lived.

Jean-Marie Villemin, Grégory's father – 'the Chief'.

The house at Paremont where Grégory and his parents lived. Still visible outside is the pile of gravel where, Christine says, Grégory was playing just before his disappearance.

A united family? The Villemins: (BACK ROW, LEFT TO RIGHT) Albert, Marie-Christine, two friends of Jean-Marie and Christine, Gilberte Chatel, Christine. (FRONT ROW, LEFT TO RIGHT) Gilbert, Jean-Marie, Ginette, Michel. Note Jean-Marie's bandaged wrist, broken when he punched the wall on hearing the news of Grégory's disappearance.

Grégory's funeral. Lépanges mourns and the police watch for suspects.

Jacky and Liliane Villemin, and
Roger and Paulette Jacquel,
leaving the gendarmerie on the
night of 16 October. The first
suspects emerge into a cauldron
of hatred and suspicion.

Jean-Michel Lambert, 'the little
judge'. He was soon to become
France's most famous
magistrate, as he became
involved in the emotional
entanglements of the case.

A lynch mob outside Epinal's Palais de Justice: an ordeal for witnesses
and investigators alike.

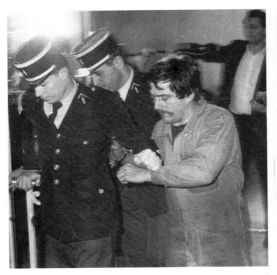

Bernard Laroche: 'I know they'll be coming to get me,' he said, shortly before his arrest, on 5 November 1984, for the murder of Grégory.

Marie-Ange, Bernard Laroche's wife, who tirelessly protested her husband's innocence.

Muriel Bolle (LEFT) with her mother Jeannine, and Louisette and Chantal Jacob. Muriel was a key witness, but her contradictory statements were the cause of confusion and acrimony.

'They needed some poor fool, and they found Bernard.' Marie-Ange bids farewell to her husband, the second murder victim in the Little Grégory affair.

Monique and Albert Villemin, Grégory's grandparents. Victim's of the Crow's hate mail over a number of years, their position at the head of the Villemin family made them central to the mystery surrounding Grégory's murder.

Christine Villemin shows the strain of the protracted case.

Grégory's tombstone in Lépanges. 'In memory of an angel.'

would be alone against not only the gendarmes who had interviewed her, but also their superiors; Tanguy, Chaillan, Sesmat. This was her last chance to redeem herself in the eyes of her family, to be reconciled with Marie-Ange. Muriel still could not understand why the gendarmes had not simply released Laroche the moment she retracted. After all, it was her confession that got him imprisoned. The law was an illogical thing.

Outside the *Palais de Justice*, the Bolles were waiting, willing her to hold out. Encouraged by her lawyers, Marie-Ange had begun to hope. They were joined in the cold air by Monique and Albert Villemin. A little later, Jacky and Liliane also turned up to swell the ranks of the sympathisers. The couple had just been 'passing by', they said. And while Muriel faced the gendarmes, the Bolles went for drinks in a nearby café with Grégory's grandparents. Monique was in a conciliatory mood. 'Anyway, Bernard is innocent,' she assured. 'I'll have a word with Jean-Marie.' Jean-Marie had decided not to attend.

At first, it looked very much as if it would end in stalemate. While the gendarmes stuck to their righteous guns and insisted on the impeccable decency of their behaviour, Muriel demonstrated what Lambert called an 'impressive resistance' in refuting their statements. She did not yield an inch. 'They frightened me, they shouted and threatened me,' she insisted. The gendarmes had 'manipulated and forced' her to make her statement. She had not even realised that Bernard would be arrested.

'They just continued typing when I said it wasn't true . . . When they came to get me on Monday, the gendarmes told me I'd be in deep trouble if I didn't repeat what I told them to the judge . . . It was the same when we went out in the cars. It was the chief gendarme who told the driver where to stop. The court clerk was in the car behind.'

And now the gendarmes were forced to admit that, rather than let Muriel spend Friday night in special officers' quarters, they had merely given her a camp bed on the floor. It was a small detail, but it opened a breach. And the breach was widened when one of the gendarmes, Burton, admitted to having drawn a map to 'help' Muriel remember. Then, as Welzer and Prompt were quick to point out, there was the vocabulary used in Muriel's statement: 'Consult . . . in the upper zone of Lépanges . . . rapid sketch . . . route taken . . . in

123

the process of renovation . . . recollection.' The words sounded much too official and abstract for a fifteen-year-old, especially one who attended a special education centre.

You could imagine it: the gendarmes leading a fearful and intimidated Muriel by the hand until she produced the right answers. Once she had 'confessed the truth about the school bus', the rest was merely a matter of finding what the questioners were so manifestly looking for. It was the bewildered schoolchildren syndrome. Perhaps all the physical details – the two roofs, the low wall, the building works – really had been put into her mouth as well. The gendarmes had lied, and confessed to a little arm-twisting. It was enough to undermine the rest of their arguments, especially given the 'nerves of steel' displayed by Muriel.

Assuming, of course, that her solidity was based on conviction, and not on tranquillisers or family terror.

After the face to face, Welzer and Prompt had every reason to feel optimistic about their renewed appeal for the release of Laroche. They knew that, on the day before the confrontation, Lambert had tried out the route 'mentioned' by Muriel, and found it extremely difficult to cover in the time Laroche would have had at his disposal.

As they left the *Palais de Justice*, Lamirand and his men looked dour. But no one was admitting even the possibility of defeat. Muriel, they maintained, had been confronted with her contradictions and had confessed. Confessed what? That they were contradictions, no doubt. Although lacking clear motives and irrefutable evidence, the case was at least rich in those.

15

It was a routine visit that Marie-Ange Laroche had prepared to pay her husband on Monday 4 February. As usual, she went alone so as to spare her son, Sébastien. He was a sensitive boy, and his father's absence was bad enough without the gloom of prison. So she told him, Papa is in hospital. Later, perhaps, he would understand.

Marie-Ange pushed her way through the heavy doors and towards the noisy waiting room.

But this time her husband was not there with the other inmates. Instead, he appeared in his own clothes. Smiling. Marie-Ange thought for a moment she was seeing things. It was all that nervous tension. But no, Bernard really was free, even though no one had told her. After ninety-one days of solitary confinement, Bernard was free . . . Well, she had never doubted.

Just before 2.00 p.m. Bernard Laroche was out on the streets of Nancy with Marie-Ange, looking dazzled. Marie-Ange suddenly seemed to have relaxed, gone soft. At last she could sink against his weight after holding up for all those days. And she had had no time to prepare herself. Gérard Welzer had not even been able to inform her that the appeal made on 30 January had been successful: third time lucky. Muriel had shaken the judge's intimate conviction and the nightmare was over.

Laroche did not seem to have changed much. There he stood in his blouson with his patterned jacquard sweater and cord trousers. Big Bernard. But his face bore the marks of his suffering, it had that quizzical, suspicious look you associate with someone who does not understand what has happened to him. And he seemed stunned, punch-drunk. His hair had grown lank and mop-like on top, and he had put on weight. Laroche had always been a hearty eater; in prison, food had been his only consolation.

The Laroche who came out of Charles III, smiling, with his arm round his wife, spoke with the same halting and reluctant voice as before. He seemed incapable of shouting as he replied to the radio reporter from a 'pro-Laroche' station, RTL. (Welzer, who knew the ropes, had at least managed to notify them.)

'It was hard, very hard. Some days I really wanted to kill myself. But I resisted – for my wife, for my son Sébastien and also, most of all, because I'm innocent. Innocent.'

The last word of the declaration was heavily underlined. That was as near as Bernard Laroche got to violent indignation. It carried all the suffering accumulated over the past three months. There was not much that could break Laroche's spirit, but there had been the hatred of the other prisoners, the feeling of impotence, the absence of his family and the loss of his friends. Worst of all for the proud, loving father of Sébastien was to hear the rumours about his son's mental handicap and not to be able to reply. 'How can people dare to say such things?' That was what hurt most, the violation of his family happiness. Suddenly, people who had never met you were making your life a failure and your son some kind of monster.

Bernard had been upset, too, by the behaviour of his 'milk brother'. Michel Villemin had never visited him or written. 'He didn't try to understand what was happening. They must have been relieved when I was put in prison, the Villemins. A bit of peace at last.'

But Laroche was not the kind of man to bear grudges. 'Now I want to do all I can to help the Judge.' And injustice? 'It's a shame they had to keep me in prison three months when I was innocent.' It was a shame too that the handwriting analysts had been influenced by the gendarmes. Laroche had learnt from Welzer that, among a total of 295 documents submitted for analysis, the gendarmes had included 45 from Laroche. The ways of Justice are impenetrable.

Now, Bernard Laroche wanted to get back to normal and normality meant work – the old references.

First, though, a short rest. 'It feels really strange to be out again,' said Laroche. He needed to acclimatise. And, what with the tension in the valley, it would be wise to keep a low profile for the first few days.

After his short statement to Welzer's selected group of journalists, the prime suspect was driven off in his barrister's white Porsche to what would be his refuge for the next few days. Offers had come in from sympathisers everywhere, but Welzer had chosen a friend's house in the Burgundy countryside, near Dijon. Unlike most things in the affair, the exact location was secret. 'He needs to rest for a few days in a quiet place, away from everything else,' insisted Welzer. Now they had succeeded in getting Bernard Laroche out of jail, he and Prompt would be pressing for the withdrawal of charges. The case against the burly technician appeared to have deflated quite suddenly, like a balloon. Said Jean-Michel Lambert, 'On 5 November, I had no choice but to put Bernard Laroche in prison. On 4 February, I had no choice but to release him.' Or, as Welzer and Prompt put it, with disingenuous tact, the case had been presented to Jean-Michel Lambert 'all wrapped up', except that when he opened it he found a jumble of tangled and disconnected threads, 'tendentiously held together by the gendarmes' lies'. Lambert would be staying on the case, so why knock him.

As for the gendarmes, their days were numbered. Henri Garaud repeated his demand that the case should be transferred to the Judiciary Police while Prompt demanded an explanation for their 'irresponsibility and incompetence'. The defence had found its scapegoat.

Like her brother-in-law Muriel Bolle also needed to rest. After failed suicide attempts, the girl had sunk into a sullen apathy. She saw no one, was no longer interested in the animals she looked after in Rue de Maroc, and had stopped playing records. 'Luckily, she's young,' said her mother Jeannine. 'She'll grow out of this.' But now Muriel did not even dare go out to buy bread, for fear of meeting the gendarmes. Or perhaps because she had been traumatised by the hate letters that followed her confessions and retractions: 'I'll gouge your eyes out,' promised one. 'Girls like you should be burnt alive.' And, for a moment, she had known what it is to be rejected by your own family. The Bolles were too fiercely united not to punish in some way the girl who had done them so much harm by 'betraying' Bernard.

All that could be forgotten now. That night, the whole of the Bolle family, some forty-five of them, were in Laveline to celebrate Bernard's freedom: all of them except Bernard, that is. It was a noisy evening in Rue de Maroc. Jeannine was in tears of joy. She kept repeating 'I always said he was innocent.' Now her family could hold their heads high. People would stop looking down on them.

But the festive spirit could not last. Each arrest and each liberation of suspects in the Vologne had inflamed a wound and fanned family passions. Roger and Paulette Jacquel had spent only a few hours in the gendarmerie, but since then their friends had grown distant, and everyday transactions were tinged with suspicion; untouchables. They spent their days in fear of the next rumour. The handwriting tests of 24 January had plunged them back into the nightmare. 'We've stopped living,' despaired Roger Jacquel. 'What have we done to deserve all this?' The couple had set up an altar to the Virgin Mary in one of their rooms. In the dark, candles were burning. Every day they prayed to God for the arrest of the assassin. 'Otherwise this thing'll kill us.'

In the absence of a new suspect, Laroche still carried the stigma of crime. Everyone knew the charges had not been lifted, and each could draw his own conclusions. 'It's extraordinary,' fumed Gilberte Chatel. 'They get an assassin and then they release him. It wasn't us who put him in prison, it was his sister-in-law. And you can't tell me that she made it all up. Besides, justice will be done with or without the police.'

Grégory's grandmother had expressed what many others in the valley thought, or feared. It was hard to say which was more intolerable: the thought of injustice, or the idea that an atrocious crime should go unpunished.

Jean-Marie Villemin had heard the news of Laroche's release from a journalist – just as he had with the arrest. But now the shock was even greater. Three months of stagnation, three months of increasing harassment from the investigators, and the gathering cloud of gossip about him and Christine, had worn his nerves thin. He seemed to shift between apathy and despair. The gendarmes were conspiring to make a mockery of his grief. 'If he is innocent, then why has he gone into hiding?' The question was asked in a flat, toneless voice, beyond hope. Christine sobbed when she heard Laroche was free. The couple knew what lay in store: more moral torture. Jean-Marie took the phone off the hook.

Everything told them it was unjust. When they heard Laroche speaking on the radio after his release, they knew it was the voice of the

Crow. So did Jacky and Liliane. The thought that he might now be considered innocent was like having a wound reopened.

'I don't understand,' repeated Albert Villemin. 'Does this mean we'll have to start all over again?' The machinery of justice had gone wild, its effect being not to find the killer but to maintain a state of profoundly uncomfortable suspense. Albert was too civic-minded a character to become bitter or cynical. 'We have to put our faith in the law,' he urged, as if to overcome his own doubts. Meanwhile, he put a notice on the front door: 'No comment.'

The law was confused. The gendarmes felt they had been let down by Judge Lambert: after all, the prosecutor had been against releasing Laroche. And Lambert felt he had been let down by the gendarmes: they had got the investigation into a mess by failing to observe proper procedure.

Lambert and Sesmat gave widely differing accounts of the crucial events of 2 November. Lambert was curt, sarcastic: 'While the gendarmes phoned Captain Sesmat from Bruyères to tell him about Muriel's revelations, I, strangely enough, was not invited to attend the interview.' He had to wait seven hours to be informed.

Not true, said Sesmat. The captain claimed that when he phoned Lambert to inform him of Muriel's sudden confession, the judge said he was about to go away for a weekend of walking in the forest. 'It can wait until Monday,' he concluded, peremptorily. So Sesmat continued, according to procedure. The Muriel he discovered in the gendarmerie was 'calm, and quite sure of herself'. She spoke without emotion. 'I can say with confidence that Muriel was never intimidated. The interview took place in good conditions and in the presence of two gendarmes and one woman gendarme. The young woman was given the statutory rest period. She even watched television during each pause so as to relax. We didn't question her through the night. And at the end of the questioning, when I asked her "Are you aware that you are accusing your brother-in-law, Bernard Laroche?" she said "Yes, I know. And how do you feel? Are you happy about that?" "Yes, I feel relieved."'

When Sesmat took Muriel back to her parents' house, he remembered, Bernard Laroche and Marie-Ange were there, sitting round the kitchen table. 'Laroche looked at us without saying a word. We spent a quarter of an hour with Muriel's father and when I left, I told her to be discreet. She would be seeing the judge on Monday.'

On Monday, when Muriel confirmed her statement to Lambert, Sesmat remembered her adding, 'Yes, I'm sure about the date because of my homework. You always write the date on your homework. It was Maths and French. I found out about Grégory's death the next day. In the photo I recognised the boy Bernard took in the car the day before.'

Sesmat's account was sincere, and full of conviction, but he had forgotten one thing. Muriel had started her confession before he arrived. What he heard was a warmed-up version. What about the subordinates who had done the original cooking?

'We know exactly what we have done, and we are optimistic for the future.' Besides, they pointed out, the Crow had stopped writing or phoning during the period of Laroche's imprisonment. Yes, but then, if you discounted all his emulators, he had stopped writing for a year and a half before the murder too.

Arguments of this calibre were not enough to make up for the gendarmes' loss of credibility. On the afternoon of Laroche's release, Judge Lambert had a long talk with SRPJ Superintendent Gérard Andrieu and his assistant, Jacques Corazzi. It was agreed that their men would start work on 18 February. By then, Françoise de Ricci and Alain Bucquet would have sent in their reports on the latest dictation and the investigation would be able to make a fresh start on the stale events of 16 October. Any new statements would inevitably be subject to the caution required when working with fading or confused memory.

In Burgundy, Bernard Laroche was discovering the reality of freedom. On 5 February, Sébastien and Marie-Ange came to join him in the countryside. Marie-Ange looked radiant. She had had her hair feathered. The three months of strain had been washed from her face. Laroche was an undemonstrative man, but when his son threw himself in his arms he could not hold back the tears. There was a silence, then the boy said, 'You were in prison, Dad. You're fat.'

But fatness was a positive sign for Bernard Laroche: he knew that the warders in prison had softened to him when they started giving him seconds. The cook had become his best mate. 'It was very hard at first, but then what can you expect? They're all family men.' Prison reactions were one thing, but what the gendarmes had done to Muriel was 'unforgivable. I don't hold it against her. But I don't know what I'll do to her when I see her, whether I'll kiss her or slap her. Whatever I do, it'll be spontaneous!'

If anything, the experience of prison had deepened Laroche's capacity for sympathy, especially since he had received such tokens of it himself: the petition from Ancel, signed by a good two thirds of the hundred-strong workforce, had deeply moved him: 'I never realised I was so well liked.' Laroche's voice trembled as he spoke. 'I'll keep it for ever.' As soon as he returned to Aumontzey, the piece of paper would be given pride of place on the sideboard. Like a charm to ward off the maleficent suspicion that still hung over him: 'I won't be a free man until the charges are lifted,' he declared. And even then, 'What happened to me can never be repaired.'

As he walked through the winter countryside, the smile captured by the 'invited' journalists could not hide the frown in his eyes: the expression of a man who had discovered the strangeness of things. And who had been changed by his sufferings.

'I'd like to get back to work as soon as possible, but these last three months I've been thinking. I don't want to live like before, spending all my time between the factory and the woodcutting. We haven't even had a holiday all these nine years we've been married. Now I'm going to take better care of my wife and child. That's the positive side of prison.'

The couple now planned to have a second child: 'We never wanted one before now, but I've understood that it's what Sébastien needs.'

At the meal around the table of the *Toison d'Or* restaurant in Dijon, life seemed full of promise. Laroche sipped Burgundy wine and smiled around the well-set table, sating himself with Sébastien and Marie-Ange's presence in the warm, luxurious dining room. He was lost for words when a waitress tapped on his shoulder and said, 'I just wanted to tell you I always believed you were innocent.' A lump formed in his throat. The words would not come. He was so exposed, he had not formed a new skin for this world.

'We'd be so happy if we could be sure it wasn't him! After all, he was my best friend when I was a child.' When he wasn't bogged down in his own need to find a culprit, Jean-Marie Villemin, too, hoped that the effects of the last few months could be overcome. But Laroche was still under charges, and the two men could not meet. So a national daily, the *Parisien Libéré*, took it upon itself to act as go between in what it called 'the terrible dialogue'. The barristers agreed, and so, on 6 February, Christine and Jean-Marie Villemin drove to Epinal and made their way to a room in the *Cadet Roussel* hotel in Epinal. There, with the help of a journalist, they wrote their questions, Christine in her careful, elegant hand. They were pensive and eager. Photographs. Then the journalist took the questions to a secret meeting place on the road between Epinal and Nancy, and Bernard and Marie-Ange Laroche came and gave their answers. More photographs.

The exclusive was well worth its three and a half pages of newsprint – especially with a confidence from Christine Villemin slipped in as a bonus: she was pregnant. Acts had followed words with impressive alacrity. The child would be called Jonathan, or Fallon – after *Dynasty*. Of course, Jonathan or Fallon was expected for October; some time around the sixteenth.

The 'terrible dialogue' was straightforward: the Villemins presented their grounds for suspicion, or some of them, and the Laroches denied some and disproved others. Detail clashed with detail, the whole thing somehow bodiless, petty and bloodless.

QUESTION: Why did Bernard go to sleep at Louisette's and Marie-Ange go to Laveline just after Jean-Marie had declared he knew who the killer was? Were they afraid of something?
ANSWER: No, they never did sleep there: it was all lies.
QUESTION: Why had Muriel given such a detailed account to the gendarmes, with all those intimate details, like the name Popov and the view of the two roofs?
ANSWER: (predictably) The gendarmes made it all up. Muriel was fragile and impressionable.
QUESTION: Why did Marie-Ange denounce the Hollards?
ANSWER: She didn't, it was the gendarmes who suggested the name. Marie-Ange had simply not ruled out the possibility.

QUESTION: Why didn't Bernard try to speak to Jean-Marie when he was released on 1 November?
ANSWER: When Bernard saw Jean-Marie in Aumontzey, Jean-Marie turned away as if he wasn't there. Bernard had got the message.
QUESTION: Would Bernard meet Jean-Marie in person?
ANSWER: Yes, if Jean-Marie made the first move.
QUESTION: What about the murderer?
ANSWER: A swine!
QUESTION: Would Laroche sign a petition in favour of the death penalty?
ANSWER: No.

So much for this strange meeting of childhood friends. Jean-Marie and Christine Villemin were satisfied, but not completely. Or rather, they were appeased. Denials though were not always enough, and every answer ushered in a new question. Still, perhaps the journalists had brought a bit of calm to the situation, for a while.

One thing was certain, the exchange marked the beginning of a long series of journalistic scoops that grew out of the media's massive presence in the small villages of the Vologne.

Could journalism do something to bridge the gaps that rumour and misunderstanding had opened? It was naïve to think so. The simple fact that several papers had started portraying Bernard Laroche as the new victim of the Little Grégory case, and showing photographs of the ex-prisoner bushy-whiskered and smiling in an expensive restaurant, was a provocation for Grégory's parents. As if their own plight was being sneered at or, worse, forgotten. Laroche banqueted while the victims mourned.

As for Laroche, he could forgive, but he would never take the first step towards the man who had signed the petition for his death and whose accusations had been spread across columns of the national and local press. 'Too much has been said about us . . . We have been sullied. But if he wants to see me, I'll receive him.' Laroche had a snail's pace temper, but enough was enough.

Bernard Laroche was going on thirty and Jean-Marie was twenty six. Both were husbands, fathers, breadwinners and home owners: they had all the trappings of responsible adulthood. But just as their environment had remained unchanged, so their adolescence survived within them, like a substratum. Sometimes it showed on their faces, and now it emerged in Jean-Marie's nostalgia for the days when he and Laroche were still friends.

'Bernard was a great lad, the kind of friend you dream of having – calm, sincere, always honest. We were inseparable as kids. We spent all our holidays playing Cowboys and Indians, hunting for treasure and stealing fruit from orchards. We built a house in the woods. We made coffee there and potatoes . . . It lasted a long time, our friendship. I still haven't forgotten our rides in Bernard's Simca. We did all the restaurants in Gérardmer. We were always out. Towards the end, he was already with Marie-Ange but I still hadn't met Christine.'

The high noon of this fraternal idyll had lasted until July 1984, when the whole family got together for a barbecue in Granges, at the home of Monique's brother André – 'A magnificent day . . . We spent it all playing boules and then we had a huge fight with wet towels . . . '

Three months later, Grégory was dead: the brutal, unmentioned fact cast a melancholy hue over Jean-Marie's remembering. Such boyish light-heartedness seemed aeons away now. The adolescents who still lurked in Bernard and Jean-Marie had been swallowed up by events that neither could understand, let alone control. And Jean-Marie was too deeply sunk in his sorrow to comprehend. He spent his days combing through Laroche's statements, subjecting them to his own stubborn notions of psychology and plausibility. When Bernard came out of prison, Jean-Marie heard him declare that what shock l him most were all the rumours about Sébastien's mental handicap. And what about being accused of killing your friend's child? As Jea - Marie saw it, it was as if Grégory's murder meant nothing to Laroch - just like his arrest: 'I know I would have been less calm, less imperturbable in the same situation.' Had Jean-Marie forgotten Bernard's calm as a youth?

But Jean-Marie was lost to nuanced judgement. After going back to Autocoussin for a spell, he was now off again on sick leave: pale, weary and desperate, like Christine. He kept having breakdowns, bursting into tears. His memory had begun to fail and he had started doing everything twice. Everything was festering: the investigation, with its pestering of Christine, and the simple fact that they still hadn't found a buyer for their home, after three months. As if they were condemned never to get away.

And to cap it all, one of the marble funeral plaques containing a photograph of Grégory had been stolen from the tomb. The Crow back to his tricks? No, just a journalist looking for a good visual: a colleague returned the object to the couple with apologies from his embarrassed associate. But it was as if everyone and everything was conspiring against the Villemins. Just like Muriel, who had run rings around the gendarmes and stirred up bitterness in the valley with her declarations. 'It's not right. Sometimes, I think of taking justice into my own hands,' admitted Jean-Marie, 'but I want the real culprit. I've nothing left to lose, I don't care if I make a mess of my life.' His life was already a mess: no home, no child, and an inability to work properly.

On 9 February, Bernard Laroche met Muriel in Pellegney, at the home of her sister-in-law. There was no slap, and no kisses either, simply a long, earnest conversation. 'I understand everything, and I have forgiven everything,' concluded Laroche with biblical simplicity. Three days later, he was ready to take up his position at Ancel. Life really was beginning to take on the appearance of normality. 'I don't see why I should hide,' he answered every time his lawyers or friends advised him to keep a low profile. Besides, it was being bruited around that the handwriting report entrusted to the Parisians Bucquet and de Ricci categorically excluded Laroche from its list of possible Crows. Jean-Marie of course was unconvinced. His cousin was still a suspect, *the* suspect.

Judge Lambert was in fact still waiting for the report from Françoise de Ricci and Alain Bucquet. After four months on the case, he was finding it as difficult as ever to understand the people he was dealing with. Muriel was an enigma: 'You tell me what goes on in the mind of an adolescent.' And Laroche a wall of silence: 'A man who has always presented the same psychological profile. I never saw him get worked up. I took him his release order in person. He seemed indifferent.' Lambert found it hard not to receive some form of personal recognition from the people whose fate, as he often liked to repeat, was in his hands. Call it a sense of communication, if you will. 'What do you think of me?' he once asked Bernard Laroche, whom he had arrested and now imprisoned. 'I don't know,' replied the suspect. 'I suppose you're just doing your job.' Lambert seemed disappointed. There was a certain naïvety in the way Lambert approached his suspects. 'If you can bring me a better culprit,' he told Laroche after the confrontation of 29 January, 'I'll release you.'

Had Lambert got a better suspect?

On 14 February, the news was made official. Bernard Laroche was not the Crow. So said the experts, whose full report would soon be on Lambert's desk. It was the nearest Laroche could get to an official acquittal without actually receiving one – in the public eye at least.

As Laroche left the case, so did the gendarmes, suspect and suspectors. Four days later, Jean-Michel Lambert summoned Etienne Sesmat to his office at the *Palais de Justice*. For the last time, judge and gendarmes rehearsed the events of early November 1984. Then proceeded to formalities, Lambert's courtesy taut with resentment, Sesmat at his most clipped, bristling with his unchanged convictions about Bernard Laroche.

Lunch, with Pierre Richard and Gérard Andrieu of the SRPJ, was difficult to digest. The SRPJ and the gendarmes had never been the best of friends. While the Judiciary Police looked down on the gendarmes as amateurs, collectors of gossip all too eager to get involved in community affairs, the gendarmes resentfully kept a list of SRPJ failures – including their inability, with Lambert, to track down the killer of three young women in Epinal only a year earlier. But that was forgotten now.

Surprisingly, Henri-René Garaud, the gendarmes' most persistent critic, was in a conciliatory mood. 'You can't really say the gendarmes have failed,' he pointed out. 'It's just they haven't succeeded.' Garaud was a master of the barrister's euphemism, and obviously wanted to avoid alienating anyone.

Lambert and the SRPJ were also cautious. The judge now got down to a good close reading of the graphological reports, and prepared his next steps. Lambert was also becoming interested in other forms of expertise. On 1 March he paid a visit to Monsieur Claude in Epinal. Monsieur Claude was a medium. Not that the affair had driven

Lambert to the occult arts, he just happened to know that Monique and Albert Villemin were regular visitors to Monsieur Claude's salon, and was hoping to glean some interesting family information. Claude told him that Jacky and Liliane Villemin had also been for a consultation, driven like their parents by the Crow – by 'the curse' they felt hanging over them. Claude had foreseen a 'grave danger' threatening Grégory two days before his death. True, he had also predicted a successful future for the child. Still, Lambert felt tempted to ask how the investigation would end.

It was all good publicity for Epinal's own practitioner of the occult arts. And no great help to the investigation.

The affair had entered a transitional phase – at least as far as declarations or arrests were concerned. Anxious to avoid the media pressure that had beleaguered the efforts of the gendarmes, the police had asked the Judge not to communicate to them the conclusions of the handwriting experts, and not to make any public statements about the course of investigations. Gérard Andrieu's men wanted to abstract themselves from the thick, rumour-filled atmosphere of the Vologne. Four months after the crime, they needed to re-establish a sense of perspective.

For three weeks, the police shut themselves away in their offices to sort through the 600 statements gathered by the gendarmes from interviews with some 200 witnesses. Everything was put on a card index system and the investigators began a meticulous search for inconsistencies. It sounded more like scholarship than police work, but the method had paid off in the past.

By early March, just as Lambert had to take a week's holiday to go into hospital for a benign surgical operation, Corazzi and his men had come up with a list of five leading suspects.

The Judge knew when to make himself scarce. Hours after he left the *Palais de Justice*, a telegram arrived on his desk from Welzer and Prompt. Copies had also been sent to Jean-Jacques Lecomte and the Minister of Justice Robert Badinter. The telegram demanded that the report by Bucquet and de Ricci be made official.

For whatever Lambert had declared, Bernard Laroche was still living in the uncomfortable skin of number one suspect. It showed in his language, in spite of himself. When asked to explain why he had had to take so many dictations, Laroche said: 'Well, after all I was . . . I mean, my writing was pretty close to the Crow's.' It was close to self-accusation: 'I was pretty close to the Crow.' It sounded like that other phrase: 'I think the experts are mistaken.'

On her side, Marie-Ange was constantly having to counter allegations that she or her family had intimidated Muriel before the retraction of 6 November. Rumours were going round about the Bolles threatening one of Muriel's classmates to make her withdraw her statement about the school coach. Why else would she have done so?

Laroche was at least fortunate to have his family and workmates behind him. When he went back to Ancel on 19 February, it was as if he had never left. There was no reception, no speeches – just vigorous handshakes and winks of friendship: normality, the way Bernard would have wanted it. It was not like that with everyone. Elsewhere, Laroche was stared at, former friends ignored him. 'Even Michel Villemin. We used to see each other twice a week before all this. We were brought up together. I even gave him wood from my tractor. I really am disappointed. It's all over with them now.'

Of course, gossip did not wait for the police to act or for Lambert to divulge the names of the main suspects. Already, by 18 February, it was being said that Bucquet and de Ricci's report pointed to three possible suspects, three women: Marie-Ange Laroche, Liliane Ville-min, and Christine Villemin. The faces of the unofficially accused appeared forthwith in a national newspaper – the very organ that had arranged the Laroche-Villemin dialogue. They made up a gallery of types from the Vologne, ready made for roles in a drama that would run and run. There was Liliane 'the intellectual', Christine 'the passionate' and Marie-Ange 'the fighter'. As the paper put it, the experts were 'almost convinced' of their guilt. Moreover, if the article was to be believed, Lambert had already communicated the name of the prime suspect to 'supercop' Pierre Richard, the deputy national director of the SRPJ whose presence seemed to endow the new investigators with an awesome authority (judging by some reactions).

By mid March, when the police were ready to go out into the streets, talk of a 'new certainty' went before them.

Liliane Villemin was aghast at the thought of reliving her overnight arrest. 'It's horrible, I'm at my wits' end. I've just had some medical examinations and the doctors say it looks bad. They mentioned a brain tumour. I'm sure the events of the last months must have something to do with it.'

A solid alibi was not enough to protect Liliane's health. Nor could it shelter Marie-Ange. But both women could consider themselves safe. Of the three, only Christine Villemin had not produced a convincing alibi. And could not.

'If people suspect me, then they should tell me so to my face, otherwise the rumour should be officially denounced. If someone is trying to create a climate to make me crack, then they're wasting their time. I won't break. They can take me into custody, my conscience is clear. This is no way to find the person who killed my son.'

Christine Villemin was not the sort of woman to let herself be intimidated by hearsay. Where Laroche was passive, resigned, she was combative and provocative. If the experts said her handwriting was closest to that of the murder note, then she and her barrister would demand a counter-expertise. What was happening to her, with the active complicity of the press, was 'disgusting', and she would not just sit back and let it go on.

On Thursday 21 March, Christine and Jean-Marie were summoned to Nancy for their first, individual interviews with the SRPJ. Although they could have insisted on being accompanied by their lawyer, Garaud advised the couple that they should cooperate and agree to field the questions on their own. At this stage of the investigation, it was important to show good will.

Christine seemed nervous. She was fatigued, pale in her black coat, her face unprotected by make-up. She and her husband were held for nine hours. Once again, they were asked to remember the slightest details of 16 October, and to give their impressions of the atmosphere in the Villemin clan. Jean-Marie relished the chance: 'I let them have it, all the family quarrels.'

While Christine and Jean-Marie were answering Andrieu and Corazzi's questions, other members of the SRPJ were interviewing more witnesses: Gilbert Meline and Bernard Colin, the neighbours, Christine Jacquot and Michel Villemin. Why was it, they wondered, that neither Colin nor Meline had seen Christine's car, or Grégory, outside the house? And why had Michel been unable to identify the voice that he heard on the phone announcing Grégory's death?

This time no one was going to leak anything important. As Jean-Marie told the pack of reporters, the police wanted to work in the strictest secrecy. But some of what Jean-Marie told the SRPJ was reproduced in another form in the press. *Paris Match* was, as ever, an obliging forum for the chief's solo denunciation of his brother Michel, and even of his parents. He told how much Monique and Albert used to dislike Grégory's liveliness, and how hard Michel and Ginette were with the chief's son. 'If ever he forgot to say hallo or goodbye to them, all hell would be let loose. But Daniel, Michel's son who's the same age, was allowed every little caprice. But then,' said Jean-Marie, 'Michel's children Daniel and Crystelle are both retarded, like Sébastien.' There was another link with Laroche. Jean-Marie remembered how Grégory had spoken to Daniel on 10 October, six days before *they* killed him: 'You talk like a baby. I don't understand you.' Ginette had been very upset, he recalled. And with Ginette, upset soon turned to spite. Add to that the opulence of the new three-piece suite they had seen at Paremont and you had a powerful charge of resentment.

There was also Michel's possessiveness. Whenever Jean-Marie came over to Aumontzey to eat with Monique and Albert, 'Michel was never there. He wanted them for himself alone. Michel has never cut the umbilical cord with his mother. At school, he was a dunce. He had convulsions and he was expelled when he was fifteen for punching the headmaster.' Monique had always protected him. Now Michel had bought the house next door in Aumontzey, and in one of those moments of candour where love meets hate, he had told Jean-Marie, 'I want all this for me when they die.'

And, finally, as Jean-Marie had noticed, 'Michel and Ginette are never mentioned in the Crow's letters.'

But Jean-Marie's tirade met with a resounding silence. Michel had alibis. Ginette had alibis. All he could do was accuse, and no one seemed to be taking much notice. Not even Michel.

It was not the couple's accusations that attracted attention so much as their confessions. Asked for a few words about her pregnancy, Christine obliged with the information that, 'I took my cap out two weeks after Grégory's funeral.'

There was nothing like a little earthiness.

Behind their declarations to the press, Christine and Jean-Marie were trying desperately to live for the future, for the child they were expecting in October. All the rumours about Christine were plunging them back into their suffering, like a punishment. 'Luckily we trust each other,' added Jean-Marie. 'That's the source of our strength of character.'

They would be needing it.

Christine and Jean-Marie Villemin spent the whole of that weekend at home in Bruyères. They had no social life, and their family circle had contracted to themselves and Gilberte Chatel. Outside, the bleak drizzle of late winter. Christine, two months into her second pregnancy, was knitting baby clothes while Jean-Marie repelled the occasional group of journalists who clambered up the stairs with an obstinate silence. Their only outing was the regular visit to Lépanges cemetery.

Grégory's parents had been hurt by the 'torrent of mud' that had been channelled through the media. 'They've even started casting doubt on my sorrow,' complained Christine. It was a betrayal. And there was more to come. Christine was due for a second hearing on Monday, this time with Lambert. The Judge had been seeing René Andrieu that Saturday to prepare his questions.

On Sunday night, Christine was listening to the radio. She was used to hearing announcements by now, but that didn't stop her growing tense when she heard those first syllables: 'Little Grégory case.' She caught her breath. Then, quickly, bluntly, the news: 'The Crow's handwriting belongs to the mother.'

It hit her in the gut. She felt sick. Her 'guilt' was out there, a public object, beyond her power, nauseating.

At eleven o'clock that evening, Jean-Marie was driving to the *Roseraie* clinic in Epinal. His wife had internal bleeding. Christine Villemin had a fissured placenta. She was in danger of losing her child.

Her visit to the *Palais de Justice* would have to be postponed. Christine Villemin had cracked.

And she had managed it badly. As if she were giving in to rumour. Or playing for time.

The week began as the weekend had ended. Gloomily. At 9.30 a.m. on Monday Jean-Marie was in Judge Lambert's office to be told that Bucquet and de Ricci's report was faithful to its radiophonic preview. The experts had whittled the original 148 scripts down to nine, and then analysed the remaining copies using two different methods, the 'statistical' one, and that of 'discordances and concordances'. The latter found an 80 per cent resemblance between Christine's writing and that of the Crow's four letters, and the former a correspondence of 99 per cent. It sounded dauntingly scientific. None of the other candidates, Bernard Laroche included, rated much higher than 50 per cent. And, unlike their predecessors, Bucquet and de Ricci had been free of pressure from the investigators.

Jean-Marie was even paler than usual when he came out of the magistrate's building at eleven o'clock. Everything was collapsing.

It was Garaud, of course, who spoke most eloquently in Christine Villemin's defence. 'The assassin must be rejoicing. He doesn't need to send any more anonymous letters to torture Grégory's parents. This is a fine result!'

In response to pressure from Garaud – and remembering what had happened with Laroche, Jean-Michel Lambert decided to order a second test for the eight witnesses of 24 January. Immediately, the machinery was cranked up again. At 2.00 p.m., Jean-Marie was back in the magistrate's building with Jacky and Liliane Villemin. He was the first to finish.

At 3.15 p.m., two Renault 4s drew up outside *La Roseraie*. The delegation had arrived from across the river, accompanied or antici-pated by a scrum of journalists. With Lambert and his clerk were Lecomte, Garaud, Jean-Marie Villemin and the two handwriting experts. For Christine Villemin it had been a day of good and bad news: the good was that her baby was no longer at risk. The bad news, or rather the bad confirmation, was that 'science' designated her as the Crow.

On her hospital bed, Christine Villemin found the strength to be bitterly defiant: 'You can make me do the dictation and say the result is 100 per cent: that won't change either the truth or my behaviour. You know perfectly well I never wrote those letters. Why are you persecuting me like this?' Jean-Michel Lambert was not used to such personal hectoring from his clients. But, like a good girl, and with all the hopefulness of someone filling in a lost property form for a stolen wallet, Christine Villemin did take the new dictation.

'No comment,' said Lambert as he scrambled past the thrusting microphones on the clinic steps. There would be a month of waiting before the new test confirmed or undermined Bucquet and de Ricci's initial conclusions. A month in which rumour could only swell, and in which Laroche's lawyers would be pushing vigorously for charges against their client to be lifted. Bernard and Marie-Ange Laroche knew peace of mind was only days away. They were radiant as they left the magistrates' offices at 6.00 p.m. after talking to the judge and taking the new dictation. Bernard could begin to enjoy his freedom, almost.

The Laroches were followed an hour later by the two experts. Naturally, the journalists were there to meet them. De Ricci, who cut a sophisticated figure with her Parisian-blonde hair and fur-trimmed coat, seemed to be enjoying the attention. 'We are sure of what we are saying, but never sure enough.' After the new dictation, she assured, 'I and my colleague will be working day and night, taking every safeguard to preserve objectivity and anonymity.' In the meantime, though, 'Christine Villemin's writing comes by far the closest to the Crow's.'

In other words; the law might not have realised it yet, but Christine Villemin's trial by rumour had already begun. Thanks to the expert's disregard for *sub judice* information and to media disregard for investigative reality: graphology can confirm, it cannot prove.

Guilty and innocent: in the Vologne valley, as much as in the media, the two terms had set up a binary system that doubt could do nothing to prise open. You were Laroche or you were Villemin, and if you belonged to the latter camp, you were losing ground.

If you were the former, you could relax, as Bernard Laroche did on

23 March, his thirtieth birthday. At a celebration dinner with his family and friends, Nanar was happy and confident. He declared the affair out of bounds for the evening: 'The law will take care of that,' he insisted. Laroche was more interested in the pleasures of freedom and friendship.

If Bernard Laroche had faith in the law, Jean-Michel Lambert was determined to ignore rumour and unofficial justice and let the investigation cool its heels. His mind was set on the walking trip he would be going on at the end of the week. He had chosen the Algerian Sahara. 'A place where there are no rivers,' he said.

16

Friday 29 March was the first real day of spring in the Vologne, it brought the first warmth since October the year before. Jean-Michel Lambert was in Paris, ready to board the plane to Algeria. Christine Villemin was preparing to leave the *Roseraie* clinic. The photographers were all there, waiting and watching the early-morning ins and early-afternoon outs of Jean-Marie. That day, they observed, he looked particularly puffy, his eyes especially sleepless and small.

Bernard Laroche was coming to the end of his second week at Ancel. He was growing more confident each day. Although his friends and family still spoke of danger, the only risk as he saw it was from Grégory's killer. There was certainly no reason to be worried by the hate letter that arrived from Rosny-sous-Bois, near Paris, on 27 March:

> If you have tortured the young couple to death, if the police, or rather the rotten magistrature we have in France now, have allowed you to assassinate not only Grégory, but also the child that Christine bears, remember that even from death the beauty of the child killed by your dirty paws shows up the ugliness of your stringy-haired runt.

The 'vigilante Crow' knew Laroche's sensitive spots well enough. But Bernard knew the fools and hotheads would one day forget, or find another cause. His name would be cleared. What is a letter after three months of prison? Nothing certainly, compared to the news that Marie-Ange had just given him; she was expecting a second child. So soon. It had to be a sign. The future was welcoming them.

At 1.30 p.m. the grey-green Peugeot drew up outside the garage of the chalet at Le Bois du Creux. Marie-Ange had fetched Bernard back from Ancel: her continuing unemployment did at least allow her the luxury of moulding her life to Bernard's newly-savoured routine.

Lucien, her brother, came to the front door with Sébastien and Laroche emerged from the car, holding two baguettes and a lunchbox. He and Marie-Ange were about to go into the house when suddenly a man ran out from behind the trees above the garage. He was carrying a gun and wearing dark glasses: but Jean-Marie Villemin was not trying to disguise himself. Perhaps the glasses simply made him feel less vulnerable, helped him point the gun at Laroche without flinching.

Lucien stepped forward.

'Get out of the way, or I'll shoot.'

The gun was still levelled at Laroche. Why the gun?

'Hey, Jean-Marie!'

It was the two men's first meeting since October. Not much was said. Jean-Marie barked out something about Muriel and Michel and experts; Laroche denied, reassured, made defensive sounds. Marie-Ange pleaded.

It cannot have taken more than a minute, half a minute.

And then Jean-Marie Villemin fired, point blank.

The bullet pierced Laroche's right lung. Blood spattered on the ground. Blood stained Sébastien's sweater. Laroche was floored by the impact. Sébastien had seen it all.

As Jean-Marie Villemin hurtled back through the woods, Lucien dashed inside to fetch his brother-in-law's gun. The blood was beginning to trickle from Bernard Laroche's mouth. Marie-Ange lay beside him, not believing yet knowing that his life was ebbing quickly. In fifteen minutes, it had gone. And Lucien gave up his chase.

17

Bernard Laroche was dead. After eight weeks of liberty, he had received a summary and unexpected execution.

Marcel Jacob, Laroche's uncle and neighbour, was the first to arrive. He knew; the gunshot could only mean one thing. Minutes later, he was joined by other members of the family, other neighbours: Muriel. They gathered in grief, rage and impotence. Marie-Ange could barely stand. Sébastien was wailing, inconsolable.

They carried Bernard inside. Something had to be done. And then they saw the gendarmes and the journalists appear and they picked up stones. Here was an object for their hatred. These people too had killed Bernard Laroche.

But there was nothing Lucien and his sons could do. All through this business they had had to look on powerlessly: Muriel's questioning, Bernard's arrest, and now this.

At 1.45 p.m., Jean-Marie was back in room 70 of *La Roseraie.* Beyond their reach. Christine was sleeping when he dashed in. He looked strange she thought, as she opened her eyes: 'Hallo Teddy,' she said, waking up to the nickname she and Grégory had shared, 'are you all right?'

'I've killed Laroche.'

Christine says she was sure it was some kind of bad joke. But Jean-Marie was now on his knees. And Christine burst into tears.

Then Jean-Marie told her what had happened. Then he picked up the phone. He dialled Garaud's number. It was his associate, Maître Salomé, who answered. 'Hallo, I'm Jean-Marie Villemin. I've killed Bernard Laroche. Tell Maître Garaud I'm waiting for him.'

It only remained for Jean-Marie to turn himself in. The police did not have far to come. The van left *La Roseraie* for Epinal prison at quarter past two. Less than an hour after the murder.

There are two versions of the exchange that may have determined Jean-Marie to kill his one-time friend. Or that may simply have slowed down the execution of a long-matured plan. In Aumontzey, Marie-Ange was telling hers to the TV cameras, her diction interrupted by spasms of convulsive sobbing. And in Epinal, after five policemen had led Jean-Marie away from the clinic, Christine Villemin was preparing to confide in a journalist friend.

As always, you had to choose your camp.

'I'm innocent, I had nothing to do with it.'

According to Marie-Ange, her husband's parting words were the same as those he had spoken when he was hauled into the *Palais de Justice* at Epinal. And when he had been released, for that matter. He was innocent, and that was what her account of his death showed him to be.

Marie-Ange was looking for her front door keys, she said, when she heard running behind them. She looked up and saw Jean-Marie with his gun.

Bernard was the first to speak: 'Don't be a fool, Jean-Marie. I understand how bad your suffering is, but it wasn't me who killed your kid, I swear.'

Jean-Marie was exasperated, white hot.

'I hear you don't want to talk to me. But I want you to tell me something about you and Michel.'

Now it was Marie-Ange's turn to try and calm things down. 'All right, Jean-Marie, but first put your gun down and come inside.'

Marie-Ange saw Jean-Marie lower the barrel, but the reflex was short-lived. The next second, he was back to his pressing questions:

'Why did Muriel say all those things, then?'

And as if he hadn't heard Marie-Ange's promise of explanation, he continued:

'It's your fault if they're all after Christine.'

Then he pulled the trigger.

As Lucien dashed forward, Laroche had just enough energy to breathe out the words, 'the .22, in the wardrobe'. But it was too late to fire back; Jean-Marie had got away.

Marie-Ange was convinced Jean-Marie had come to kill. He didn't want explanation, he wanted revenge. It was the gendarmes' fault: after the SRPJ had taken over, they had continued to encourage Jean-Marie in his convictions. Sesmat kept telling him: 'It's Laroche, we're sure of it.'

Christine, of course, maintained the contrary. Jean-Marie had wanted to talk.

Christine and Marie-Ange were exemplary wives.

When Jean-Marie had been led away by the Epinal *Sûreté*, Christine picked up the phone and dialled a Paris number: *Europe 1*, the radio station. 'I've got something to say.' She waited for the journalist to call back, and then started:

'When he came this morning, Jean-Marie told me he had been to see the gendarmes to ask about Laroche and about Muriel's deposition. He was obsessed with the thought that they might have influenced her, and had found out the name of the doctor who examined her on Saturday morning: Rousseau. The gendarmes told him: "In any case, it's him, but we don't have enough evidence to arrest him. The Judiciary Police'll come to the same conclusion in the end, and they won't be able to get him either." '

A few minutes later, Christine Jacquot arrived and the two left Christine's room in order to let the nurses carry out their morning inspection. When they came back, said Christine, Jacquot had been crying, and Jean-Marie was white as a sheet. He phoned Maître Garaud and said 'I'm sick of it all. They keep trying to bring down Christine. I just can't take any more.' Jacquot had told him that the police were hoping to expose Christine by working away at all the witnesses she had cited for the evening of 16 October. 'They'll do all they can to get you,' said Jacquot. 'They told me you were guilty. That the statements in your favour didn't stand up, that they'd destroy them all.'

Jean-Marie left saying he would go to the flat in Bruyères and then to the Judiciary Police, 'to see if they're really trying to demolish your statement.' He promised he would be back by two o'clock, after a visit to the cemetery. When Christine phoned him in Bruyères at lunchtime, he sounded weak and distant.

It was Laroche's attitude that had provoked her husband to pull the trigger.

Jean-Marie said: 'Laroche just kept mocking me. Laroche said "We've nothing to say to each other."' And when Jean-Marie questioned him about Muriel, he sneered and said: 'Muriel, I don't know why she said that.' And when Jean-Marie mentioned the experts, Laroche just sniggered. 'The experts, they were paid to do down your wife.'

According to Christine Villemin, that was when her husband pulled the trigger.

It was a story she would have numerous opportunities to repeat, starting with that Friday afternoon, when Jean-Jacques Lecomte and Gérard Andrieu came to *La Roseraie*. Surely, they pressed, Christine must have been expecting something to happen. Andrieu wanted to know if Bernard Laroche had ever been her lover. The SRPJ seemed obsessed with her sexual relations.

At Epinal prison, Jean-Marie was given a medical check-up and then driven to Nancy for questioning by the SRPJ. Now that the shock of events had passed and the tension had gone out of him, Jean-Marie Villemin cried uncontrollably: now, he measured the full meaning of what he had done, and could see what lay ahead of him. Perhaps, somewhere, there was a trace of mourning for Bernard Laroche. In a sense, Jean-Marie had just killed his youth. But tell him that and he would not know what you meant.

His response to the investigators was unequivocal: he had acted alone. 'She didn't know about it. I chose Friday because it was Christine's last day at the clinic. I didn't want her with me.' This was more a proud declaration than a confession: 'I promised that I'd kill my child's murderer the night they found him in the Vologne. I had to do it.' Now, at last, Jean-Marie Villemin had proved himself. He was, as the local expression had it, *un glorieux*.

And, contrary to what Christine had just claimed, Jean-Marie freely admitted that he had always been out to kill. Unlike his wife, he had no interest in the effects of such nuances on courtroom sentences. There was nothing calculating about the murder.

In fact, Jean-Marie had wanted to do more than avenge his son. The second part of his plan was to kidnap Marie-Ange and Sébastien in order to force the truth out of them. He had taken a tape recorder along for the confessions. The 'chief' was going to prove that he was right and, in the process, show up the weakness of institutional justice, which had so lamentably failed him. The presence of Lucien Bolle had made this impossible.

Jean-Marie's interview with the SRPJ lasted until two in the morning. Then, on Saturday afternoon, Christine arrived. The police took particular interest in the fact that the murder weapon had been paid for by one of her cheques.

'I always make the cheques – ever since we got married.'

Before Christine Villemin was released she was allowed a brief meeting with her husband. Then Jean-Marie was marched off. Just before he disappeared down the corridor, he turned back to her: 'I love you. I did all this for you. I hope you won't forget.'

Christine did not go back to Bruyères. Her new destination was Petitmont, the home of her grandmother, Jeanne Blaise; and in happier times her own. Jeanne used to look after Christine and her siblings when her mother was at work. Christine Villemin was retreating from the Vologne. She had never liked the place anyway.

The little judge was in Paris, about to board the charter to Tamanirasset when he heard the news over the radio. The trekking holiday would have to wait. Jean-Michel Lambert had begun to regret the release order he had signed for Bernard Laroche, against the wishes of his colleague Jean-Jacques Lecomte.

The river had a hold on him. Arriving back in Epinal, Lambert knew he would be held responsible for Bernard Laroche's death. He could not afford to make any more mistakes.

The Jean-Marie Villemin he saw in front of him on Saturday night in his office in Epinal was haggard with the strain of the last two days. His eyes were red, he seemed overwrought. But Jean-Marie Villemin also seemed strangely relieved. Killing Laroche had been a catharsis. Or, as one newspaper put it: by killing Laroche, Jean-Marie had 'killed his own doubts.' Jean-Marie had no regrets. After his interview with the judge, he was led away to Epinal prison, where he was charged and sent to the Charles III in Nancy. The same jail as Bernard Laroche.

Jean-Marie Villemin's guilt was so clear and freely admitted it was

151

almost pointless to discuss it. Prompt saw things differently. If Jean-Marie had pulled the trigger, someone else had driven him to it. If there was one thing Christine and Marie-Ange agreed on, it was the role of the gendarmes. Everyone knew Bernard Laroche had been their suspect. Had he been the victim of a rivalry between two different arms of the law? Paul Prompt had no doubt. He immediately accused Captain Etienne Sesmat of being Jean-Marie's director of conscience. According to Prompt, Sesmat and his colleagues had knowingly encouraged Jean-Marie in his convictions, and they had done nothing to communicate them to the Judge. Worse, they had refused when Marie-Ange or the barristers approached them for protection. There had been no reaction to their letter to Prosecutor Lecomte on 6 March. Prompt was filing a charge against the gendarmes on behalf of his clients.

Prompt was at fever pitch of anger and agitation. Leaving Lambert's office, he ducked and looked tensely up at the surrounding rooftops. Snipers, he was sure there were men on the roofs ready to pick off the supporters of Bernard Laroche. A Villemin guerrilla. The case had gone to his imagination. But Prompt was not totally out. A few days later, the handwriting expert Alain Bucquet received an anonymous letter. 'Laroche bribed you,' it said. 'You've seen what happened to him. Arsehole. The same will happen to you.'

The gendarmes lost no time reacting to the accusations made against them. Although Etienne Sesmat was bound by his function to silence, both the head of the Lorraine gendarmerie, Colonel Fressy, and the National Director of the service, Oliver Renard-Payen, leapt to their colleague's defence. Captain Sesmat had done nothing that was not in keeping with his duty. Besides, as Jean-Marie had testified, Sesmat had not been present to receive him on the morning of 29 March. It was an unfortunate irony, however, that the only thing Christine Villemin and Marie-Ange Laroche could agree on was the role of the gendarmes in exciting Bernard Laroche's killer. 'He used to see him regularly, just to keep him on the boil; it's Laroche, it's Laroche,' railed Marie-Ange. Everyone knew that Jean-Marie had always been on good terms with the force, that he had trusted Sesmat and that

Sesmat, with his own family, was a ready sympathiser for the bereaved father.

On Monday 1 April, Etienne Sesmat spent two hours with Jean-Michel Lambert. Sesmat and his colleagues found themselves in the middle of a national *malaise*. In Paris, the gendarmes of Vincennes had come in for fierce criticism over their treatment of a case involving suspected IRA terrorists. In the Vologne, rumours were beginning to go round to the effect that the SRPJ had tapes of conversations between Sesmat and Jean-Marie after 18 February, conversations in which Sesmat gave free reign to his opinions.

Not that anyone ever questioned Sesmat's integrity. But he could hardly continue in the Vosges after the affront he had suffered. The Saint Cyr graduate lost no time in applying for a transfer.

For Garaud, the death of Laroche had a sad inevitability about it. It was the result of the moral torture inflicted on his clients. 'The anger of the meek can lead to anything,' he said, hiding the exaggeration behind his emotional forcefulness. Jean-Marie, meek?

Garaud had already called upon an associate to assist with the ever-complicated case of his client. Marie-Christine Chastant-Morand was his spiritual daughter, and as close as he was to *Légitime Défense*. Her first declaration was brutally unequivocal: 'There is only one victim in this affair so far.' So much for the grief of the Laroches and the Bolles.

In Aumontzey, Laroche lay at rest in the living room of his chalet. His wife had dressed him in his best suit, a grey three-piece, with white shirt and dark tie. In his big, rough hands, she had placed a yellow rose and a rosary. About them she had wound thick strands of silky hair. Marie-Ange's hair. She had shorn her locks with clippers as a sign of mourning, or grief-stricken self-mutilation, and wound them about his hands in final tribute. Laroche had always loved Marie-Ange's long hair. Never again would she wear it like that.

Around the body, Marie-Ange laid the red flowers offered by the family, together with five funeral plaques and photos showing their wedding day and their child, Sébastien: Sébastien, his big liquidy eyes staring out at the camera; Bernard standing stiffly in a big velvet bow tie and one of those flared, high-waisted black suits that were fashionable in 1976, his arm round Marie-Ange in her full white dress – like figures on a cake. Nearly ten years ago.

Although he had witnessed his father's death, had been splashed by his blood, Sébastien had needed hours to take in what had happened. He was in a daze. Three long months of absence, and now this.

For the Bolles, Laroche's death was a raw wound. In the chalet, the painful sequence of mourning and last respects had begun. Marie-Ange did her best to receive her visitors with dignity, but the misery and the anger were almost tangible: they clenched the men's fists, made their movements restless, twisted their faces. Lucien Bolle, Laroche's father-in-law, was rabid with grief. 'I'm going to get my gun and shoot into the crowd,' he warned when he saw the journalists and onlookers on the slope below. And when one of his sons tried to calm him down, he punched him with all his strength. 'You're no better than the others. You're worthless. Get out!'

Nearby, in another room, Muriel Bolle was pale and silent. She had 'killed' her brother-in-law. There was nothing she could do now. It made no difference that the others all tried to avoid the subject. She could feel it like a burn spreading inside her, hot and cold.

As for Marie-Ange, she struggled between dignity and vituperation. If, as was said, she had always disliked Christine Villemin, her hatred could now come out into the open. 'She's the one who made him kill Bernard! She's a bitch, a liar. She plotted the whole thing.'

The Villemin family were no better. 'They didn't lift a finger when the whole thing started.'

But unlike her father and brothers, Marie-Ange knew that revenge was no solution. 'I hope they'll control themselves. If they don't, they'll kill Jean-Marie's wife, and there'll be no end to it all.'

'Jean-Marie's wife.' At that moment, the woman's name would have felt like an obscenity in Marie-Ange's mouth. Christine Villemin, the witch.

Like Grégory's, Bernard Laroche's death had been announced well before the event. Jean-Marie had made his threats, after Laroche's arrest and after his release. So, Lambert and the gendarmes could now remember, had Gilberte Chatel. Looking back, it was all horribly obvious. After his arrest on 29 March, Jean-Marie freely admitted that he had prepared it all. 'I didn't want Christine with me because the other times, when she was there, it went wrong.' It was no use blaming Laroche for wanting to come back to the valley earlier than advised.

Evidence found by Marcel Jacob brought further confirmation – if it was needed – that Jean-Marie had planned his move carefully. Jacob had come across an alarm clock and a half-finished bottle of wine among the trees, only 15 metres away from Laroche's chalet. An observation post. Jacob thought the two items made up a primitive bomb. In fact, the clock was there simply to time Laroche's comings and goings. Jean-Marie never wore a wrist-watch.

Jacob had warned Bernard. He pointed to the wooded track leading up from the chalet and said: 'If they come, they'll come from there.'

Other neighbours told Marie-Ange they had seen Jean-Marie Villemin prowling round the house. She immediately called the gendarmes at Bruyères. 'We're not on that case any more.' The voice at the other end was abrupt and refused to identify itself. 'Is it our fault if something happens to your husband?' Marie-Ange was told to contact the gendarmes at Corcieux. She also informed Welzer and Prompt. When Bernard Laroche's representatives wrote to Jean-Jacques Lecomte on 6 March, they were certainly given consideration, but there were no gendarmes to protect Bernard Laroche.

Marie-Ange kept telling her husband about her anxieties. Laroche was sceptical, especially about Jean-Marie's intentions. 'He simply couldn't do such a thing. Everyone would know!' Killers, it stood to reason, were secretive people.

In fact, like most men convinced of their righteousness, Jean-Marie was perfectly open about his intentions. And, being isolated from his family, he did a good deal of his confiding to journalists. By now, of course, he and Christine were beginning to get an idea of which journalists were on their side, and which against.

Jean Ker, a photo-reporter from *Paris Match*, was emphatically pro-Villemin. He had even spent long hours going over Muriel's statements with them, talking through their obsession with Bernard Laroche.

Ker knew what a state they were in – perhaps better than anyone else. Ker had seen the dress rehearsal for Bernard Laroche's death.

On 26 February, he had a rendezvous with Grégory's parents in the afternoon. Sipping cold beer, they talked their way through every aspect of the case. Ker was astonished at the couple's grasp of detail, their in-depth knowledge of the press coverage. He noted, too, that Jean-Marie seemed particularly tense.

Ker did not really feel like spending his evening in the small flat in Bruyères, but when Jean-Marie invited him to dinner he knew better than to turn him down. When they had chomped through the pork chops cooked by Christine, and after a painful discussion of the hypotheses concerning Grégory's death, it was obvious to Ker that Jean-Marie was unmovable. Laroche was guilty.

But this was more than a conviction. It was a manifesto.

'Yesterday, a gendarme came round,' said Jean-Marie. 'He told us that if Grégory had been his son he'd have killed Laroche a long time ago.'

Upon which, he brought out a 12-calibre hunting rifle: enough to slay an elephant. He handed the weapon to Ker. It was loaded. 'Ready to kill Laroche,' he said. He told Ker he and Christine had already been to observe their target up at Bois du Creux twice in the two weeks since he had come back to his chalet. 'But he's on the lookout and never goes alone.' From their hiding place in the wood, they had seen him with Marie-Ange and, on the other occasion, Lucien Bolle, Marie-Ange's brother. Lucien was a self-appointed strong-man with the Bolles' special brand of family feeling. He was often at the house, ready to protect his sister at the slightest sign of trouble.

Jean-Marie and Christine had it all planned. Ker saw two plastic bags lying ready on the floor. Jean-Marie opened one of them: it contained photos of Grégory and daily necessities; underwear, toiletries. Christine had the same in hers. Once they had accomplished their act of execution, the couple intended to hand themselves over to the police. Did they fully realise that killing Laroche would mean separate prison sentences – the destruction of their life together for as long as the court judged necessary? No matter. Prison with justice done would be better than their false freedom and the unbearable sentiment of wrong. 'Justice has done nothing to help us, and yet I swore on Grégory's tomb I would avenge him.'

They had imagined several scenarios. Laroche could be killed in front of his home in Aumontzey, when out shopping, or on his way back from the night-shift, at 5.00 a.m. Christine was to block his car in the Renault 18 while her husband took aim.

As Ker left them that night, Jean-Marie took his hand. 'If we do go to prison, I'd like to think you'll stick by us. Will you do that? We are so alone.'

It was touching, this mixture of ruthlessness and vulnerability. Jean-Marie did not show it often.

'All right . . . Sure, of course I will.'

'Thanks.'

'Jean-Marie . . . Don't do anything foolish now!'

'No, don't you worry. Good-night.'

Back in Epinal, Ker found it hard to believe what he had just seen. As he turned it over in his mind, he could feel the worry rising up in him. After all, if Jean-Marie and Christine had just revealed their secret plans, then . . .

Later that night, Ker decided to phone the couple back. It was Gilberte Chatel who answered. She said tetchily, 'They're asleep.' Her voice was wrong. Ker didn't like it. He hurried outside, jumped into his Citroën and drove back to Bruyères. When he got there, Jean-Marie's white Renault was nowhere to be seen.

That week Bernard Laroche was on the night-shift.

In Aumontzey, Ker found the Renault 18 parked by a crossroads, lying in ambush. Laroche was due to pass through in the next ten minutes.

When she saw Ker, Christine calmly told him to leave before he fouled things up for them. Ker stayed where he was. Then he stationed himself in front of the Renault to stop her driving out and blocking Laroche. Now Christine started swearing. 'Fuck off, Ker. Fuck off, bastard. You'll fuck it all up.'

Christine Villemin was hysterical.

When, at last, she had calmed down a little, Ker invited the couple back to his hotel in Epinal.

'Come on, let's talk.'

They nodded, got into their car and followed. Ker gave a puff of relief – he had won. But then in his rear-view mirror he saw the Renault 18 suddenly fork off up the road leading to Laroche's house. Christine and Jean-Marie were going to ambush him outside Louisette's place. Ker screeched up the road behind them, headlights full on. Now Laroche really was there; two car lights suddenly flicked on. Then, just as suddenly, they went out again. Had Laroche seen the Renault?

Ker tried again.

'Come on Jean-Marie, Christine, let's go . . .

This time, the couple did follow their reporter friend to his hotel. Over coffee and croissants, Jean-Marie announced that they had set themselves a deadline: the end of March. 'If the law hasn't done anything by then, then we'll do something.'

This all happened three weeks after Laroche's release. Of course, Ker told Judge Lambert and Captain Sesmat what had happened. Otherwise, he kept the incident to himself. Publication in *Paris Match* would only get the Bolles on the war path.

So Ker's article was published after the true event: 'The night I prevented Jean-Marie Villemin from killing Bernard Laroche.' Truly posthumous glory.

18

'**N**o, my darling, no!'

    The same cry had stabbed the air in Lépanges five months ago. A mother's howl of disbelief and pain. This time, it was the cry of a woman torn by the death of her lover and husband. Marie-Ange, her voice unsteady with the continual sobbing that had racked her body for four days, sent up a piercing wailing that faltered and grew faint with her own physical weakness. Then she leant for comfort into the chest of her brother Lucien. Bernard Laroche's body was lowered into the earth of Jussarupt. From the cemetery outside the pink granite church, you could look down to Aumontzey and see the Laroches' chalet. Beyond lay the glistening silver of the Vologne. Children were playing in the meadows. Beyond, for Marie-Ange, lay the prospect of solitude and the rearing of two orphans. She would be giving birth at the end of the year.

Ever since she had witnessed the shooting of her husband on the afternoon of Friday 29 March, Marie-Ange had been unable to sleep. The doctor had been a regular visitor to the chalet at Aumontzey where her brothers and sisters kept her company. How many times did she relive those last few moments? How often did she reckon up the incalculable loss for her future and the massacre of her fragile, present happiness?

    Now, the rough, short mane around her lined, fleshy face was like an exclamation mark to the pain imprinted there. But Jean-Marie Ville-min's vengeance had created more than suffering in the Bolle family. Marie-Ange was haunted by the fear of retaliation from her brothers and sisters, and their righteous anger was only exacerbated by the sight of the gendarmes patrolling the heights around Aumontzey. The gendarmes were there to protect Marie-Ange from kidnapping, but it was the gendarmes who had pushed Jean-Marie into killing Bernard. The Bolles were all convinced of that.

At least Marie-Ange had two immediate, concrete problems to occupy her: keeping Bernard's funeral dignified – 'We don't like making a spectacle of ourselves,' she said, and keeping it free of the violence that hung so thick in the air. Three things were clear – three exclusions. Neither Muriel, nor the Villemins, nor the gendarmes should be there. 'They mustn't come: please no!'

Marie-Ange made herself heard. The only Villemins present at her husband's funeral would be those dozen or so already buried in the cemetery. Jussarupt was one of their strongholds. And the only uniforms present would be those of the firemen whom the mayor had ordered to regulate the flow of traffic.

Tuesday 2 April was a spring day, with the sun darting its warmth through intermittent clouds. In Aumontzey, however, Monique and Albert's home looked set for a hard winter. At midday, the blinds were closed, and the metal screen protecting the front entrance had been left down from the night. It was the same at Jacky's house in Granges. Even if clans had never existed in the valley of the Vologne, then the events of the last few months would have sufficed to invent them.

Bernard Laroche had been lying at rest in the lounge of his chalet since Sunday. Marie-Ange had been accompanied all through her vigil by her brothers and sisters. Now, on Tuesday afternoon, she was alone with him for the last few minutes before the funeral procession took him to Saint Gertrude's church.

Just as it had in Lépanges, the knell began to ring at 2.15 p.m. The final tête à tête was interrupted by the arrival of the hearse. The undertakers loaded on board the varnished oak coffin: Bernard Laroche, 1955 – 1985, said the diminutive plaque. Marie-Ange set off with her brothers and sisters. 'It can't be,' she kept moaning. 'It's just not possible.' Christine's words.

At Jussarupt, Bernard's colleagues from Ancel had come to pay homage to their friend and to act as stewards. They were carrying branches of boxwood. Among them, many Muslim immigrants, bringing a note of industrial exoticism to what was more like a peasant funeral. In recognition of Laroche's popularity, Ancel had stopped its timekeepers from from 12.00 p.m. to 4.30 p.m. so the employees could offer their final respects. Laroche would be a loss to the company. On 29 March, three hours before his death, he had been unanimously elected as a CGT delegate to the company works council. At the door to the church, on the marble slab given by his workmates, could be read:

'Since your eyes closed, ours have never stopped crying.'

Next to it lay the offering from Laroche's lawyers, Welzer and Prompt:

'To Bernard Laroche, the innocent victim of blind hatred.'

And Sébastien's:

'To my father. I shall remember you for ever.'

But Marie-Ange did not want her son to remember the trauma of his father's funeral: with or without violence. Sébastien stayed at home on 2 April.

There was no word from Monique, who had raised Bernard, or from Michel, one of his best friends: but, with the insistent parallelism of the affair, there was the same number of mourners, six-hundred. Laroche had even become a political symbol as left-wing militant and martyr; a victim of the right wing, Legitimate Defence movement. However genuine their sympathy for the man, that was the meaning of the presence of two local Communist leaders: the prospective candidate for Bruyères and the federal secretary of the party.

Paul Prompt was there too. He was crying. His emotion had gone beyond the confines of professional or political activity.

As the Bolle cortège approached, the whirring of the cameras dazed and frightened Louisette and her daughter, Chantal. It was all so different from their life before the affair.

Marie-Ange walked with difficulty, held up by her family. She was wearing navy blue and black, and with her as she entered the small church were her father and mother, and Isabelle her sister. Isabelle could easily have been mistaken for Muriel. She had the same flamboyant mane, and dressed in boots, black jeans and jacket: the same freckles and chubby protuberant cheeks. These days, the resemblance was no gift.

Marie-Ange was also shadowed by a plain-clothes agent of the special police. The bodyguard had been watching over her since Monday night in case Jean-Marie's allies decided to try an abduction, or finish off his handiwork.

The coffin was borne in by Bernard's colleagues from Ancel. An elderly woman churned out Bach on a harmonium and the male-dominated singing was broken by the priest's lesson. Abbé Duval had chosen a text whose pertinence could not fail to be noticed.

'I have not hidden my face from the outrages and I have been spat upon. My face has hardened. My face shall remain of stone. I shall not be confounded.'

Events in the Vologne had moved the Bishop of Saint-Dié to make a new declaration to the embittered members of his diocese:

'Once again,' he mourned, 'the tragedy of a valley resounds through a whole nation. Violence so great that it has destroyed life. There is in stored-up bitterness, in gossip and rumour, a mortal venom. At the heart of this tragedy which has brought us together here, there are men and women who suffer. They are our brothers and sisters, bruised in the depths of their being. We want to respect their dignity.'

Echoed by her sisters, Marie-Ange wrestled with sobs as the service proceeded with the breaking of bread, 'the bread which Bernard worked to earn'.

Someone had taken note of the bishop's reminder, for most of the journalists and cameramen had been kept out from the cemetery. They stood on its low protective wall, looking, from a distance, like scarecrows or gargoyles. As the coffin was carried up the main alley to the freshly-dug hole, the stewards from Ancel braced themselves. Nothing, nothing but subdued sobbing could be heard, with the whirr of camera shutters, softer this time. Marie-Ange endured the giving and accepting of condolences without faltering. Then, as she saw Bernard descending into the ground, she broke down: 'No, my darling, no!' She hugged the coffin one last time, and once it had reached the floor, she bent down to deposit a red carnation on the top.

Although most of the photographers were all at a respectful distance, there was a group of journalists standing opposite the family mourners, a row away. Suddenly, one of them pulled out a camera and took two snaps of Marie-Ange. Immediately, another photographer followed suit. As he was about to get up, a steward approached and seemed to beckon. But instead, he caught the man by the lapels and gave him a solid head-butt. Back on the cemetery wall, it was only the fear of violence that held the other photographers back.

The moment was a symbol: gossip, and the avidity of the press, had done enough damage. The Laroche funeral could not undo it, but it might give some people pause for thought, and re-establish a little dignity. Certainly, among the journalists assembled at Jussarupt that day, there were few who had not known Laroche; and few, no doubt, who did not feel uneasy about trying to justify their work.

Bernard Laroche, 'the monster', had enjoyed liberty for only eight weeks. Not long before his death, Judge Lambert had written to Welzer and Prompt declaring his intention to withdraw the charges against him in the very near future.

19

Ten days after the murder at Aumontzey, Christine Villemin gave an interview to *Paris Match* magazine.

'Laroche,' she declared. 'I couldn't care less,' she declared. His death had been too sudden, too clean for Christine Villemin's liking. 'He said he was innocent just to stick Jean-Marie and me in the shit.' That kind of person deserved a bit of agony. At least now, Jean-Marie was relieved. He had got rid of the tension. 'He used to chain smoke, but he told me he's stopped. He said "I feel fine, even if I have this heavy feeling on my chest."'

Christine Villemin herself had never been so worked up, or so full of hate. Everywhere, she found proof of Bernard Laroche's guilt. For example, she noted that, since Grégory's death, Laroche had been especially careful not to let Sébastien out on his own. As if he were worried the boy would give something away. Never mind the common fear of violence, or Jean-Marie's repeated threats: every observation was grist to the Villemin mill.

Especially observations of Marie-Ange. 'If Marie-Ange really is pregnant, then her husband's death doesn't seem to have upset her too much. She's already been to the hairdresser's twice since he was buried.' Marie-Ange had suddenly become a free woman with £3,000 of insurance money to play with: now she had only to speak into a microphone for the windfalls from press exclusives to come fluttering down into her outstretched palm. 'She's the Merry Widow.' In short, the death of Bernard Laroche had ushered in not mourning but the good life. In short, she had every reason to be grateful to Jean-Marie for bereaving her.

What in other circumstances might have passed as small-town cattiness was printed a week after Bernard Laroche's funeral. Christine's recriminations were set against Marie-Ange's in a diptych of hate. The affair had become a clash of men driven by the mutual hatred of their wives. As if Bernard and Jean-Marie were mere executants.

Marie-Ange returned the same treatment. The story Christine told about Bernard trying to play footsie was a fabrication, she protested: for a start, Jean-Marie had not been on parole from military service at the time, and she and Bernard were already married. 'Bernard always told me everything.' Christine was a liar, she said, always making things up.

It was like a schoolgirls' squabble, more appropriate to the days when they were both neighbours in Laveline and pupils at the Lycée Jean Lurçat in Bruyères. Except that now the two women were arguing over two corpses and a dozen or so ruined or mutilated lives.

On the day of Jean-Marie's incarceration, Christine phoned Monique Villemin.

'That'll make a few people happy,' she insinuated.

'I suppose you're talking about Michel.'

'Him and the others.'

Michel was the other, associated obsession.

Christine pointed out that her brother-in-law had lost more than 10 kilos since 16 October. Why? Perhaps he was feeling uncomfortable about something? And then who could prove that the Crow really did call him that afternoon to announce that Grégory had been drowned? The whole thing could have been a ploy he had agreed upon with Bernard Laroche, his close friend. Laroche could easily have planned the whole operation with Michel: hence the afternoon they spent together just before the crime.

Neither she nor Jean-Marie cared what the family thought of their suspicions. Anyway, Jean-Marie had refused to see his parents in Nancy. He needed them earlier. Now it was too late.

If the couple had been misunderstood, then it was for others to change, not them.

In the Charles III prison, where he was sharing a cell with two other prisoners, one accused of a hold-up, the other of murdering his wife, Jean-Marie told Garaud: 'The judge just didn't understand us. He's not a father. That's what made me despair.' Despair, and outraged family feeling, had killed Bernard Laroche.

Christine Villemin's new existence was almost as confined as her husband's. Some 80 kilometres from Lépanges, she spent most of her time indoors, obeying police instructions to avoid journalists. They said it was for her own protection. But at least she had the moral support of her grandmother Jeanne Blaise, and her protective brother, Alain. Petitmont was a Blaise stronghold, Christine's birthplace, and the last resting place of her father. She had always preferred the area to the Vosges. It was as good a place as any to hold out against the ever-ready cameramen without and the sadness within. There would soon be a support committee too, organised by the mayor, Bernard Teisworth, who circulated a petition with the words: 'It is intolerable that an individual's freedom should be so impinged upon that they cannot lead a normal life in the calm and peace of the village.'

Christine's health was still a source of worry: her pregnancy was precarious. The bleeding that took her into Epinal came back twice after Jean-Marie killed Laroche, like an index of fear or excitement. This was her third month, one of the most crucial and the most difficult. Christine was being closely followed by a gynaecologist in Lunéville and she was forbidden to travel. In her state, visits to Grégory's grave in Lépanges were out of the question. And as for going to Nancy, Lambert had not yet granted her permission. At Easter, however, Christine made a short journey to spend the weekend with her sister, and, sure enough, the bleeding started again. A few days later, Christine Villemin made the news official: 'I have lost one of the twins I was carrying.' She was none too sure she would be able to travel to Epinal on 17 April for her interview with Judge Lambert.

What excuse could be more legitimate or more heart-rending? Christine Villemin was not expecting the doctors at *La Roseraie* to issue a formal denial stating that she had not been carrying twins.

It was not the first time Christine Villemin's version of reality had been contradicted. Her partial use of truth was beginning to alienate people. Even her good friend, Christine Jacquot, seemed to have changed her attitude since the murder of Laroche. 'Of course,' said Jacquot, she continued to believe in Christine's innocence, 'but then one does see such strange things.' Jacquot had no intention of contacting her former flat-mate; she was too afraid of getting caught in the position of prime witness again, as she had on 16 October and 29 March. 'I'm not going to put myself in the shit for them,' she said.

But that did not stop the SRPJ wanting to talk to her. As a concession to the Jacquot family's fears of getting involved, Christine was driven out of the Vologne in the boot of her brother's car. When she emerged, smiling, she was transferred to a police vehicle to be taken to Nancy. It was all getting a bit ridiculous. But by the logic of previous events, a key witness was a hot target.

Jacquot's seven hours with Corazzi and his colleagues yielded a contradiction and a confirmation. On 29 March, Jean-Marie was indeed worked up because he knew the SRPJ were interested in his wife and could not bear the doubt. And secondly, the contradiction: 'Christine must have been dreaming. I absolutely wasn't crying when I came into Christine's room that morning. Why did she go and make that up?'

So, as one journalist put it, on 29 March, Jean-Marie killed his doubts. And, as Marie-Ange claimed, 'Christine Villemin was always making things up.' Perhaps she read too many romances.

The contradiction reminded the SRPJ of another difference between the two Christines. This one concerned an exclamation made on 16 October: 'I'll never see the boy again.' Whereas Christine Villemin claimed she said those words at Paremont at about 6.00 p.m., Christine Jacquot remembered hearing them at Gaichamp, around 5.30 p.m. If Jacquot were right, that would mean Christine Villemin had foreseen her son's death before anyone knew what had happened to him. The premonition was disturbing, to say the least. Seen in that light, it was strange that Christine Villemin had never warned her friend of the danger hanging over Grégory.

There was something strange about the way Christine described the case, too. Referring to the fact that a syringe had been found near the scene of the crime, she recalled that only Jeannine Bolle, Laroche's mother-in-law, could use such a device, since she suffered from diabetes: but then, she admitted, the autopsy found no trace of insulin in Grégory's body. 'It is a shame, because it would have explained Grégory's serenity. If the little one had been given a jab, that would have strengthened the case against Laroche. And that would have helped us.' Christine seemed to be thinking aloud, playing with potential strategies. It was as if the case against Laroche were not strong enough on its own, or as if it needed making up. Her logic seemed to run: we have decided Laroche is guilty, therefore we must find evidence to back us up.

Christine Villemin seemed to carry her subconscious in her mouth. It was as if two women were speaking at the same time: 'La Villemin' and the 'grieving innocent'. Between them suspicion lodged. La Villemin spoke like a hard-hearted selfish creature. When she said 'I wish Grégory could come back, if only for a few minutes,' it was just so that 'he could tell me who threw him in the water'. Was that the only reason? Besides, dead children can no more come back to life than suspects in France can take the truth drug. All that was an attempt to throw the investigators off the track. Of what?

Contradictions and ambiguities are not much without concrete evidence. The SRPJ was anxious to press on with investigations. Like Christine Villemin, they seemed particularly interested in the insulin syringe that had been discovered near the Vologne two days after Grégory's death. They were also focusing on Paremont. One member of the force spent hours panning the gravel which still lay outside the house. The SRPJ were nothing if not meticulous, but the gravel kept its secret.

However, the men combing Paremont did come up with something rather more interesting: a piece of rope. They found it holding the gutter in place on the roof. It was an unusual variety, with three tightly interwoven strands: the sort you would never find in hardware shops. Its origin, they thought, was industrial – from one of the spinning mills. The SRPJ also found lengths of the same rope in the garden, and in a pair of Jean-Marie's shoes, standing in for his laces. A sample was immediately dispatched to Lyon for laboratory analysis.

On 25 April, Jean-Marie and Christine were summoned to Epinal to be shown the new evidence. Jean-Marie recognised the rope: it was his. When he saw the cord that had bound Grégory's wrists he just went pale: lost for words.

Christine was blank. 'I've never seen it before. It's Jean-Marie who does the handiwork around the house.' He must have used it the previous winter for some repair she didn't even know about.

The three minutes the couple were allowed to spend together before Jean-Marie returned to prison were their first for four weeks. Their joy was muted. Jean-Marie left Epinal tight-lipped and frowning. This time, there were no words, no trenchant declarations for the perennial journalists.

Following her interview, Christine was taken up to Paremont in the company of Maître Garaud. The police were carrying out a second search. She stood and watched as they discovered more lengths of rope under the radiator in the sitting-room and under a pile of wood outside.

In Grandvilliers, the home of the Villemins' friend Martial David, police searchers found two more pieces of the same rope among belongings the couple left there when they moved from Paremont. In Gilberte Chatel's flat in Bruyères there was no rope, but there was an interesting cassette in the hi-fi system. The SRPJ had every reason to believe their collection of Crow recordings was complete. But here, quite by surprise, they had stumbled upon something new. Jean-Marie had received it at work, a message to be savoured with hindsight. 'And as for you, chief, I'm going to put a bullet in your back. But you'll get over it and I'll come and bring you oranges in hospital. You won't recognise me. I'd rather get at your brat. You'll find him stagnating down below.'

A few days later, Judge Lambert summoned Christine Villemin to Epinal for the results of Bucquet and de Ricci's new handwriting analyses. The message was simple: no change. She was still the possible author of the Crow's letters. In what was becoming routine, Garaud immediately demanded counter-expertises and Lambert obliged by appointing two new national experts. Roger Larfer and Jean Glénisson. A month would go by before he could be sure of bringing new scientific evidence to the case.

Christine could not wait that long. After the meeting with Lambert, Garaud came out onto the steps of the town hall to read the declaration from his client:

'I can't take any more,' she pleaded. Being judged by the press before she had even been charged was 'torture'. If she continued to fight, it was only because Jean-Marie needed her. 'I'm sure there are people who would say: if she killed herself, then she's guilty.' Christine Villemin, who had made the mistake of giving dozens of interviews, was sick of having her private sorrow paraded around the market place: 'Grégory has become a new kind of lottery. The assassination of my son is a gold mine that must be exploited every day.'

Her own personality had become part of the game, too. The interest of understanding it had not escaped the SRPJ. They had taken on a psychologist to analyse Christine's words, reactions and behaviour.

There was plenty for him to get his teeth into. For in spite of her secluded existence, La Villemin was still managing to make herself heard, and to answer some of the questions incessantly thrown to her by journalists. She might have done better to unplug the telephone and refuse all meetings.

Just before her audience with Lambert, Christine gave a new demonstration of her sharp tongue. In 'Christine Villemin's Confessions,' as it was entitled in the *Parisien Libéré* (which accorded her two and a half full pages), she re-formulated her statement on the gendarmes' role in Laroche's death: 'They said there wasn't enough evidence to charge him but there was enough for Jean-Marie not to be condemned if he knocked him off.' Then she vented her sarcasm on the 'extremely well paid' handwriting experts and insisted that Laroche had killed Grégory out of jealousy of her marriage to Jean-Marie: 'I know that their union was hardly a great success.'

It was the usual Villemin tone: the mixture of petty aggression and heart-rending sorrow. And the constant readiness to describe the slightest details of her emotional life. It was hard to forget that it was Christine who had brought Bernard Laroche to the attention of the gendarmes with her talk about playing footsie: and that it was her cheque that had paid for the rifle that killed him. And so what if, as Christine stated, she had always held the purse strings for their purchases. Everyone knew that Jean-Marie at first refused to believe in Laroche's guilt, then suddenly became obsessional about it. All Christine had ever expressed was certitude.

For those predisposed to notice it, there was something offensive in Christine's brutal frankness: in the way she both insisted on the strength of the love between her and Jean-Marie and admitted: 'If I didn't love him, I'd have divorced him ages ago.' Or quoted Jean-

Marie's letters from prison: 'For me, Grégory was of that same pure gold as you are, my treasure.' Where was the modesty and restraint you expect from a grieving mother?

Of course, it was just as simple to see these statements as the attempts of a solitary woman with a clear conscience to relieve the nervous tension that had accumulated over the months. Or as no more than childish fits of bad temper. After all, Christine remained defiantly unafraid of her interview with Judge Lambert – or so said Henri Garaud.

Events, or this event at least, proved her right. After four hours of questioning from the 'Little Judge', without the assistance of Henri Garaud, Christine was cleared of complicity in the events of 29 March. It would come as a surprise to Marie-Ange, who could not understand why Christine had not been 'troubled'. For the Bolles, 'the witch is responsible for everything'.

Christine was therefore left to continue on her own particular war-path: Laroche, and Michel Villemin.

Laroche was still very much on Lambert's mind, too. As he told Marie-Ange: 'You know, I can't get your husband's death out of my mind. When I charged him, it was on trust. I didn't have the gendarmes' records.'

The least he could do was give Bernard Laroche – or his death – a proper reconstruction. The event was set for 20 June.

Viewed from a distance, there was something grotesque about the exercise. The journalists started to arrive on the night of 19 June, like shoppers at the opening of Harrods' sale. Some slept in cars, others found lodgings with local residents. The less devoted started turning up early the next morning. It made no difference, though. Nothing happened.

Then, at two o'clock in the afternoon, a convoy of police vans drew up. Two hundred men in uniforms began to fan out around the Laroche chalet, some of them with dogs, as if in a belated attempt to protect the dead man, exaggerated by bad conscience. Negotiations were started up with photographers and commonly acceptable positions were found. The better equipped crouched behind telescopes on the top of their vans. Others pressed against the security cordon in the hope of catching an emotional word or two.

Inside the security cordon, Jean-Marie waited, his face gaunt from loss of weight, highlighted by an austere prison haircut. He was wearing a bullet-proof jacket: even with all the policemen, he was a sitting target for the better marksmen in the Bolle family.

Against him, against the black and blue of police uniforms, Marie-Ange looked a fragile, incongruous figure in her blue, floral-patterned maternity dress. She was bitterly indignant at the 'special treatment' being meted out to the Villemins. What did Bernard get? He had been dropped by the gendarmes just as suddenly and brutally as they had taken him in. He had never had a single bodyguard, let alone two hundred.

To Jean-Marie, the whole exercise was absurd. He had never intended to deny a murder he considered both justifiable and honourable. So why all these policemen and questions? It was a side-show. The choreography of a death announced, rehearsed and, now, commemorated. And Grégory's death?

The event took one and a half hours. Judge Lambert repeated his instructions like a patient director and the lawyers took notes and consulted or comforted their clients. Five times, Jean-Marie advanced from the trees with his gun, and five times Marie-Ange wanted to change a distance or the height of the barrel. Every time Villemin lifted the butt to his shoulders she flinched and looked away. She kept drawing a small white handkerchief from her pocket, and Welzer hastened to console her. Jean-Marie dutifully executed, he even found it in himself to smile at Garaud. He had not come to contradict Marie-Ange or Lucien, except on one point – the murder that started it all. When Jean-Marie repeated his convictions about the man he had killed, she was overheard shouting back: 'Shut up! You know perfectly well who killed Grégory.' Jean-Marie went pale: 'Christine! No! She loved Grégory.'

Jean-Marie would never admit to doubt if you put the question point blank. However, evidence had come to light suggesting he was not quite as rock-like as he appeared. A few weeks earlier, the killer of Bernard Laroche was transferred from the Charles III prison in Nancy to Saverne, a more modern and intimate establishment. The official reason was that he would be nearer Christine. Others said that he had been involved in fights with the other prisoners and warders had found razor blades and rope under his mattress. Jean-Marie had written to his mother: 'I doubt, and I who never used to pray have started praying.'

20

By the end of June, Jean-Michel Lambert found himself staring at an uncomfortable conclusion: Christine Villemin had killed her son.

An intimate conviction of this sort is hard enough to admit to, let alone to act upon. But Lambert felt he had no choice. Before him, the SRPJ synthesis report and the latest expert analyses all pointed in the same direction: Grégory's murderer was his mother. This was not titillating, chilling press rumour, but a list of facts and probabilities.

First of all, the analysts in Lyon had reported that the rope found at Paremont was 'rigorously identical' to that used to bind Grégory Villemin. Left in a jar of Vologne water, the strands behaved in exactly the same way. No other member of the family possessed any lengths or balls of such rope: they had all been shown it and failed to recognise it. It was a rare variety – masons' rope most likely.

Second, but of increasing importance, the graphological tests. Larfer and Glénisson confirmed what Bucquet and de Ricci had already concluded on two separate occasions: Christine Villemin's handwriting was most probably the Crow's. Laroche's came nowhere in sight.

Of course, these discoveries could be written off as coincidences. But there were many others. From an analysis of the Villemins' depositions, the SRPJ had realised that Jean-Marie had nearly always been on his own when the Crow had called. Even with the daily reality of shift work, it seemed remarkable that Christine should never have been there, and that she too had always received calls when she was on her own. About the only call they had been together for was from a man asking for a 'Monsieur Villemin', the local bone-setter.

Another discovery was more serious. When they analysed the

couple's phone bills, the police noticed that their expenditure had nearly quadrupled during the period of the Crow's peak activity. Neither Jean-Marie nor his wife were the chatty sort, but no one else in their entourage had spent as much on telecommunications.

Christine of course could explain: she had been phoning around for a second-hand car. Unfortunately, two witnesses from outside the family circle had also identified her as the Crow. One of them, a workmate, had been harassed on several occasions. Marie-Claude Magron remembered buying an item on credit at the MCV shop because she was short of cash. Before she had paid back the loan, Magron received a couple of anonymous phone calls: 'Thief!' the voice accused.

Christine Villemin had been in the shop when Marie-Claude bought the goods. And Marie-Claude Magron's husband Bruno was Christine's former boyfriend: their relationship had ended unhappily for Grégory's mother.

But what of the day itself, the crucial and mysterious half hour? Christine's four workmates continued to insist that they had seen her on her way to the post office on 16 October. Maria Leite, a young Portuguese woman, had seen her car heading towards Bruyères, the opposite direction from home. Sandrine Loupes had seen her stopping outside the post office and Anne Marie Texeira had seen her putting a letter in the box, while Marie-Lise Blondel remembered seeing the Renault 5 doing a U-turn outside. Could they all have got the date mixed up, and remembered Christine's visit of Monday 15 October? It seemed unlikely. Marie Leite always caught the train to Laveline just before five, and Christine had already stated that she went to the post at 5.30 p.m. on Monday: Maria could not have seen her that day. Sandrine Loupes confirmed. She remembered getting a phone call from her aunt in Lépanges, just after the murder was known. 'Oh no! It's horrible,' she exclaimed. 'I saw Christine tonight outside work. She was posting a letter.' The aunt also remembered her niece's exclamation.

How was it that Christine's visit to the post office could be so strongly attested, and her presence at Paremont so little perceived? Neither Bernard Colin nor Gilbert Meline, the nearest neighbour, had seen Christine, or Grégory, or the car, outside the house. Christine said she was listening to the *Grosses Têtes* on a medium wave station,

RTL, but the radio was found to be set on FM. Besides, the *Vâche Grosjean* advertisement she claimed to have heard was not broadcast after 5.00 p.m.

All this made for a lot of inconsistencies, especially when you added them to the other contradictions or half-truths: the invention of the lost twin, the embroidering on Laroche's death which even Jean-Marie had contradicted, and the discrepancy between her memory and Jacquot's: that elusive phrase she pronounced at Gaichamp about never seeing Titi again.

Could Christine Villemin have planned the murder? Certainly, she could give no convincing explanation why she had taken time off during the weeks preceding Grégory's death. At first, she had said it was because she needed to see the gendarmes at Corcieux about the Crow, but she soon admitted this was untrue. The investigators were still waiting for her to supply a better reason. Funnily enough, Christine had also planned to take the morning off on 17 October: that of course was when the murder note would arrive. Christine would thus have been in an ideal position to intercept it should the assassination fail. Yet another coincidence. Naturally the SRPJ had noticed that the note was addressed to 'Monsieur' and not 'Monsieur et Madame' Villemin.

Of course, that still left the question of motivation. An answer was surely not far away. The press had already quoted the SRPJ psychologist's description of the subject as 'an intelligent, cunning, tough and choleric woman'. The SRPJ expert was particularly interested in her statement about not 'cracking before Laroche confesses'. And then there was the strangely double-edged reaction to rumours of her impending inculpation: 'If they haven't got further than that, then they really are a bunch of fools.' Fools not to judge her, or fools not to look elsewhere? The French word was *con*; it had also been used on the note sent to 'Monsieur Villemin' on 16 October: '*pauvre con*' it said.

'You can't imagine how lonely an examining judge can be when he has to take his decision. You're alone, absolutely alone.'

Jean-Michel Lambert had entered the most solitary phase of his career, the loneliness being magnified by the celebrity of the case. The press had been hinting at Christine Villemin's possible guilt for months now. Arrest was in the air, and yet to take the step was to plunge the affair into a new dimension. Whatever happened, he alone would be held responsible.

Of course, there was no lack of advice. Many told him to let the case sleep for a while. But there was also duty, and personal conviction. And the memory of Bernard Laroche. It was the fear of repeating his mistakes of eight months earlier that made Lambert conduct a new series of interviews with key witnesses, and that drove him to insist: 'If you have any doubts about what you say, please abstain.'

No one did. Neither did the experts in Lyon, nor Larfer nor Glénisson.

Lambert did not want to carry the burden of decision alone. He phoned the public prosecutor at Nancy, Roger Descharmes, and explained. 'Yes, obviously it is difficult,' he was told. 'But you must do what you think is right.'

On Thursday 4 July, Lambert returned late as usual to his flat, just across the Moselle from the magistrates' offices. He was agitated, bursting with his unhatched decision. He put on a record, a protest song by Léo Ferré called 'Can't take no more!': something from the 'hard period'. Then, like an adolescent, he burst into tears. The next day he would be accusing a young woman of infanticide. And putting her in prison. He knew too that the prosecutor, Jacques Lecomte, was against him, just as he had been against releasing Laroche. Lecomte had orders from very high up in the chancellery.

And Lambert, like everyone else, had read Christine Villemin's declarations in the papers: 'If they put me in prison, they'll have to carry me out feet first. I'm not going to just sit there and let them wash, feed and launder me. I'm not going to let them accuse me of a thing I haven't done.'

The next day, the atmosphere in the *Palais de Justice* was electric. One colleague pointed to Lambert's tie and said, 'Arresting today, are you?' Lambert only wore ties on big days.

At 9.30 a.m., Lambert summoned Gérard Andrieu and Jacques Corazzi to his office. He made out an arrest warrant, and then they set about planning the best, most discreet way of taking their suspect. The last thing anybody wanted was a scandal.

Then Lambert was left alone to flick listlessly through other files. And to wait, rehearsing the scene he was about to play – trying to calm his nerves and strengthen his convictions. At lunchtime, he was back in his flat, back to the cathartic dramatisation of Léo Ferré's song about a judge. 'Integrity is what counts,' it said, and Lambert felt, poignantly, that he had no lack of that.

At 2.00 p.m., Christine Villemin arrived in Saverne with two of her cousins to visit Jean-Marie. Her black dungarees showed off her swelling, six-months pregnant belly, her cheeks had grown fleshier. Christine Villemin seemed relaxed. She joked with the photographers who pursued her down the street, and then entered the prison.

She never got to her husband. Inside, the warders told her to go back to the governor's office. There she was met by Andrieu and Corazzi. Outside, impatient visitors were told that there was a technical problem due to a jammed lock: they would have to wait a few minutes before seeing their loved ones. But the real technical problem was how to get Christine Villemin out of Saverne without attracting too much attention.

When Christine Villemin saw the men from the SRPJ she thought she understood:

'Are you arresting me for the murder of Bernard Laroche?'

'No Madame, for Grégory's.'

'You're joking.'

'Not really, Madame.'

21

It would have gone like this:

She was born one of six children in the Meurthe and Moselle. It was a happy childhood, shared between the affections of her mother Gilberte and her grandmother Jeanne. The children used to play in the woods where their imaginations could roam at leisure. Christine dreamt of being a missionary in Africa, caring for little children.

She did not see her father often: he was a hard-grafting woodcutter who usually came home late. But that made their outings together such special occasions, the stuff of childhood fantasy. One day, when he returned from work his foot was blue and they had to take him to hospital to have a plastic artery put in. It was brutally sudden, and it was not enough. Two days later, they had to amputate up to the knee. Soon, the second leg was infected. This time it was too late to amputate. Lucien Blaise died in hospital after weeks of atrocious pain.

Christine Villemin was six at the time. The image of her father's agony would forever be coming back in her nightmares. The child was suddenly exposed, her world made insecure.

Then came the next shock. After a short and unhappy second marriage, Christine's mother had to move to Laveline-devant-Bruyères in the Vosges; there was a job going.

Christine was approaching her teens. She found that whereas the Meurthe and Moselle were picturesque, life in the Vosges and in Laveline was harsh and unadorned. The people were more brutal.

In the ugliness of her environment, Christine sought refuge in the world of dreams. Romance. She was a shy, sensitive girl, and could never get used to the brutality of school life, although she was an outstanding pupil. A first brief relationship ended unhappily for her.

Then, at the age of sixteen, she met Jean-Marie. He seemed different from the others. He had ideals, he was gentle but strong, sensitive but resolute: the nearest to her ideal. Still, Christine was anxious not to get too involved too quickly. She had seen her mother divorce and an older sister maltreated by her husband. The idea of such mediocrity appalled her.

However, Jean-Marie had begun pressing her to become a part of the family. Soon, he had her staying with them for Christmas. That was when they first slept together.

The family: All workers, tied to the Vologne and to their lowly lives. Christine felt lost among the crowds of relatives, of brothers and sisters, and she could not hide her distaste. And they of course found Christine pretentious with her social aspirations, with her careful dressing, her dreams of kinder landscapes.

At least Jean-Marie shared them.

But then Christine had to leave school in order to earn money. The relationship was becoming serious. They were going to live together. They spoke of going away to find jobs in the south.

But then Jean-Marie got a job at Autocoussin.

And now he wanted a house in the Vosges.

A job came up in the Camargue, minding horses. They were tempted, but it passed them by. Jean-Marie had just been promoted and there was no question of forsaking his career. He was so proud: success at work, an attractive wife. She felt like an object.

The couple got married. It was a joyless, almost furtive ceremony. Just five of them. No romance. And she was his. Jean-Marie was a man of law, his law. He spoke of his work, his family, his possessions – of strict certainties.

Christine's yearnings were pushed aside, into a corner of her mind. In their place, a quiet desperation grew. She was stuck in a dull job. She found herself caught in the machinery of a vast family with its interminable meetings, its bickering and small envies: she was a reject – 'the snob'. Christine grew bitter. Sometimes there were rows with Jean-Marie. One night, he slapped her. She tried to run away to the south: he caught her.

And now she was pregnant. Pregnant without desire for the father.

Without desire for the child. Made with child as cattle are branded: his. 'That'll stop you running away,' he said.

And now they were moving to *his* house, up on the slopes, in the middle of nowhere. Her solitude was starker here, and her thoughts stretched out into the nights and the forest. She thought about the family, their ugliness, and their mediocre ambitions. And she saw the child before her, the proof that it was all real, inescapable.

What she could not say, what Jean-Marie did not want to hear, she kept to herself. Then started saying it over the phone, making sure no one recognised her, no one saw. She was often alone. And she wrote. And watched what happened.

The desperation did not go away. The child grew to be a man's child: Jean-Marie's thing, his deputy.

Already, he had the certainties and the intolerance of the father. He made the father's demands on her.

She saw the years ahead of her and knew it would never end. Look at Monique.

Sometimes the thoughts subsided, sometimes they swelled up. And the idea of freedom kept prickling her mind. But there were the obstacles. The obstacle. She knew without knowing, it was a matter of time. And she learned to dissimulate, to manipulate and spread doubt, to turn the family against itself: by phone, first, and even by letter.

When it came, it was blind haste. Absolute urgency. That day she did everything as usual. Until she posted the letter, the letter she had written like a speculation. Until she took the boy, not home, never home. To the river. And phoned, as she had imagined it so many times, not believing it. And now she had all her life to wake up to it . . .

That, as some people saw it, was how Christine Villemin became an infanticide. Those who believed conclusively that she had killed her healthy, smiling son.

Christine Villemin was now in prison. And journalists and writers were all trying to understand her guilt, her possible guilt, or her possible innocence. It was no simple legal debate, but the public construction of a character: innocent, crucified mother, or diabolic infanticide.

The fascination was taken to its height by an article in the daily *Libération* by Marguerite Duras. Duras had just won the nation's prestigious literary prize, the Goncourt, and sold nearly a million copies of the prize-winning book. She was everywhere. And so was the clinching phrase from her portrait of Christine Villemin, the woman who, Duras believed, had killed her son. This was no sordid crime, but an act only other women could understand, an act of a woman crushed by the law imposed by men. Like Medea, a tragic heroine of elemental proportions, a part of all women. This crime was '*sublime, forcément sublime*'.

The phrase has entered the French language.

22

I t was 3.00 p.m. when Christine Villemin was handcuffed and led out of Saverne prison. She had a black cardigan over her head, but she was not trying to hide herself: she was not 'ashamed to have disfigured myself with crying'. It was the SRPJ who made her use it. They were finding her singularly uncooperative that day. She had also refused to sign the arrest warrant.

In Epinal, the unfailingly debonair Judge Lambert was going through a severe attack of nerves. He was as pale as a corpse. At 2.30 p.m., Andrieu phoned from Saverne to tell him that Christine Villemin had been arrested. Now he had an hour and a half to imagine how it would feel to confront a mother you have just accused of murdering her own child. He was looking through the eyes of an executioner.

At 4.10 p.m., Christine Villemin was escorted into the building. Lambert began sobbing. Perhaps a little emotion was justified. He had known her for nine months now. He had found himself calling her 'my little Christine.' or 'my dear Christine'. His little Christine had killed her son. Fortunately for Lambert's professional composure, though, Garaud arrived in his office a few minutes before his client. There was nothing like a good heated discussion of procedure to clear the mind.

When Christine did come in, Lambert did not look at her. He was trying to concentrate on the task in hand. He would not look at her. He heard her repeating 'It's disgusting, my little one, disgusting!' He knew the mixture of anger and supplication that came into her eyes. Lecomte was there too, stiffly hostile. So Lambert rehearsed his arguments and read the official accusation.

Christine Villemin cajoled and threatened. She warned him she would not go passively. She would be an embarrassing prisoner. She would go on hunger strike. And if Jean-Marie committed suicide because of what he'd done, he, Lambert, would be responsible. 'You haven't heard the last of me!' she said.

Practical arrangements. Lambert phoned the prison at Metz Queuleu. 'What treatment are you on for your pregnancy, Christine?'

'What does that matter to you if you're putting me in prison!'

'Don't be silly, Christine.'

Metz Queuleu prison is about two hours' drive from Epinal. It is a modern establishment with crisp white corridors and glossy painted doors. Clinical. Outside, it has the cold, hostile, rectangular look of a building designed for only two functions: the storage and surveillance of human beings. But Metz Queuleu has a centralised electronic monitoring system for every cell, as well as special facilities for pregnant women.

Lambert had chosen it with care.

Christine Villemin arrived at 8.00 p.m. She was told to give up her clothing and even her Grégory medallion for keeping by the prison staff. And, while she was allowed to keep her wedding ring, she lost her married name. Now she was no longer Villemin but Blaise; as if her maiden name stripped her of her rights as mother and wife. As a protective measure it was half-baked. The prisoners all knew Christine Villemin was coming, and they had no trouble identifying her. Still, Christine did not suffer from the hatred that had greeted Bernard Laroche in Nancy. As the affair's second suspect, she had the benefit of the doubt and, as a mother, the understanding of her fellow prisoners. It is a shared, if taboo knowledge, the maternal urge – not to kill, but to no longer have a baby. Even the happiest mothers can feel it, if only for a few seconds. The rest is a question of circumstances.

Christine Blaise spent her first night awake. It was a chance to get to know her mates in cell 210. Martine and Sylvie were around the same age; one was awaiting trial for a hold-up and the other, a battered wife, for an attempt to take revenge on her husband. Out of despair, she had killed her child by suffocation.

It was despair, now, that led Christine Blaise to keep her promise. That evening she began her hunger strike.

186

Lambert had chosen prudently. Not only was Christine Villemin carrying a baby, she also had to worry about a possible new attack of phlebitis, as well as the state of her kidneys: they had been infected when she was a child.

But never mind the medical surveillance. Christine Villemin was clinging to death, dragging her unborn child with her. The infanticide had been tracked down and cornered: the innocent mother had reached the last phase of her martyrdom. Around her, ruins.

For the price of a small investment on the news-stands you could make your choice between these two options, between 'martyred angel' and 'Machiavellian demon'. Everywhere, 'reason trembled before the terrible suspicion'. Christine Villemin was on the way to supplanting royalty as the staple of the sensationalist press. One magazine, *VSD*, conducted a survey on the affair and found that more than eighty per cent of the population were 'interested', half of them 'intensely' so. And more of them believed the truth would never be known (42 per cent) than were confident in the ability of the police to find the answer to the crime (40 per cent).

Locally, the sale of newspapers had tripled. 'Everyone is asking: is she a monster?' titled one of them. But in the Vosges interest was mixed with shame, lassitude, or disgust. People preferred to talk about the *Tour de France*, which was due to pass through Epinal that weekend. The combination of folklore and sport was a fine idea, and this year it was salutary. A touch of gaiety under glorious sunshine would perhaps wash away the bitter taste. Not that everyone reacted in the same way: one local newspaper births column informed readers that 'the Laroche family' were happy to welcome their new-born son: Grégory. It was becoming a fashionable name.

Grégory had put Lépanges on the map. The Vologne had become an obligatory detour for tourists. Couriers mugged up on the sensational details of the saga in order to pep up their guided tours of the Vosges, and coaches of holiday-makers started following the goods vehicles along the D44. In the cemetery, families took photographs of Grégory's tomb and the more sentimental laid down the odd posy. Others went up to Paremont and came away with a bit of gravel as a souvenir, or meditated by the river. The place had become a sort of morbid theme park, complete with farouche rustics and fun activities such as posting a letter at Lépanges post office or phoning from a local call box.

Among the protagonists of the affair, reactions were naturally much more down to earth. 'It's not the first time a mother has killed her child.' While Marie-Ange was 'objective', the Villemins were strangely silent. 'Well, you see,' explained Jacky, 'it's been such a talking point.' They had got used to the idea. And then, did they really know Christine Blaise?

It was left to Garaud to thunder against the 'irreparable' damage that had been done, and to press for immediate release.

In Saverne, Jean-Marie lost no time in manifesting his solidarity. On 8 July, he too went on hunger strike. 'I shall refuse to eat until I can see her again. She's a wonderful woman. I can't live without her,' he protested.

He would have to learn. Whatever he thought of Christine's merits or her hunger strike, Jean-Michel Lambert decided to reject Garaud's appeal, because of the needs of the judiciary. Garaud and Chastant, now joined by Thierry Moser, a barrister from Mulhouse, therefore took the case to the Appeal Court in Nancy. And Lambert instructed Corazzi and Andrieu to conduct further investigations.

The legal battle was growing ever more complex. As if she had at last found a way of avenging herself, Marie-Ange now chose to become *partie civile* against Christine Villemin, for her alleged role in the killing at Aumontzey. And, four days later, on 12 July, Albert and Monique Villemin arrived at the *Palais de Justice*. They too were becoming *partie civile*. Their chosen barrister, Paul Lombard, was one of the most distinguished and best known in France. On behalf of his clients and two colleagues, Maîtres Lagrange and Bourdelle, Lombard declared that the grandparents' action had been taken merely in the name of the truth, and was directed against no one in particular. The aim, he said, was to exert pressure on the investigation so that proper light could be shed on both cases.

Of course, Jean-Marie could hardly be expected to take it that way. Nor could Christine, who had heard the news on an 'enemy' radio station, RTL. Lombard's lofty declaration was a fine thing, but why hadn't the Villemin family intervened earlier; when Laroche was still alive for example? Or right at the beginning, when Jean-Marie and

Christine invited them to? Worse, Albert and Monique had been joined by Jacky and Michel and their wives Liliane and Ginette. Michel had been Laroche's 'milk brother', and Jacky the first suspect. Jean-Marie knew they were not benevolent neutrals. The family was split, with only Jacqueline and Gilbert and their spouses remaining on their side. Monique and Albert's action was a betrayal that Jean-Marie would never forgive.

At least he was no longer on hunger strike when the news came to him. Christine had started accepting food on 10 July, when she heard that the Nancy Appeal Court had brought forward their hearing of her case to 15 July. Her husband followed as soon as he had gathered the news from Garaud's telegram. Christine had lost 5 kilos, but her baby was safe. Garaud had warned her that to continue her protest would look like a very crude attempt to put pressure on the judges in Nancy. A tactical error as much perhaps as a medical one. But then the two were intimately linked for Christine: 'I want my innocence to be recognised. If it isn't, I'll die.' Judging by past performances, the threat was to be taken seriously.

The same emotional logic governed Marie-Ange. As Gérard Welzer hastened to make known, Laroche's widow was capable of anything if Christine Villemin were released. Her health was fragile, and she had threatened to kill herself if she lost her baby. So much for the Merry Widow.

Christine's twenty-fifth birthday was on 13 July. From Paris, to find a motive for murder, came two psychiatrists commissioned by Judge Lambert, Serge Brion and Jacques Leyrier. From Nancy, a bouquet of twenty-five red roses and a small parcel: it contained a heart-shaped wooden frame carved by one of Jean-Marie's fellow prisoners. From the scrolls and flourishes wrought by the craftsman beamed the smiling image of Grégory.

Two days later, Jean-Michel Lambert arrived at the prison to sneak an interview while Garaud, Moser and Chastant were busy in Nancy, arguing the case for Christine's release in front of the Appeal Court. But Lambert ran into the same adamantine rebuttal as ever. And when the little judge held out his hand in farewell, his 'dear Christine' refused to take it. That seemed to surprise him.

A day after being snubbed by Christine Villemin, Lambert was given a slap in the face by the Appeal Court. Or so it was described. They had decided that Lambert's presumptions could not, in the circumstances, justify keeping a six-month pregnant woman in jail: especially when she was as famous as Christine Villemin. *Le petit juge* really was on his own.

As the magistrates admitted, Christine Villemin might have had the time to kill her son, and the investigators had uncovered numerous clues pointing to the possibility of her guilt: but there was still no convincing motive, and the evidence needed to be more thoroughly checked. Meanwhile, Christine would be placed under police surveillance and confined to her residence.

For a slap in the face, it was very gentle. As a victory for Christine Villemin, it was makeshift.

But such considerations were for another day. Once the news had reached Metz, Christine's fellow prisoners cheered and embraced her. It was as if she had won a prize. Release for one was a victory for them all. Such unanimous sympathy was a novelty. It was echoed by Garaud and Chastant's high spirits as they embraced her and escorted her to the car.

It was 7.00 p.m. when Christine Villemin left Metz Queuleu.

Outside, the crowd of journalists had to make do with a half-baked photo-opportunity as Garaud's white Renault 25 drove through the gates of the prison and whisked its passenger to Petitmont. Christine was paler, thinner, but smiling. There was no declaration. Those dedicated souls who followed her to Petitmont were greeted by Christine Villemin's brother, Alain Blaise. 'The first one who touches her gets his bones smashed.' It was not a good day for the press.

However, beyond the relief at leaving prison after so short a time behind bars, Christine Villemin had little to look forward to. Certainly not in the immediate future. She might be among her family, but she was unable to leave the Meurthe and Moselle *département* where they lived. She would need the judge's permission every time she wanted to cross into the Vosges to go to Lépanges cemetery. And if Lambert had transferred Jean-Marie back to the Charles III in Nancy, which was in the same *département*, the prison was a much grimmer and more inconvenient place to visit than Saverne.

In addition to her territorial confinement, Christine was duty-bound to make herself available for any interviews or tests thought suitable by Lambert, not to mention medical treatment.

But Christine Villemin had got off relatively lightly, and she was safe. In Petitmont, a team of four gendarmes was on the watch outside her grandmother's house. There had already been threats from the Bolles, and the privileged treatment that Christine was receiving, when compared to Laroche's, was enough to inflame their already overheated passions. Marie-Ange, as the pro-Laroche press was quick to point out, was unemployed and without a home – or at least, looking for a new one, and Gérard Welzer had to make regular phone calls to ensure that none of her brothers and sisters were preparing for some kind of revenge. The gendarmes had not seen fit to accord Laroche emergency protection. Now, as a direct consequence, Welzer was playing the gendarme with the family-in-law of the deceased.

Protection, though, also meant suspicion. What Garaud described as a sanction had done nothing to shake Jean-Michel Lambert's conviction. 'I shall continue with my work on the case,' he said tersely. And it was clear that the SRPJ would be with him, their convictions unchanged. 'They should have told us before if they wanted to kill the case,' said one policeman.

Nor could Christine expect much support from her family-in-law. When she was released, their declaration as *partie civile* was not exactly cordial. In fact, Christine Villemin was not even mentioned: 'This freedom, which we do not oppose, will do a lot of good to Jean-Marie. It will also mean that the new child will be born elsewhere than in a prison. It was a prospect that broke our hearts.' Apparently, the imprisonment of their daughter-in-law did not upset the emotions of Monique and Albert Villemin to quite the same extent. It was as if they had disowned her. Well, the Villemins had a long history of falling out together.

23

'Judge Lambert's file is like one of those Brazilian motorways that sets off in all directions and then stop dead at the edge of the virgin forest.'

They were Henri-René Garaud's words. But the virgin forest was much less unexplored fact than lost time. The death of Grégory was fast coming to resemble an original manuscript that had been lost, and for which there remained only commentaries and footnotes – just like the murder note of 16 October, whose secret had been effaced for ever as a result of manhandling by numerous experts. The general opinion was that the truth would never be known. But that was not enough to deter Lambert.

'There is absolutely no question of me giving up,' he declared, his tenacity well hidden behind his smooth, rounded features and over-grown Beatles haircut. 'What counts,' he insisted, 'is to do all you can to maintain your self-esteem.' Lambert felt he had, and his first grey hairs were there to prove it.

Still, he would be regretting the interview he had recently given to the women's magazine *Elle*, and which came off the presses just before Christine Villemin came out of Metz Queuleu. Next to artfully posed photos of the young judge strolling in the forests of the Vosges, the budding star laid bare his heart and admitted to the pain left from the break-up with Chantal, the love of his life.

'I am Taurus, rising sign Scorpio,' the little judge told the young female readers with assurance, 'so I always see things through to the finish.' That of course meant the Villemin case. Had he made any mistakes? 'I think a magistrate of fifty could have made the same ones. I count myself lucky that it's happened to me at thirty-three.'

Of course, there were times when the pressure had been too great.

'Some nights I used to have fits of bulimia and throw myself uncontrollably on my store of cocktail snacks after dinner.' And when the affair was at its height, 'I had periods of sexual atony, sometimes for weeks on end.' The little judge had been having trouble with his erections.

After the turn-off of 16 July, Lambert would be feeling a bit foolish. 'All that's left to do now is pose in *Playboy*,' they quipped at the *Palais de Justice*.

Etienne Sesmat was just as sure of his moral integrity as the judge. At the end of August, he would be leaving the Epinal gendarmerie for Berlin. It was a promotion, the next step in what his superiors called a career that promises to be brilliant. Sesmat bade farewell to his comrades with the sense of a mission properly accomplished. 'Gentlemen, I hope you will continue to hold your heads high, as I shall do when I leave here.'

In Petitmont, hidden behind a hedge of fir trees, and guarded by her four gendarmes, Christine Villemin began to prepare for the birth of her second child. As well as letters of support and encouragement, the mail regularly brought her cheques and presents from unknown sympathisers – clothes for the child, and even a gold watch. It was a stylish kind of captivity: every time she moved she was followed by a little Renault 4 with three men in uniform. However, her visitors were restricted to a list of fifteen people approved by the judge.

Everyone was interested in Christine Villemin. And especially 'the shrinks'. According to the psycho-portraits premiered in the press in the weeks following her release, Christine Villemin was 'of superior intelligence and very calculating. Madame Villemin,' they said, 'is totally lacking in maternal instinct and has a personality capable of beating her child.' According to Leyrier, 'Madame Villemin has a potential tendency towards mental states of confusion which could cause neurotic disturbances due to a perverse type of hysteria.' Or as she had once told Lambert herself, 'Sometimes I get these blackouts. I can't remember what I've done.' The blackouts were due to her poor circulation.

Never one to miss out on an opportunity of conducting a counter-expertise, Henri Garaud promptly got in contact with Jean-René Lavoine, the general secretary of the French Association of Criminology. Lavoine was a renowned figure, a familiar of the best in deranged criminality. He had been to America to visit Charles Manson, the killer of Roman Polanski's actress wife, Sharon Tate, and, more recently, had been consulted for an analysis of John Hinkley, the man who tried to assassinate Ronald Reagan.

Petitmont was a somewhat more humble setting, and Christine Villemin was said to have murdered only her child, not a film star or president. Nevertheless, Lavoine arrived with Garaud on 19 July and spent an hour tête à tête with his client. His first conclusion was that 'Christine Villemin is not mentally ill. There is nothing incoherent, delirious or pathological about her denials.' Or, as Christine put it: 'The people who think I'm mad are bonkers.'

It was unprecedented in French legal history for a barrister to commission an independent psychiatrist for his client. Garaud had a simple explanation. 'I knew it would suit everybody to declare Christine Villemin mad, so I decided to anticipate a bit.' Madness, as Garaud well knew, is the next best thing to a motive.

In fact, neither of Lambert's appointed psychiatrists had either completed or presented their official report.

Christine Villemin was tired. It did not take long for the euphoria of freedom to wear off, leaving only the stress of solitude and suspicion. On 24 July, she had her first meeting with Lambert and was asked to give blood so the experts could ascertain if it belonged to the same, non-identifiable 20 per cent found on the envelope of the murder note. At least it gave her a chance to go and see Grégory's tomb. Four days later, it would have been his fifth birthday. She put down a new plaque: 'In memory of an angel,' said the gold lettering. It would fill the space left by Monique and Albert's memorial 'To our grandson'. The offering had been stolen.

It was altogether a hard time for Monique and Albert. Since they had become *partie civile*, Jean-Marie had written forbidding them to touch their grandson's grave. 'I never want to see you again,' said the last letter. If Christine Villemin had wanted to escape the milieu of her parents-in-law, then perhaps she was on the way to success. Monique, the matriarch of the clan, seemed impotent. She was not given to public declarations, so the appeal she made through the press was all the more pathetic:

'We knew Bernard well, and not for one moment did we think he could kill Grégory. How was it that Jean-Marie could decide to kill him? If only we'd known, we'd have talked him out of it, and he wouldn't be in prison now.'

But he was. And Monique and Albert are like all parents overtaken by events and powerless over children who seem suddenly to have metamorphosed into hostile strangers.

It would be no consolation for Monique to realise that Jean-Marie and Christine Villemin were too fraught to see the difference between benevolent neutrality and outright hostility. The couple saw enemies everywhere, especially in the press. They had just sued *France Soir* and *Le Figaro* for articles implying Christine's guilt. The approach seemed to pay off. Their first offender, *Paris Match*, had now started producing articles pleading their cause. Big names would set their signature to heart-rending portraits of Christine Villemin and her trials. Among them, Yann Queffélec, another Goncourt Prize winner. In addition, the magazine had begun to re-explore the Laroche enigma.

The press was less interested in Muriel Bolle. The chubby, sullen Muriel was not photogenic enough. But she too felt persecuted. In early August, she was interviewed by an insistent freelance journalist. Later, Jeannine hit upon a small electrical device when she was vacuuming the house. At first, she thought it was her daughter's Walkman. It was in fact a transmitter, capable of broadcasting conversations for a distance of 100 metres. Muriel was being pursued by a small-time scoop hunter. On 2 September, her parents went to Epinal to lodge a complaint against the amateur spy, for breach of privacy. And also for the threats to their daughter's life. 'Don't cry victory yet. Grégory's murderer is dead, and that's a start. But Muriel will have to talk sometime, and she'll die too. I hope it all comes down on top of her.'

Not surprisingly, Muriel still hadn't gone back to school. She remained listless and uncommunicative. As if to make herself less conspicuous, she had cut her thick red mane. It was ten months since her interview with the gendarmes. She might just as well have spent them in prison for all the good they had done her.

At the beginning of September, six weeks after their unofficial airing in the press, the psychiatric reports reached Epinal. After the preview, this was a disappointment, In fact, it was Jean-Marie Villemin who came out of it worse. He was described as 'intolerant and always sure of being right', in spite of 'contradictions that he might himself be unaware of'. In fact, said the report, Jean-Marie was a mixture of superiority and inferiority complexes. On the one hand, he appeared cocksure, a strong man with his martial arts and body building. On the other, he was prone to persecution mania and was easily influenced. He was also extremely materialistic. In short, he was something of a hot-tempered brat, perfect justification for the hatred of chiefs.

Everyone knew how proud Jean-Marie was of his possessions, and how rapidly his convictions could switch from one suspect, Jacky, to another, Bernard Laroche. How he could not bear doubt. Had he brought his fate upon himself?

As for Christine, she got off relatively lightly. There was no sign of her being 'hysterical, perverse and lacking in maternal instinct'. Nor did she show any clinical symptoms of 'developing or congenital mental illness'. At the most, she was 'a woman perfectly at ease in her imaginary romances for whom Grégory could have been a disruptive presence'. She was 'intelligent and calculating, a highly complex woman with two levels of personality'.

It was anyone's guess if that made her a potential child-killer.

Lavoine, not surprisingly, went further. After a total of three meetings with the subject, he asserted that Christine Villemin was fully responsible for her actions. She had never wanted to leave the Vosges. She was and always had been attached to her husband. 'I found nothing abnormal about her,' he concluded.

In short, Judge Lambert would find it hard to argue that Christine had killed Grégory in a state of dementia. Christine could still be the killer, but it was no more likely than before. Investigation by expertise had not got anyone very far. Lambert would have to find another motive, or more opinions.

It was the *partie civile* that gave the investigation its new impetus. On 5 September, Lombard, Bourdelle and Lagrange deposited a request for twenty new tests and procedural measures aiming at greater thoroughness. Beside a blood test, which was already underway, they called for a reconstruction of 16 October and a general confrontation. They also wanted a new flotation test to be carried out with a model exactly equivalent to Grégory, and Lagrange suggested recreating the precise conditions of the Vologne in a laboratory.

Another key request was that the police should make up a chart showing the activities and whereabouts of the family for each of the eighty-seven Crow calls recorded by Monique.

The SRPJ would be happy to oblige.

Meanwhile, though, Lambert's office was to house the latest confrontation, this time between Jean-Marie and his family. It was a rare occasion for Monique to try to reconcile her son. Once again, the papers obliged: 'Jean-Marie, I am your Mum. You know very well that we are not your enemies, your father and I, nor Christine's. I loved Christine as my own daughter. Our house and our larder were always open to her. You must try to understand. We never meant to abandon you.'

Monique's willingness to reveal her maternal wound paid off. For, if no revelations were dredged up from the meeting in Epinal a week later, Jean-Marie did at least throw himself into his mother's arms. He was enfeebled, hardly a chief any more and at times more like a child. But he maintained his position on Laroche, and his parents maintained theirs: the reconciliation depended on avoiding the subject, and so was unlikely to last. Especially since the family now agreed that the Crow was a woman, and that she had started calling after Jean-Marie and Christine's marriage.

Christine Villemin was not present in Epinal that day. Her pregnancy made it dangerous to travel or experience stress. On the evening of Monday 30 September, the pains started. At 9.00 p.m., she called a doctor, and then the gendarmes: 'Don't forget to tell Jean-Marie why I can't come tomorrow!' At 9.30 p.m., with the squad car trailing behind, she arrived in the special maternity wing at Lunéville. The child was born twenty minutes later.

Visits would be strictly filtered, and the nurses kept a sharp eye out for photographers trying to pass themselves off as members of the family. Monique and Albert Villemin would come to the bedside but, in spite of appeals by his lawyers, Jean-Marie did not obtain special permission to see the child born at 10.00 p.m. on 30 September – his own date of birth. For once, Lambert's decision was supported by Jean-Jacques Lecomte. If the killer of Bernard Laroche were let out, it might do terrible things to the fragile nerves of Marie-Ange Laroche and trouble her pregnancy.

In fact, it was from the radio that Jean-Marie Villemin heard that he had become a father for the second time. The warders had 'forgotten' the message carefully passed on by the gendarmes.

Julien Jean-Marie Gilbert Villemin weighed in at 3 kilos, and blue, being three weeks premature. Christine had decided against the name Jonathan, which Jean-Marie – and the journalist – preferred. Besides, they had not done so well with Anglo-Saxon names in the past. As for Gilbert, the name was a tribute to the father's only 'faithful' brother.

Julien was the star of that week's *Paris Match*. Julien and his tenderly smiling, rosy-pink mother in the warm and flowered hospital room. The magazine had purchased exclusive photographic rights for 650,000 francs as part of the outside court agreement reached with Henri Garaud.

The lawyer, who had handled all the arrangements with the magazine, would at last be receiving some form of payment. And Grégory's mother would be able to claim her share in the Grégory gold mine exploited by the sensational press. Christine Villemin's spell as media star had begun.

Three weeks later, it was the first anniversary of Grégory's death. Christine could not go to Lépanges. And there was no commemorative mention in the church. 'Angels don't need them,' said the priest. In the cemetery, Grégory's grandparents stood before the beautifully-decorated grave amidst indifference and resentment. 'Christine Villemin is as famous as Caroline of Monaco,' was the local gripe. 'It's ancient history,' said another variation. In Lépanges, Grégory was losing his reality, even if his school friends, encouraged by their parents, continued to bring flowers to the tomb. Besides, there had recently been another event to occupy attention. An old woman of seventy-seven had been burnt alive in her bedroom. Everyone knew it couldn't be an accident.

In Brazil, of course, no one could have been expected to realise all this, so the camera crew sent over by a national channel must have wondered what all the fuss was about when they arrived in Lépanges that day. No blood on the streets, no distressed women or assassinations, no processions.

They would have done better to come a week later, on 22 October, for the latest confrontation in Epinal.

Christine Villemin's contribution to the new instalment of family suspicion was confined to a brief interview with Lambert in the morning. She was, according to her representatives, disappointed that she could not stay for the afternoon session. But even without her, it went on until just before midnight. They sat there stealing uncomfortable glances at each other, Monique always ready to 'save' the family name, Albert terse and reserved while Lambert probed them all with the age-old question, trying not to get exasperated. 'Who do you think could have killed Grégory?' Only Jacky replied, 'It's not for me to have an opinion, it's for the law to find the culprit.' Jacky, it was true, had also been a suspect, and almost killed by his brother because of opinion.

But Lambert's method was a little more than inspired guesswork. He could now reveal the comparative timetable plotting each member of the family's activities when the Crow called. Of the 87 calls noted by Monique, Christine Villemin would have been free to make 80. No one else came anywhere near this mark.

Lambert also had a chance of proving exactly how much time Christine Villemin would have had at her disposal on 16 October. The secret was locked away in the tachograph belonging to the bus driven by Marcelle Claudon's son, Gilbert. As Marcelle remembered, the bus driver Christian was already home by the time she came back and saw Christine outside her house. Now the SRPJ was on the trail of the black box. At present, they were trying to find it at a depot in Paris. This was not as easy as it sounds. French bus drivers had not taken kindly to the introduction of the timekeepers they called 'informers'. In early 1985, they demonstrated their unhappiness by sending them back to Paris. The Ministry of Transport's cellars now contained some 400,000 of these unwelcome objects. It was to be hoped that the SRPJ's effort would be worthwhile.

Apparently, the *partie civile* thought it would be. 'In two weeks from now, the Crow will have a name,' promised Paul Lombard. 'Only Bernard Laroche and Christine Villemin looked likely suspects,' he continued, 'and the evidence against Laroche was slim.' In other words . . . Lombard knew there was another reason for suspecting Christine. She had always said that the note she found against the window after a night alone at Paremont, the one which said 'I'll get your skin, Villemins,' had been slipped between the shutters. The police had tried to do just that. It was impossible.

Naturally, Garaud was not impressed. 'We haven't advanced an inch,' he groaned.

It is what the French call a dialogue of the deaf.

According to the Judiciary Police, who might be trusted to know about such things, the dossier was now solid enough to take Christine Villemin to court. 'With all the evidence we've gathered any suspect in any other affair would already have been condemned.' Like the gendarmes before them, Andrieu and Corazzi's men were beginning to chafe at the bit.

But Judge Lambert had already been stung once and a half. He wanted to test his conclusions against the reconstruction he had set for 30 October. The grand return to Lépanges.

The exercise took four and a half hours in all. In the presence of Christine and Jean-Marie Villemin, and safely out of earshot of the journalists, Lambert tried Colin's walk with his Dalmation and Claudon's with her cows. Confrontations were held, gestures repeated and explained.

Christine Villemin was almost unrecognisable as the young woman of only a year before. Her hair was longer now, her features still carried some of the weight she put on during her pregnancy. She walked hesitantly, as if closed in on herself. And Garaud, like a protective father, stood beside her, hand on her shoulder.

But this Christine was no more cooperative than before. She was not the sort to break down when confronted once again with her workmates on the subject of her supposed visit to the post office. 'They never liked me anyway,' she said. When Bernard Colin more or less accused her of being the Crow she merely shrugged it off disdainfully.

Jean-Marie was equally stubborn in his response to his parents. 'I 'don't want to see them,' he warned. The period of grace had been short.

But the reconstruction did afford him and Christine a rare moment of intimacy. The police had the delicacy to leave them alone for an hour in the house on Rue des Champs – just like the old days. The longest they had been together for more than six months.

It was the day's most tangible result. Lambert nevertheless declared himself satisfied, and so did the defence and *partie civile* while sharp observers declared that Christine Villemin was less serene at the end of the day than at its beginning. It was a meagre harvest, but one that everyone could make their own, like politicians after an election with massive abstentions. More than a year after the event, the art of lawyers and judges was to a great extent that of making the absence of negative proofs into the presence of positive ones.

Two weeks later, Christine Villemin was called upon to explain some rather more disturbing and substantial evidence. First, the feverish rise in her and Jean-Marie's phone bill during the Crow's periods of activity. She had now resorted to three separate explanations for this fact: the attempt to buy a second-hand car, a sister ill in an Epinal hospital, and a simple mistake on the part of the telephone company. It was unfortunate that Epinal was in the same tariff zone as Lépanges, but that Aumontzey, the home of Albert and Monique, was not. Inconvenient too that the second-hand car was purchased before the period in question. And bad for the suspect's credibility that she should have to fall back on a vague conspiracy of fate and the telephone service.

These embarrassing facts were nothing compared to the cassette found among Christine and her husband's possessions. The audiometric experts had concluded that this supposed recording of the Crow contained no signs of taking place on the network: no click as the receiver was picked up or put down. It was a simulated call: Christine apparently talking to Christine. And, in the background, the voice of a child. Jean-Marie insisted it belonged to Michel's son, Daniel. The words were certainly difficult to make out, but the child was saying something like 'Mummy' or 'Come on Teddy'. Teddy was Jean-Marie's nickname. For the police, the voice was Grégory's.

Finally, there was the tachograph, the needle in the haystack of

400,000 black boxes. An initial analysis by a Monsieur Lévy of the *Ponts et Chaussées* ministry revealed that the coach had stopped between 5.36 p.m. and 5.38 p.m. (the meter having only two-minute graduations). If that was so, Christine had had ample time, nearly twenty-five minutes from her arrival at Paremont to seeing Claudon.

Strangely enough, neither Moser nor Chastant were present to receive this new information. The former had been doing cartwheels in his Volvo, and the latter was ill. 'I hope they soon get over their emotions,' commented Lombard wryly.

From the SRPJ laboratory in Paris and the sound research centre of Orly airport came confirmation that Christine's voice was the closest to the one recorded on Monique and Jacky and Liliane's cassettes. Garaud's reminder of the expert verdict designating Laroche met with no echo: that report, commissioned by the gendarmes, had been cancelled.

Jean-Marie and Christine simply denied. Christine, according to the men of the SRPJ, had 'seen nothing, heard nothing, knew nothing and had nothing to say.' Paul Lombard described her behaviour as the 'Shepherd of Manosque syndrome': a shepherd accused of murder protested that he was at the cinema when the crime occurred. When told that the film he had supposedly seen was not showing, he insisted: 'I was at the cinema of Manosque.' When told that the cinema was closed that day, he still replied: 'I was at the cinema of Manosque.' And when judged, he was acquitted, for lack of hard evidence.

From his prison cell, Jean-Marie went back on the offensive. His parents were trying to 'do down' their daughter. The Crow timetable drawn up by the SRPJ with Monique's help was 'glaringly inaccurate'. Monique bemusedly pointed out that her son had said nothing when she first showed it to him. Besides, Jean-Marie had never been able to give a satisfactory explanation for the rope. It was all bark and no bite.

Lambert, on the contrary, seemed to be growing in assurance. He put off the family confrontation scheduled for 29 November until 20 December, when he would be in possession of his new handwriting analyses from Geneviève Gille, Eliane Petit-Mirbeck and M. Ourliac. Ten experts had now pored over the handwriting of France's most famous suspect: the courts would be running out of specialists. If the new analysts confirmed their predecessors, then seven of them would have condemned Christine Villemin. A respectable score, especially when you considered the pressure brought by the gendarmes on the two others, Berrichon-Seyden and Jacquin-Keller.

The Villemins next counter-attack was an attempt to wrench the course of the investigation back towards Laroche. Jean-Marie and Christine Villemin were attacking Muriel Bolle for 'complicity with assassination, non-opposition to the crime, and failure to denounce the crime'. It was 29 November, exactly eight months after Laroche's death. And, as Muriel's lawyer, Jean-Paul Teissonnière, pointed out, this new burst of aggression carried a distinct echo of Jean-Marie's behaviour when suspicion first began to thicken around his wife. Only this time he was trying to assassinate Laroche's memory.

In this new ordeal, Muriel would not be getting much support from her sister. Marie-Ange was continuing to ignore her when they met at Laveline, and all Muriel could do was remain mute, as if she was not there. Anyway, Marie-Ange had other preoccupations, material ones. She was living on the money sent by Bernard's factory mates, and her unemployment benefit would soon be running out. Like Christine, she had also received donations and gifts from sympathisers but she refused money. Never one to be in debt, Marie-Ange. She was thinking of moving back to Aumontzey, once the baby was there. Her second, difficult pregnancy reached its conclusion on the evening of 7 December, in Epinal, where she brought into the world the child she conceived two or three weeks before Laroche's death. The Laroche-Villemin symmetry was as powerful as ever: it was boy. 'I am happy,' said Marie-Ange, 'but not joyous.' The new arrival could not help but make her husband's absence more painful, all the more so since it was a son. She called him Jean-Bernard. Bernard was obvious, but Jean, as in Jean-Marie? Marie-Ange had shown she could be as tough a fighter as Christine Villemin. But if she was now dreaming of reconciliation, Marie-Ange had become an idealist.

An idealist, and a 'woman of dignity' who had ample opportunity to prove her superiority to La Villemin. She had never signed any lucrative contracts with Parisian magazines. Marie-Ange had simply ordered one professional photograph of herself and her baby and insisted that it be distributed to the press so as to avoid 'an unhealthy rush'. So much for the glamour star in Petitmont. There she was, her rival, dressed in black, the face looking into the distance as its lips touched the child's head.

The wave of interest for the other woman in the affair did not last long. On 18 December, Gilberte Chatel became the third *partie civile* for Grégory Villemin, bringing with her François Robinet, a specialist on legal procedure from Nancy. Chatel was throwing her weight into the effort to force the police back onto the tracks of Bernard Laroche. It was her way of saying how much her grandson's death had affected her, claimed her representative. Sincere, certainly, but rather belated.

Meanwhile Garaud had left documents about the truth drug on Lambert's desk and was threatening to take his client's case to the European Court of Human Rights if Lambert refused. Which he duly did.

The only truth drug available in the Vosges was the adrenalin stirred up by family confrontations, and it did not seem to produce very spectacular results. After Lambert had ploughed through the cassettes with Christine on 19 December, and gone over her contradictions and obscure points, he kept her for ten hours the next day in the company of her parents-in-law: from until 2.30 p.m. till after midnight, with only one short break. It was a tense, gruelling session. Monique had brought a list of thirty-five questions: she and her lawyer had a lot of doubts to lay to rest.

Why, they asked, had Monique not noticed any evidence of the laundry Christine claimed to have been ironing on 16 October? Why did Christine leave Grégory outside for a whole half hour, in spite of the anxiety she said she felt? Did she go to the Vologne that afternoon? Why did she lie to justify her absence from work? What was behind her persistent demands for the truth drug? Why did the Crow only start his activities once Christine and her husband had moved into Paremont?

And what did Christine have to say about the time the family had wanted to phone Bernard Noël from Aumontzey? Since Bernard was not on the phone, they used to leave messages with the neighbour, a music teacher. That night Christine suddenly volunteered the information that the teacher had stopped taking messages. No one else knew, except the Crow, who had been shouted at when he tried to avail himself of the facility a few days earlier.

At first, Christine simply refused to answer, or insulted Monique and Albert, or kept demanding the truth drug. Then, after the break – and a talk with Garaud – she was serene, almost affable; almost schizophrenic, if you like. Christine was too volatile, too fluent in her shifts from laughter to tears and back again, from groaning to swearing. And she was careless with her declarations: 'I swear on Julien's head that I am innocent.' Christine Villemin continued to put herself before her child, as she had when she went on hunger strike. It was not enough to deny the audio-metric analysis, or to reject Christine Jacquot's statement that she was crying when she arrived to ask about Grégory that evening, fourteen months ago now. Jacquot, after all, was Christine's friend. Was, or had been. But no: 'I can't have been crying because I didn't know then that he was in the Vologne.' Exactly. Christine's memory had perhaps been blurred by her suffering, or her present desperation. You cannot expect a wounded animal to be rational. Christine's mistake was to counter-attack. But then why did she provoke her father-in-law with her comments about Jacky's illegitimacy, or insinuations about the time Albert beat his wife in the middle of a choleric drinking bout? It was no good, in these circumstances, stirring up the murky depths of Villemin family life.

The case had reached a kind of deadlock in which Lambert's carefully-constructed hypothesis was continually lashed by the indignant tirades of Henri Garaud. In which Christine Villemin had given up her intensive press coverage to read only the newspapers and magazines favourable to herself. In which Jean-Marie Villemin was consistently refused the liberty demanded by his representatives. And in which everyone shouted their desire for justice. 'If she did it, then she'll have to pay,' asserted Marie-Ange, who had just laid a new plaque on her husband's tomb: 'Daddy, my name is Jean-Bernard. I was born on 7.12.85.' Like Christine with her medallion containing a photograph of Grégory, Marie-Ange still wore her gold chain with the name Bernard. Emotions were not like facts, and those generated by 16 October 1984 were still painfully present. They were their own irrefutable proof.

But behind them, behind the judge, the prosecutor said nothing, in spite of exhortations that he should accept his responsibilities.

In fact, Jean-Jacques Lecomte was going to accept his responsibilities: elsewhere. The prosecutor had been nominated for a position in

Mayotte, in the Comora Islands. He would be replaced by André Simard, an outsider with no knowledge of the affair, early in 1986. Perhaps it was a good thing. Since July 1985, Lecomte's relationship with Lambert had deteriorated to the point that they now communicated solely with memoranda circulated by their secretaries.

Movement was on the cards in the SRPJ too: Gérard Andrieu was heading for Lille. And if Henri-René Garaud had got his way, Judge Lambert would also be leaving Epinal. Garaud had filed a request for the Little Grégory affair to be taken out of the little judge's hands. Lambert, like Garaud before him, blamed the gendarmes. 'If this investigation had been better conducted at the beginning, the affair could have been tied up in three or four days.'

No one would deny that the investigation had suffered from its botched beginning. Worse than the procedural irregularities, there had been numerous oversights. The failure to conduct thorough searches during the first days of the inquest. The failure to conduct a thorough autopsy on Grégory, with a proper analysis of the water in his lungs. The archaic and damaging treatment meted out to the Crow's letters. The attempts to direct the experts. The fact that no reconstructions had been staged immediately after the event and no confrontations either. The lack of cooperation between the gendarmes and judiciary police, two rival forces. The constant leakage of information to the press. The fact that the tyre mouldings were too small for the investigators to distinguish between two different models. Lambert, apparently, was not responsible for any of this.

And, in spite of it all, he believed he held enough evidence to make a case. Andrieu had left him the report synthesising the results of his new investigations. In a nutshell, Christine Villemin was still the number one suspect. And Bernard Laroche was still out of the running. And so said the handwriting experts, still. In their sixty-page synthesis, Laroche was given twelve pages and Christine seventeen. The rest was shared between seven other candidates. 'But,' concluded the authors, 'our observations can be said to constitute presumptions sufficiently serious for the litigious documents to be attributed to Mme Villemin.' So, would Lambert be winding up?

While he waited, arming himself with expertise, the press feasted on the Villemin enigma.

It was a highly charismatic mix. Christine Villemin had star potential, if packaged rightly. Since Garaud's deal with *Paris Match*, she had attracted the interest of Denis Taranto, founder of the Jet Set agency, which handled the likes of Julio Iglesias, Margaux Hemingway and Caroline of Monaco. Into this glittering company stepped the 'humble seamstress of the Vosges'. Photo sessions were arranged complete with make-up and wardrobe artists. Nothing was left to chance. Of course, Christine sometimes refused to don certain outfits, and she had never been the lipstick and mascara type, let alone a devotee of professional studio make-up. But now she had a Pygmalion. 'My greatest recompense,' said Taranto, 'is to hear people who see her on a magazine cover say: By God, she really is all right, that one, I'd never noticed before.' There was Christine, groomed and softened, walking in the garden of Petitmont, or staring soulfully into the camera from the table, or smiling at Julien. A creature of modern romance, with just a touch of evil – enough to make you wonder: Could it be her?

Taranto's photos could fetch as much as £30,000. Christine, he enthused, was 'The affair of 1985 and even more the affair of 1986'. But little of the money went her way: there were barristers to pay, and intermediaries. Nor did much of the sympathy. While Lambert reminded the Appeal Court at Nancy that the suspect was showing scant respect for the obligation to keep a certain reserve on the affair, Monique Villemin was outraged that her daughter-in-law should be cashing in on Grégory's death and her son's misery: playing the pin-up while Jean-Marie was despairing in his cell.

Albert and Monique felt Christine was playing games with them all. First she would make some snide comment about them to the press, then she would phone the next day to say she didn't mean a word of it and, in the same breath, ask a favour: for example, she wanted Albert to say he was the one who lent Jean-Marie the rope found by the SRPJ at Paremont. Of course, Albert refused. Christine seemed to oscillate between two versions of reality. Sometimes, her parents-in-law were sweethearts whose kindness when Jean-Marie was away on military service she still remembered, and at other moments they were a couple of retarded alcoholics who had never liked Grégory and disapproved of the way she and her husband brought him up. It was the same with

Grégory, too: sometimes he had been wholeheartedly desired, and at others a burden imposed by Jean-Marie to keep her in her place.

It was not surprising Monique and Albert felt lost: they received all this information second hand, through the media.

While Christine's relationship with her parents-in-law grew ever more complicated, Lambert continued to dredge the psyche of 'my Christine Villemin', for a motive. On 20 January 1986, he ordered her to make her first trip to Paris to talk with two psychiatric experts attached to Sainte Anne Hospital. Eight hours of interviews. Then she was off south to Lyon, chaperoned by Garaud, for a second opinion from France's second city. Four hours with three specialists recognised by the Appeal Court: the lost little Vosgean seamstress wandering disconsolately through a hostile world of hostile experts with loaded or incomprehensible questions: being stared at in the street by people who had seen her in the newspaper.

Christine Villemin had been launched into a grotesque parody of her supposed phantasies: travel, glamour. All the old markers had gone.

And, like all modern stars, Christine had to have her book. While the little judge was rumoured to be setting down his reflections, Christine Villemin already had a contract with a Parisian publisher for her memoirs. Due out in May, the book was known to contain attacks on Lambert and the Laroche family, particularly Bernard. In contrast, life with Jean-Marie and Grégory would be painted as an idyll capable of melting even the coldest of hearts. The book would be safe, at least for Christine. Its raw material was ten ninety-minute tapes of interviews with a journalist. These had been reworked by an experienced ghost-writer and then submitted to Garaud's legal expertise for cuts and modifications.

Predictably, the family was not happy. Both Monique Villemin and Marie-Ange Laroche warned they would be taking action to stop publication. 'She has muddied the whole family,' fumed Monique. Marie-Ange's barristers argued that any revenue from the book should be seized and put to good use: the compensation of Laroche's widow. For that they required 1 million francs. The rest, they conceded, could be used for Julien's upbringing.

The Tribunal of Paris would not oblige them, although it did demand that Jean-Marie should pay 300,000 francs to the woman he had widowed. The money from Christine's book, however, would be her own. After all, no one had proved her complicity in the Laroche murder. Yet.

Nor could anyone say when Lambert would be concluding his dossier. For weeks and months now it had been almost ready. But March was a bad month for conclusions: France was in the middle of its parliamentary elections, and in France, legal authorities, like financial ones, are reluctant to stick their necks out before they know who is likely to be cutting them.

At least Gérard Welzer would have an idea. He had just been made the Socialist member for the Vosges. He promised that his new responsibilities would not mean he was giving up the case which had helped establish his local reputation. Beside, Welzer felt a genuine sense of duty and attachment to Bernard Laroche's widow.

Christine and Jean-Marie had got something out of the early spring as well. The house in Paremont had at last been sold to a couple from Alsace. For months, the place had been on offer at 450,000 francs. Now they had been forced to go down to 300,000 francs, barely more than it cost them to build.

Now at least they could stop their payments on the loan. It was by no means enough to lift the couple's depression.

For Jean-Marie the return to the gloomy brick buildings of Charles III prison in Nancy had been a painful experience. Saverne, where he had stayed up until Christine's release from Metz, was small, and its visiting room allowed a measure of genuine intimacy. There Jean-Marie could earn as much as 4,000 francs a month from packaging work: he could support his family. In Nancy, no such purposefulness was allowed. And the place was crowded. Jean-Marie became listless, started smoking a packet and a half of cigarettes a day and spent his time engraving images of his dead son or answering his abundant sympathy mail from the vicariously outraged. He was isolated. The other prisoners, with whom he generally avoided socialising, had invented a game of 'Grégory Bingo'. This involved betting on the next surprise produced by the affair. There was no respect for the wounded father.

On 15 April, though, Jean-Marie had an unusually busy visiting time. At last, he had agreed to see his parents – providing of course that Christine was there, and that they promised to support him and his wife. Monique obliged. 'I do believe Christine is innocent. After all, I'm first and foremost a mother.'

But reconciliation still did not come easy. The next day's paper contained an interview with Christine in which she accused her parents-in-law of speaking a double language, of wanting to separate her and Jean-Marie so that they could take Julien, 'whom they've never wanted to see'. And Christine could not resist the temptation of digging into the family's history. 'The mother thinks she can save her son by accusing me. Why? Because there's something she knows, someone she wants to protect. Yes, there is a clan secret.' As proof of her argument, she quoted a phone call she had received a few days earlier: 'The day you're cleared is the day you'll die.'

This was hardly appeasement. But then neither she nor Jean-Marie expected to see much more of Monique and Albert Villemin. They were dreaming of their new life: they would start anew in Australia or Canada. France had become too small for them. And besides, their image of the country had suffered. 'The French are incompetent,' said Christine.

The incompetent French were also extremely interested in what she had to say. In late May, Christine's publisher produced 60,000 copies of her memoirs, *Laissez-moi vous dire* (Let me tell you . . .). Success guaranteed.

24

'**I** needed this book, Everyone talks about me, describes me, tells stories about me, calumnies me, but nobody knows me.'

Laissez-moi vous dire was Christine Villemin's way of cleaning her image up. Whatever the truth content, the method was debatable: for it was the usual combination of soft focus sentiment and hard recrimination.

On the cover, Christine Villemin peers soulfully from one of Jet Set's photographs. Inside, other photographs by the agency show her with Julien, with her brother and sister and mother, and a few Villemin snaps show the happy times: Grégory standing in his baby walker, the holiday in Italy – Jean-Marie in cut-off denim shorts, a muscular figure with his arm round Albert, Christine fresh-faced and smiling beside Monique.

As advocacy it is a soft sell. You want to share in all the legitimate sentiment, but then you remember the photos are more often than not posed, agency jobs. Then you remember that Garaud wrote the preface and monitored the contents. You see the last photograph, 'Memory . . . Grégory', a close up of Christine Villemin holding the medallion, her face full of soulful sadness, and you see both the pose and the genuine emotion. With Christine Villemin, you never knew which came first.

Yet the image of Christine gives of herself is simple and banal when set against rumours. Point by point, these are deflated. The father's death is described but not as a personal trauma. Christine admits the shock of moving to Laveline, but it is healthily stated and shrugged off. It is the same with the question of her truncated education: 'I was never much of a genius.' Or the first boyfriend: 'A flirtation, he dropped me.' And the unromantic wedding: 'Since we'd already been living together for six months, it seemed ridiculous to go in for some big jamboree with evening dress and buffet!' And the move to Paremont: 'Peace and independence were very important to us.'

And so the book goes on, the portrait of a simple woman who aspires only to recover the sensation she lost on 16 October, 'the feeling of being in your own home with your own baby . . . absolute happiness.'

But defending such an image also means attacking those who question it, however obliquely. Christine therefore returns to the investigation. She berates the SRPJ for being obsessed with the idea of a sexual relation between her and Bernard Laroche, tells Lambert 'I shall never forgive him,' and insists that her memory of 16 October is better than Christine Jaquot's, that she was expecting twins, whatever the staff at *La Roseraie* said.

More importantly, she attacks Laroche: and here, she gets out of control. She introduces a third version of the events of 29 March 1985. Now Christine has Jean-Marie say: 'At first I just wanted to talk with him, to have an explanation.' She has Laroche say: 'We bribed the agents' and make a mockery of Jean-Marie while Marie-Ange protects him with her body.

'This tragedy,' she concludes, 'could have been avoided if Laroche had agreed to talk.'

It all sounded so simple. Yet what of the gun they bought four months earlier, and the earlier attempts. Christine says Laroche would be alive if he had talked but nowhere does she admit the possibility of his innocence or deny that Jean-Marie had sworn to avenge Grégory. She is trying to have her cake and eat it: we are kind and right to kill but it could have been avoided.

Innocent or guilty, would Laroche really have mocked Jean-Marie, especially when he was armed?

If Christine Villemin is distorting the truth here, she might lie elsewhere. And that was the trouble: you could never tell. The image of ordinariness and family happiness is overdone, the arguments weighted. And, for good measure, a legal document arguing Laroche's probable guilt is attached as an appendix.

25

No sooner had *Laissez-moi vous dire* come out than Gérard Welzer demanded that it be removed from bookshops. On 30 May the Paris Tribunal obligingly ruled that the work should be withdrawn because of the extreme gravity of the defamatory imputations it contained. Immediately, Henri-René Garaud appealed. And two weeks later the Paris Appeal Court equally obligingly ruled that the right to freedom of expression could in this case take precedence over the offensive elements contained in the book, these being judged insufficiently serious to warrant a ban. The book had its justification as the 'cry of an accused mother', even though, the court admitted, certain passages might justify compensation for 'certain persons'.

Certain persons had indeed already been awarded damages for earlier published declarations. A series of interviews in *Paris Match* judged defamatory by Marie-Ange and the Bolles had led to total awards of 600,000 francs. Libel cases had become a staple in the Grégory affair.

So of course had the appeals to free or transfer Jean-Marie Villemin, and the rejection thereof. The argument never changed. Law and order required as much, and favourable treatment of Jean-Marie Villemin would appear as pure provocation to Marie-Ange Laroche. On 22 July, the Court of Criminal Appeal in Nancy decided that Laroche's murderer would definitely appear before the Court of Assizes. His wife, though, would not. Or at least, not for complicity in Laroche's death. However, the three magistrates headed by Justice Vogtensperger – all new to the case – insisted that Jean-Marie could not be judged until a decision had been reached with regard to his wife. While he was waiting, he would at least be transferred back to Saverne that autumn. That was better than nothing.

Lambert knew that time was running out. As a result of his own decision, he had only four more months to make good his case. The little judge had obtained sabbatical leave for 1987. Two and a quarter years of manning the bridge was long enough. 'Since this began, we have had three Ministers of Justice, two prosecutors and a dozen lawyers. But I have stayed, alone, from beginning to end.' Was this a boast, a plea for sympathy or a complaint? Lambert was so anxious that people should recognise his merits, and he liked to think staying power was one of them.

By late October, he was ready to hand the fruit of his persistence over to André Simard, who would then decide if it should go to a *Chambre d'Accusation*. It was a ripe dossier, one and a half metres wide and containing 2,000 statements and interviews. At the centre of its leading argument, the image of Christine Villemin defined by one of the psychiatrists. 'On the one hand, a young girl who had remained very juvenile, well brought up, idealistic, with a gift for making herself liked. On the other, a wild woman capable of violence, vulgarity and aggression when her version of the truth is contradicted.'

This was the kind of split personality that could make Christine an infanticide. Set about this central perception were the facts, the contradictions in Christine's statements, the adverse testimony from other witnesses, the numerous experts' analyses. Lambert was sure they would be sufficient argument for the Appeal Court to send her before the Assizes, and to criminal judgement.

Like many things in the Grégory case, the session of the Nancy Court of Appeal did not go as planned. Scheduled to deliberate on 28 October, the magistrates were obliged to defer their debate by the last-minute arrival of a memorandum for the defence. This was a document in which the procedural expert François Robinet picked out all the flaws in Lambert's investigation: these, as the document's 297 pages implied, were numerous. Robinet's finely-combed analysis was accompanied by a severe critique of the handwriting experts Bucquet and de Ricci which Garaud had obtained from another expert in Switzerland. It was a digestif the magistrates would gladly have done without after grappling with Lambert's heavyweight dossier. This eleventh hour disruption was not to their liking. It smelt of delaying tactics. But the memorandum had to be read none the less, and the hearing was postponed.

Two weeks later, the two-day hearing began in earnest. The defence highlighted four main weaknesses in Lambert's dossier: the failure of one laboratory technician in Lyon to sign his analysis of the rope, the fact that the statements gathered during the reconstruction of 30 October 1985 were not signed, the unreliability of the handwriting analyses by Bucquet and de Ricci and the failure to observe the rules in the audio-metric test. Garaud had also come armed with hearsay about a friend of Muriel's. Muriel had apparently told the young girl about the family intimidation that had made her retract her condemnation of Bernard Laroche.

This was only the tip of the procedural iceberg that the defence was hoping would melt and drown the case against their client. The attacks were by no means all far fetched. Lombard and his associates agreed about the rope and the reconstruction, and even referred to 'Lambert's failure'. But Lombard had also brought with him thirty eight charges against Christine Villemin. 'If you don't send Christine Villemin before the Assizes,' he mocked, 'then you'll have to put chance on trial.' And this was not just any old barrister speaking.

For outside observers, the most likely outcome seemed to be that the magistrates would demand a new reconsruction, and a new magistrate to conduct it. The Villemin affair would run and run.

What followed was therefore a surprise. On 9 December, Vogtensperger and his colleagues presented a sixty-page document stating that Christine Villemin would be sent before the Court of Assizes and commending Judge Lambert for the unfailing objectivity of his investigations.

The little judge had succeeded.

For once, Garaud and his colleagues seemed to have been caught out. They did not appear until an hour after the judgement was announced. When Garaud, Chastant, Moser and Robinet did step up to the microphones, it was of course to insist that their client was innocent, and state that they would be appealing to the Court of Cassation. That was their last hope of avoiding a trial and Christine Villemin's second to last hope before condemnation: somehow, no one could imagine her going to the Assizes and being acquitted.

Ever since she left Metz-Queuleu prison in July 1985, Christine Villemin had been collecting reasons for hope, reasons to believe that she and Jean-Marie would one day, somewhere, have a normal life. Now those fragile hopes were shattered. Now that the machinery of justice had begun to grind into motion, nothing could stop it. It would crush her.

The news cracked open her defences. As if she were plagued by a guilt she could not even understand, a guilt that lurked in her nightmares at Petitmont.

And yet news of this import did not mean that her life would suddenly change. Things did not stop just like that. The photographers and journalists still came for the exclusive interviews: indeed, they had now added reason for doing so. There was a fresh cry of grief and indignation to be gathered and transcribed. Christine had a rendezvous with *Paris Match* on 13 December. Maître Garaud was there to reassure her.

As he left his client, Garaud felt that he had succeeded in instilling just a little confidence in her. It was a hard moment, a desperate one, but it would pass, and it could not be worse than the night of 16 October.

That was what Garaud had told her. She had already lived through greater disasters. And then there was the possibility of appeal, the Court of Cassation. Besides, even if she went to the Assizes, that did not mean she would be condemned. But Garaud knew those were only words to Christine Villemin: she had seen the bottom fall out of her existence.

Still, Christine Villemin promised that she would be brave. She would hold out, for Jean-Marie's sake, and for her son's.

The photographs of that day show a woman whose eyes are red with sleeplessness and tears. A woman whose lips buckle and hands fidget under the pressure of nerves. She chain-smokes and her eyes are pale and feverish. The young mother is in blue, and she and her mother and her sister-in-law have run out of words. Christine's gaze skates helplessly over her shrunken world.

Such a woman could make no declarations, no appeals.

Her statement took a more radical form. Two days later, at 7.30 a.m., Jeanne Blaise heard her great-grandson crying. Of course, all young children cry in the morning when they want their parents. But Julien just did not stop. It was a continuous moan.

Jeanne hurried upstairs. If she had had time to anticipate, then her worst fears were confirmed. Christine was lying on the floor, unconscious. Jeanne saw two empty Temesta tubes. Each tube normally contains fifty pills. Temesta, a sedative, can be lethal when taken in such doses.

'Oh my God, don't let her be dead!' cried Jeanne.

Jeanne called an ambulance and tried desperately to bring her granddaughter round. To her relief, Christine was not totally lost to sense.

'It wasn't strong enough,' she finally muttered.

A few minutes later, a blaring cortège of gendarmes and ambulance hurtled through Petitmont. By 8.30 a.m. Christine Villemin was in intensive care in Lunéville. She would live. By Wednesday the seventeenth, she could be let out. But she did not return to Petitmont. She and Julien were moving to Nitting, a town further north, near Sarrebourg, where Christine's sister Danielle lived. Petitmont was no longer anonymous enough. Not now that she had tried to kill herself there. Christine Villemin was going into retreat.

Of course, she had mentioned suicide before, both to her barrister and to the press. Just like Jean-Marie and his intention to kill Laroche. They were not the sort to hide their feelings. And as with Laroche's murder, Christine had foreseen everything. On the night of 14 December, she left three letters behind her. One of them begged her grandmother's forgiveness. Another, to her legal representatives, explained that, rather than face years of separation from Jean-Marie and Julien, 'I have chosen to leave them to be with Grégory. No one, not even this accursed justice, can ever separate me from my little man.' Then there was the letter to Jean-Marie. 'My tender love, you are the only person to know how much I loved our child. Unfortunately, the law does not want to believe me. We live in an unjust world.'

Christine's costly gesture had its cruel irony. If only for the space of a letter, Christine Villemin had become her own tragic heroine, and she had found the style to match: noble, plangent, with something of that 'borrowed' feeling which is often present in the sincerest of declarations made by people unaccustomed to writing.

Christine Villemin had anticipated this moment twenty months earlier. 'If I were to die,' she said then, bitterly, 'there would still be people to say that she killed herself because she was guilty.'

And sure enough there were. As one commentator put it, it did not matter whether Christine Villemin had or had not killed her child. Either way, she was in a personal hell.

'We have been kidding ourselves,' said Christine Villemin in her farewell note to Jean-Marie, '1987 will be just as awful as 1986.'

Perhaps. On 30 December, the Appeal Court refused to free Jean-Marie, for the fourth time. And in March 1987, they refused to grant Christine permission to cross over into the Vosges every month to visit Grégory's grave, 'because of the stage the procedure has reached, and for safety reasons'.

There was every reason to believe that the magistrates in Nancy did not look kindly on Christine Villemin.

Meanwhile, in Paris, Marie-Ange and her family battered the sensationalist press with libel actions, four of them, including an attack on the author of *Laissez-moi vous dire*. Christine Villemin was condemned to pay the symbolic franc in compensation for her vilification of Bernard Laroche. That meant she could not be made to pay more, but still had to make amends.

There would be no more vitriolic declarations any more from the newly reclusive subject. Henceforth, it was her sister who answered the questions put by journalists visiting Nitting in search of strong sensations. La Villemin might be glimpsed in the hall or through the window, but she wasn't talking. Since her suicide attempt, Christine had retreated into a world occupied by her son and by her three weekly visits to Jean-Marie. It was enough, and all she had. In Nitting, where the locals hardly knew her, she enjoyed a benevolent neutrality. At most, she stirred a little resentment: not all its 330 inhabitants appreciated the presence of the gendarmes.

Christine Villemin was beginning to learn that it is the role of victims to suffer in silence. Or at least, never to fight back, let alone attack. Words had a nasty habit of entangling you, like a net thrown against a contrary wind. Henceforth, she would leave the conduct of her case to the specialists in legal procedure.

The vital date was 17 March, when the Court of Cassation would deliberate on the solidity of Judge Lambert's dossier. If, as François Robinet was hoping to persuade them to do, they found it too weak, the Villemin case would be referred to another Court, where the decision whether or not to send her before the Assizes would be made again. It would at least give Christine Villemin a second chance.

What followed was as much of a surprise as the decision of 9 December. The Court of Cassation announced that the mother of Grégory Villemin would not be judged for his murder, or rather not until the Court at Dijon had examined the dossier. The case would be dealt with away from the passions of the Vosges. And, assuming the Dijon magistrates did not simply clear the suspect, another magistrate would take over Lambert's dossier and attempt to gather more conclusive evidence. Either towards the arrest of Christine Villemin or against it.

What the defence's lawyers vaunted as a triumph of good sense in fact hinged on three procedural irregularities: the fact that one of the experts examining the rope, Doctor Clément, gave only a written oath. Likewise, only one of the two German experts in Wiesbaden had signed the report: a report which itself came to no conclusions – which indeed refused to even attempt to. The final and most important reason concerned a number of documents whose validity had been rejected by the magistrates at Nancy. These documents included the voice and handwriting analyses carried out during the early stages of the investigation, and which had themselves been removed from the dossier because of procedural irregularities. None of them designated Christine Villemin as the Crow. Much to Garaud's satisfaction, the Nancy Appeal Court now asserted that they should be taken into consideration. If they were, it could no longer be claimed that Christine Villemin had been unanimously identified as the Crow.

It seemed a mild, even pedantic response, but it gave a breathing space. At the very worst, it was a stay of execution.

For Jean-Marie, too, the latest news was good. His case was being transferred to Dijon. Not that judgement was any nearer, for that depended on the fate of Christine: in black and white terms, the court would need to know if, in killing Bernard Laroche, he had been avenging an innocent mother, or just acting out his role in a plot that had been coldly prepared months before. Murder could carry a life sentence, or it could be no more than five years.

Meanwhile, though, Christine Villemin had had enough of the law. She let it be known that she would refuse to go to Dijon.

Jean-Michel Lambert was not present in the magistrates' offices to savour the unease or derision that this new judgement brought with it. He was recovering, and meditating his next career move. Lambert had made no secret of his interest in journalism, and was toying with the idea of a short training at Europe 1 radio, a channel he had had ample opportunity to get to know in the Vosges.

In the meantime, there was his book, *Le Petit Juge*, due out in May. This was the crowning moment of his celebrity and the consummation of his divorce with judicial respectability. It is not seemly to use a notorious and controversial case to satisfy a craving for fame – assuming Lambert had one: perhaps he thought he was simply improving public understanding of the law. Whatever the true motive, his authorial adventure was firmly snubbed in a communiqué from the French Association of Magistrates. With *Le Petit Juge*, said the organisation's representative, Lambert was standing on the soap box of media exposure to say 'I am the author of a great judicial catastrophe, and I am happy.'

Le Petit Juge was not a contentious book, nor did it reveal any judicial secrets. In a sense it was worse than that: it was a banal book, and its author appeared more self-indulgent than big-headed. He knew his fame as 'the best known judge in France was fragile', but he could not resist taking advantage of it to produce an autobiographical account in which personal confessions alternate with the flattest of observations on the course of human crime and human justice. Gems such as: 'It is not only the poor who commit crime,' or, 'There are some people on whom life does not smile.' And finally, 'My modest experience has taught me that most cases can be turned over as easily as a pancake.'

It was a strange thing to say when he had just spent two years working on one of the most hard-fought cases in recent local history, especially when it was precisely that case that had enabled him to write the book.

If Lambert was hoping to become a successful journalist, he would have to find a sharper turn of phrase.

Le Petit Juge is a dull book, and longer than *Laissez-moi vous dire*. Like the Villemin apology, it is half autobiography, half reflection on experience. Reading it, you would not accuse the judge of arrogance, perhaps not even of incompetence. You would say that he was inexperienced, sometimes self-indulgent, and that he takes himself too seriously. The very title of the book suggests that he is too concerned with his public image, and too complacent about it. You feel the same when he picks up the famous Marguerite Duras phrase to describe the solitude of the examining magistrate as *forcément sublime*.

Perhaps Lambert thinks he is being witty, or in the know. After all, he had met Duras. But it sounds more as if he is jealous of Christine Villemin's dark fame.

Yet Lambert regrets his indiscretion, the interview he gave to *Elle* for example when he 'stupidly gave in to a journalist'. It was a habit he had got over since.

Lambert wants to be understood. To that end, he quotes from numerous hate letters received during the investigation – those accusing him of incompetence or impiety and threatening him with death. The judge is tough. But what does shock him is the behaviour of Christine Villemin, her declarations to *Paris Match*, calling him 'an incompetent, a sponge for whom the last person he spoke to is always right'. Lambert is indignant that a suspect can get away with such 'insolence to members of the judiciary'.

But the book suggests another reason for this reaction. Recalling his tears the night he knew he would be arresting Christine Villemin, he explained, 'No suffering in love ever produced such an effect on me.'

Perhaps that was the problem: emotional involvement. For *Le Petit Juge* is also the portrait of a lonely bachelor with a lot of sympathy for his own plight. Lambert evokes his unsatisfactory, fleeting affairs 'which left me with the memory of a slight graze but also a deeper wound that only I can see.' Whatever that means. He describes his solitary walks around Epinal, returning to the flat he had filled with antique furniture whose warmth 'helped me to forget that there was no woman, no children waiting for me when I went home at night.'

This was not a sublime solitude. It was a sad but commonplace one.

It therefore came as little surprise that the little judge had now set his sights on achieving a little emotional stability. On the night before Ascension, in the Vosges town of Mazirot, he got married to a local woman and mother of two children from a former marriage. Their honeymoon trip would no doubt compensate Lambert for all those missed holidays on the Grégory case.

And then, when they got back, there would be a wife and children to go home to.

With or without Lambert, the affair limped on. The gendarmes and the SRPJ had been and gone. So had Jean-Jacques Lecomte, Etienne Sesmat and, now, Jean-Michel Lambert. Even the Vosges had gone, in so far as the case would henceforth be pursued in Dijon, and Christine and Jean-Marie had both left the Vologne. Perhaps now there could be a little serenity.

In Dijon the magistrates felt sufficiently in command of the voluminous dossier to begin their debate on 21 May. For the Villemins, the horizon seemed to be brightening up a little: Maurice Simon, the senior and betitled President of the Chamber, made a statement that was clearly favourable to Christine. And that was fortunate, as Garaud made clear: 'I'm worried that Christine will be driven to suicide, and that this time she'll succeed.'

Garaud and his client could breathe more freely. On 24 June, the Appeal Court issued a dense statement on the investigation so far and requested a supplement of information, including a new reconstruction. According to the magistrates in Dijon, Lambert's staging of 16 October had been too limited, and made no attempt to deal with movements of the participants on their way to and from the area around the chalet in Rue des Champs. Many other elements for the prosecution were declared invalid as well, including timings and the minutes of time trials. Eight of Lambert's interviews were cancelled, thus rendering a number of important statements null and void.

But this was more than a procedural rebuff: 'In the present state of investigations, it cannot be said to be demonstrated that Christine Villemin is the only person who could have committed the crime for which, as far as she is concerned, no motive has yet been found.'

In other words, Lambert and the SRPJ's conclusions were either mistaken, or at least premature, and their methods of testing them inadequate. After all the time trials it was impossible to admit that adequate proof had been advanced to the effect that Christine Villemin really did have the time needed to commit the crime of which she stands accused. Not even the time of Grégory's death could be considered certain. The autopsy, which set the boy's death at around 6.00 p.m., was not thorough enough.

Lambert's and the SRPJ's case had not been destroyed, but it suddenly appeared flimsy. Did that make Christine Villemin any less guilty, or any more innocent? The image of the infanticide that she had so convincingly been made to fit was still there, ready to superimpose itself on her slightest gesture or statement.

26

Exit Judge Lambert, exit, for a few months at least, the most talked-about case in recent French history. The unending calvary of little Grégory was entering a silent phase. Its destiny was now in the hands of Maurice Simon, President of the *Chambre d'Accusation* of the Dijon Appeal court. Having argued against sending Christine Villemin to the Court of Assizes, Simon would be directing the new round of investigations.

'With this case,' he said, 'I have ample material to get me to my retirement.' Simon was sixty-four, ready to quit the world of the judiciary. But the Little Grégory case had tempted him to take advantage of the five-year extension available to top-flight French civil servants. After forty years of career crowned with the *Légion d'Honneur* and *Ordre de Mérite* medals, Simon had nothing left to prove – unless to himself: he was drawn by the challenge: and by the desire for justice.

Simon brought with him a reputation for meticulousness and rigour. He was a man who liked to meet each witness four or five times so as to probe their personality, and then to subject their statements to ruthless cross-checking. Simon was also allergic to media involvement. He would be protecting the truth of the investigation. Neither he, nor the investigators, nor the witnesses, would be talking. It was not just that careless disclosures could upset the course of the inquiry: Simon believed in the humane aspect of this work, and the necessity to respect the suffering of his witnesses. He did not want to *make them speak* but to allow them to express themselves – to breathe.

Epinal and the Vologne had seen the last of the mad months when journalists seemed to be shaping the inquiry as much as reporting it. In those days, anyone with as much as a second cousin who had spoken for five minutes to the gendarmes was hounded for his or her opinion.

At night, working late in his office, Lambert heard groups of journalists banging on his window with the latest clue, or to confirm what they had already heard.

They had made the Vologne and the Vosges into a kind of rural, lumpenproletariat Dallas, a land of men with 'tow-coloured hair' and women 'whose language would make even a drunken trooper blush'.

No one had gathered statistics to see what percentage of the local population was interviewed on the subject of Little Grégory. But there were days when anyone would do. The headmistress of the local school had to fight off the reporters trying to get into the playground, or who were already in the corridor, notebook in hand.

Verbal and documentary evidence were like nuggets in a gold rush. Photographs were stolen from the Villemins and the Hollards. A window was smashed at Paremont in the hunt for good material. There were the stolen plaques and the wreath taken by one photographer and floated on the Vologne where Grégory was found, then dragged in after the snap had been taken: the photo was 'exclusive'.

There was also editorial involvement. Papers tended to be pro-Villemin or pro-Laroche, or two journalists on the same paper took one position each. The tendency was not without its little ironies. The Communist daily *L'Humanité* unwittingly provoked Roger Jacquel to give up his party card when it mentioned him as the first suspect isolated by the gendarmes' graphologist, Colonel Argoud.

For some journalists, though, involvement was much more personal. The freelance correspondent for *La Liberté de l'Est* reacted to Laroche's murder as if Jean-Marie Villemin were his own brother: 'Oh, why did he do it, the fool, the bloody fool!?' The same passionate writer later ransacked the offices of his 'ungrateful' employer.

Another reporter found himself having an affair with the wife of a young gendarme from Bruyères. She used to make the reporters coffee while they were waiting outside headquarters. When she invited him in one day, the couple got talking, and one thing led to the proverbial other. It was a mixture of genuine passion and a reporter's nose for inside information – like everything else surrounding the affair, a mixture of feeling and expediency.

And as if there had to be a criminal parallel to the snooping and prying of journalists, the affair soon threw up a case of stolen documents. On 4 February 1985, the notes on Bernard Laroche taken by President Alteroche of the Nancy Appeal Court simply disappeared. A few weeks later, they were found beside the motorway heading south towards Besançon. Alteroche had not even noticed their disappearance.

Christian Vigne, a thirty-nine-year-old credit card thief and maker of false cheques, was arrested, for the sixteenth time in his career, on 4 July 1985. He became the affair's third 'offender' to end up in Charles III jail. Vigne claimed to have wandered into Alteroche's office without realising it. He said he had stolen the dossier so as to sell it to Christine Villemin. He would have done better to sell it to the press.

In contrast to his predecessor, Simon would keep a tight reign on journalistic curiosity. Perhaps Lambert had been too young for the Grégory affair.

For the press, certainly, the comparison was too tempting to be left alone: Lambert was thirty-two when he took on the case, Simon was twice that age; where Lambert had acquired the odd highlight of grey, Simon had a full head of white hair. Where Lambert could be photographed smiling and elegant in well-cut jacket and polished moccasins, Simon was always seen in a trenchcoat buttoned up to the neck, an expression of profound concentration on his face. Simon was an established magistrate, Lambert the little judge.

In other words, as the press lost no time in pointing out, Maurice Simon was 'the anti-Lambert'. Of course, criticism came cheap and Simon versus Lambert made a good sub-plot to Villemin versus Laroche and the gendarmes versus the SRPJ.

But Simon, for one, was careful not to make any comments. He knew 'There'll be no forgiveness if I make a mistake. No one's going to do me any favours.' Why waste the little credit remaining to the judiciary?

So the judge began cautiously, working closely with the research department of the Dijon gendarmerie, directed by the equally discreet Colonel Gilles Lamy. Simon had a conviction that no one had a good enough memory to sustain a lie for ever. The hard part would be to decide which were the lies that really mattered. For the moment, the working principle was simple. It had been stated by Jean-Jacques Lecomte three years earlier: 'everyone is suspect'.

Simon had decided to avoid the Vologne. He conducted the interviews in Dijon or in Gérardmer and the neighbouring gendarmerie of Xonrupt – a picture postcard mountain chalet with heraldic shields on the walls bearing brightly painted police insignia. Altogether a more relaxing proposition.

It was of course only apparently so. In an interview, you knew that the judge would never make do with a half truth. He would be inviting you back – politely, firmly. For Christine Villemin, this was a new experience. She seemed fraught as she left the Dijon *Palais de Justice* on 21 July.

Of course, Simon could not keep away from the Vologne for ever. There was a new reconstruction to be staged. The judge had chosen four days in October, the thirteenth to the sixteenth; two years after Lambert's annulled effort of 30 October 1985, and three years, to the day, after Grégory's death. Simon too was hoping for a little help from circumstances. But the 'anti-Lambert' was going to take his time: three and a half days, as opposed to the little judge's four hours.

To avoid accusations of partiality, Simon was accompanied in the Vologne by two independent assessors and the Dijon prosecutor, Bruno Estrangin. Simon tried out the various segments of the fateful day before having the protagonists enact them. And to disorient both the participants and the journalists following them, Simon had decided to jumble up the order of events: that might throw out a few rehearsed responses.

Hundreds of gendarmes and flying squad police made security cordons all around the vital sites. The atmosphere, however, remained calm, and the locals chatted amiably. It was almost like old times; except that there was no longer a footbridge over the Vologne near where Grégory was found, and that Jimmy, Bernard Colin's Dalmation, had died. And of course, proceedings went ahead with a bit more restraint this time. Jean-Marie Villemin was constantly surrounded by four gendarmes in bullet-proof jackets. The only incident occurred when journalists observing from the railway line at Docelles nearly got themselves crushed by the Epinal train.

Among the participants, emotion was intense but contained. Albert and Monique had not seen Christine since well before her attempted suicide. Like Jean-Marie and his wife, they had thought of leaving the Vologne, where people threatened or looked askance at them, where Lionel was plagued with the Little Grégory pranks of his schoolmates. But they were old: Where could they go? So now they tried to make contact with Jean-Marie and observed Christine. Neither Monique nor Lambert could uproot their feeling of suspicion: 'She smiles too much for a grieving mother.'

But Christine was not smiling now. Huddled up in her raincoat, she was hunched into herself. She refused to re-enact the letter-posting episode: 'I cannot be forced to repeat something I never did in the first place.' Simon did not demur. Christine was strangely serene up at Paremont, tearful when re-enacting the visit to Christine Jacquot at Gaichamp. Grégory would have been seven now.

For Jean-Marie, it was a rare opportunity to meditate on his first son's tomb. He stood there, like a prisoner at ease during inspection, while Julien toddled around the slabs of marble, half aware that this place meant a lot to his parents, that it had something to do with his mother's tears.

Lambert's dossier had begun to take on water. His conviction that Grégory had been thrown into the Vologne several hundred metres out of Docelles came up against the expert opinion of André Marin, the forensic specialist Simon had brought in to observe and make a report on proceedings. Marin pointed out that Grégory's body would almost inevitably have been scratched as he travelled downstream. Besides, the killer would have had to cross not only the railway line but also a stream to get to the river at that point. And the body would have rolled against stones as it was swept up by the current.

This was all cheering, if belated news for Adjudant Robert Lamirand. He now had the satisfaction of seeing his three-year-old thesis confirmed: Grégory might have been thrown into the Vologne behind the firemen's barracks.

That left the problem of time and visibility, and the fact that the mannequin had neither the size or the weight of Grégory's body. It was too light. A month later, Simon was back with a heavier model. This time, however, the thing kept sinking a few metres downstream from where it was thrown into the Vologne. Was it too heavy?

Lombard, now assisted by an expert criminologist, insisted it was. Garaud felt that the new tests merely confirmed what he had always said: Grégory was put in the water in the centre of Docelles.

It was, as ever, much ado about nothing.

27

While Simon's investigation remained cloaked in discretion, personal events took centre stage. For Christine Villemin, Christmas brought precisely what Christmas should bring – hope. On 24 December 1987, Jean-Marie was released after thirty-three months in prison. He was a changed man – more sober, more thoughtful, and 17 kilos thinner than in March 1985. He had been to the depths and learnt how to live there.

For Monique and Albert, it was 'our best Christmas present ever'. Their boy, 'the one who has suffered the most in this affair', was free. But they would have to wait to see him: the condition of Jean-Marie's release was that he and Christine should live and stay away from the Vologne, in the Essonne *département* near Paris.

The couple would be moving to Brières-les-Scellés, where Auto-coussin had helped Jean-Marie find work in a local factory. For the Bolles it was all too easy, revoltingly easy. 'If he comes back here we might do what he did. Since there is no justice, we might have to make our own,' said Lucien.

Lucien Bolle's reaction could stand for the whole family. Once again, their grief had been flouted. In Biffontaine, two days before the New Year, the Bolles gave a press conference to protest. This time there were no lawyers, no professionals of communication. Just one of Marie-Ange's brothers reading awkwardly from a scrap of notepaper, appealing 'to all those who disagree with Judge Simon's decision to write to Marie-Ange'. She was edging towards absolute despair: 'I've stopped hoping . . . It's my lawyers who keep me going. If I didn't have the damages they obtained from the newspapers, I don't know how I'd cope.'

There was worse still to come. On the night of 30 December, in

Epinal hospital, Jeannine Bolle died, leaving Marie-Ange, Muriel and eight other children. Her worries for Muriel and Marie-Ange had undermined her already fragile health: the release of Jean-Marie Villemin had finished the work of destruction: 'It was as if all her efforts to obtain justice had been reduced to nothing. The shock was more than she could bear.'

Muriel was on her own now. She was eighteen, but circumstances seemed to be conspiring to keep her in uncomfortable adolescence. Every time she tried to get a job she was turned down. Like Marie-Ange, who had just been refused by Autocoussin. Muriel spent her time reading French Mills and Boons and walking her dog. She had a few friends, but it was no life for a young woman.

At least now she had been forgiven by her sister. Jeannine had achieved that at least before she died. After all, they were both prisoners of Bernard Laroche's death. Marie-Ange had abandoned the chalet in Aumontzey for good: there had been more death threats, cars in the night. And every time she walked past the garage she saw blood and her husband's last few minutes.

Sébastien was growing up with trauma. At school, he pretended that his father had died in the war. At home he proclaimed, 'When I am big like Uncle Lucien I'll avenge my Dad. Then Mummy won't cry any more.'

Others could escape the affair more easily, even if it stuck in their throat. In Bourg-en-Bresse, Jean-Michel Lambert was making a discreet return to the judiciary. And not as an examining magistrate. One thing at least would provide a little continuity: his colleague, Judge Guillemaud, had also served in Epinal. But Lambert had little desire to rake up the past.

That was the job of the press. On 20 February 1988, *Le Figaro* and the local *Le Républicain Lorrain* both produced articles suggesting that the SRPJ had tried to frame Christine Villemin by planting the rope at her home. As the articles pointed out, previous searches at Paremont had failed to yield any such evidence, and Jean-Marie and Christine would not have been so foolish as to leave it there after the murder. The articles quoted Gérard Dittinger, Christine's brother-in-law, who had tried to visit the house when the crucial search was being conducted. The police had refused to let him enter. While he was waiting outside, he saw that two roof tiles giving access to the garage had been displaced. The police told him it was the wind, and an officer immediately legged up to put them back in place. Strange. Just like the fact that, as Christine recalled, the police seemed to know exactly where to find the rope. And the fact that when the Villemins' roof was repaired in April 1984 the material used was hemp, not rope.

There was more. The police had apparently inserted a rope lace into Jean-Marie's shoes. At least that was what his brother-in-law, Bernard Nöel, thought. He always remembered the shoes being very dirty, but when the police presented them to him they were clean. Not very subtle. And what about the rumour that one of Jean-Marie's cousins also possessed a ball of the same rope, that he had given some of it to the police unofficially. The SRPJ would have been free to do as they pleased with the incriminating evidence.

It all sounded very damning. Predictably, the SRPJ took the papers to court. Equally predictably, perhaps, their good name was restored to them a year later. And in the process each of the four officers picked up 390,000 francs in damages.

It was one of the features of the affair: the constant blackening of the forces of order, and their continuing success in the courts. Muriel's complaint against the gendarmes for use of forgeries to extort her confession was equally unsuccessful. On 24 June 1988, the court at Dijon declared the gendarmes innocent of abusive procedure.

It was most intriguing. The gendarmes 'had not put any kind of illegal pressure on Muriel to make her confess.' And, at the same time, Muriel was cleared of non-assistance to a person in danger, the charge brought by Jean-Marie and Christine Villemin. In other words, Muriel's confession was obtained by legitimate means, but it was not credible, because she had not been present when Grégory Villemin was taken away from Paremont. So why had she given it?

Maurice Simon had inherited more than his fair share of misunderstandings. And of undigested evidence. As he continued his work, rumours began to circulate concerning forgotten witnesses.

The ever-vigilant *Paris Match* spoke of the statement made by Jean Descey, a Parisian house painter with a second home near the Vologne. On 16 October 1984, Descey was in Lépanges. At 5.20 p.m., he saw four people sitting in a small car by the banks of the river. He was all the more certain because he remembered thinking they had had a breakdown and had nearly stopped to offer them help. When Descey saw the car again, it was at Grégory's funeral.

Then there was the statement made by a woman who sold chips from a van parked outside Bruyères supermarket. It dated from 29 October. Like Descey's, her deposition confirmed the gang hypothesis. Three days before the murder, the woman remembered serving two men and a woman. As they stood eating, she overheard the woman ask:

'So, what do we do?'

And the bigger of the two men replied:

'Yes, we have to do something. He's really starting to get on my nerves. He has started to piss me off in a big way.'

Then, a few moments later:

'If I take Titi, I'll dump him in the Vologne, you can take my word for it.'

It was almost too convincing to be true. And four years too late.

Inevitably, the gang hypothesis brought Bernard Laroche back to the murky forefront of the affair. Judge Simon had started talking to Denis Klein, the gendarme-cum-expert taken on by Sesmat's men in 1984. Lambert had never gone further with the initials Klein had found engraved in the paper of the murder note by pressure from a pen on the sheet above. Now photographs of the sheet were published and Klein's presence was like a confirmation of Marie-Ange's worst fears.

Nothing was simple for Bernard Laroche's widow. Having lost her mother, she was condemned to watch impotently as her husband was once again linked with infanticide. *Did she realise that she had been living with a monster?*

It was enough to spoil what should have been a joyous occasion; for on 16 September 1988, Marie-Ange was married to Denis Jacob. The name said it all: Denis was a cousin of Jean-Marie Villemin. He was a thin, wiry man with sharp features – very much the opposite of his predecessor. 'I haven't forgotten Bernard,' said the moderately merry newly-wed to the few journalists interested in the brighter side of the affair, 'but life has to go on.'

As if to illustrate Marie-Ange's statement, Muriel was present at the celebration. She had even got herself a boyfriend. 'He's from the Vosges,' she said. 'He protects me.'

Muriel needed protecting, especially after her mother's death. Her behaviour had been showing signs of strain. One newspaper, the extreme right *Minute* – a natural if not desirable ally of *Légitime Défense* – had mentioned two bizarre incidents a few months earlier. On 23 June 1988, Monique and Albert Villemin narrowly avoided being run down by a car. Muriel was at the wheel. Three weeks later, the same thing happened to Lionel Villemin.

It was true that Muriel had only just learnt to drive. Accidents do happen.

And especially to Marie-Ange. As part of her fresh start in life, she had been planning to manage a restaurant with one of Denis Jacob's sisters. The place burnt down a few days before the wedding. It was enough to make you superstitious.

Marriage did nothing to weaken Marie-Ange's vigilance. On 28 November, she wrote to President François Mitterrand (at least he was still there) urging him to do something to protect Laroche's name and to bring Jean-Marie Villemin to trial.

But as everyone knew, that depended on Judge Simon.

During 1988, Simon held three major get-togethers with the Villemin family: in March, they listened to the tapes of the Crow; in May, a reconstruction was staged in Aumontzey to try to fix the precise time of the phone call to Michel, and in November there was a general confrontation in Dijon. None of these events produced any new revelations.

In Aumontzey, however, Simon did at least have the chance to observe a surprising inconsistency. With the exception of his under-standable confusion about the TV image corresponding to the Crow's call, Michel and his younger brother Lionel had always taken the same line on the events of 16 October: when he heard the phone ringing in his parents' house, Lionel had tried to climb through the kitchen window before the caller hung up. When Simon asked him to repeat the action, Lionel was incapable of getting up to the window. By now he was fifteen, nearly four years older than at the time of the murder.

He was also healthier, for he had recently been operated on for a hip problem.

Perhaps Lionel, like so many other witnesses, had just got confused. Had taken his intentions or his imagination for reality. There was no way of telling.

Simon kept coming up against the same obstinate detail: time. According to a statement by Professor Leauté, the reconstruction in Aumontzey did at least tend to confirm that Michel Villemin received the Crow's message at 5.33 p.m. rather than 5.26 p.m. But what about the drowning? Lambert had always pinned his hypothesis on the testimony of Josyane Guyot, who saw the blue object in the river at 5.30 p.m.

And yet Lambert had never checked Guyot's statement by showing her Grégory's anorak. When Simon brought out the exhibit, Guyot told him that the blue she had seen was of a lighter shade. And then Grégory's anorak had fluorescent armbands: she did not remember seeing those either.

Of course, Guyot had had ample time to forget. Her mental image could have grown blurred. Besides, it is hard to get a precise idea of a shade of blue when you only glimpse at it in running water. Guyot may not have looked long and hard enough to register the armbands. But if her memory could be trusted, then there was no reason not to believe that Grégory had been thrown in the river much later than 6.00 p.m.

That in turn made the hypothesis of a group effort much more likely, and the tyre treads and syringe much more significant. Especially with the discovery Simon had made when flying over the Vologne in an army helicopter. In the centre of Docelles, there was a secluded, overgrown bridge that the killers could easily have crossed without being noticed. Once on the other side of the river, they could have waited with the drugged child until it was dark.

If Grégory had been killed later, a lot of alibis would be worth re-examining.

And Christine Villemin was innocent.

28

The odour of guilt is tenacious. Today, there are still plenty of people who believe that Christine Villemin killed her son. They point to her lies, her enigmatic behaviour, her hysterical gaiety or savage aggression, and her seeming detachment, those moments when she seemed to be contemplating the affair from outside. More than the material evidence, those traits are forever ready to merge in the dark, perfect image of mother and infanticide. It is more compelling than daylight reality, this dark spot of the psyche, Christine Villemin's sublime flaw.

Naturally, other explanations are less sensationally attractive: to consider that Christine Villemin has been the victim of her media image, of her own foolish declarations and naive lies; that she has clumsily succumbed to the binary logic of a floundering investigation – Villemin or Laroche. It is of lesser interest to consider that her suggested motive remains vague, and that material proof is lacking. Judge Lambert's tissue of presumption has a fascinating weft.

Nevertheless, Christine Villemin, the creature of evil, has for many been reduced to more fitting proportions: she has become the humble seamstress of the Vosges, silently and docilely awaiting the acquittal that Henri Garaud has been publicly anticipating since the summer of 1989. She is silent now, like her husband: they have withdrawn from the web of poisonous words spun in the Vologne. Their silence, and the 'positive evidence' found by Maurice Simon's investigations have done their work.

But Simon did not take on the Little Grégory affair to produce an accumulation of negative proof. He came to the case to restore a vision of the crime, to set the Villemins and Bolles to rights, to act as a confessor.

On 10 September 1989, Maurice Simon surprised the media, and perhaps himself, by giving an interview to French television. The Little Grégory affair was back, but more as oracle than revelation. Simon was laconic, guarded, his silences heavy with the unsaid:

Q: Have you found the motive?

A: I cannot tell you what I've found.

Q: Will the truth ever be known?

A: I think so, yes.

Q: Is something about to happen?

A: Quite possibly.

Q: Something surprising?

A: Perhaps, yes.

Q: The whole thing leads back to a motive and a person?

A: A motive, and one or several persons.

It was an overture, surely, but to what?

In the Vosges, there was a flurry of excitement, talk of imminent charges. And, on 11 September, Michel and Ginette Villemin were summoned to Bruyères gendarmerie by Commandant Lamy, Simon's right-hand man.

Perhaps, then, Jean-Marie had been right all along: Michel and Ginette were the couple who manipulated Bernard Laroche. The crime was as Marie-Christine Villemin once imagined. 'If Bernard Laroche did it, then he must have been with Michel and Ginette, because they are evil people.' Look closely: you could see the spite on their twisted lips, which seemed constantly tempted to grimace; in Ginette's narrow eyes, in Michel's empty gaze. They would make the perfect man-and-woman Crow suspected by Jean-Marie, the long-neglected source of revelation. It was significant that, up to now, Michel had never taken part in the dictation tests because he 'couldn't write'.

As they got out of their car to enter the gendarmerie, Michel and Ginette were frowning. Michel had changed: his lank hair was cut short, his stomach was getting a little barrel-like. Ginette had changed less: she still wore her hair low and bushy over her forehead, shading or hiding her eyes.

This time, Michel Villemin did take a dictation. He and his wife stayed in the gendarmerie for six hours. Outside, the journalists were back. But when Michel and Ginette emerged, they parried questions with a smile: "We've had a good day," they stated.

That is not everyone's definition of six hours of close questioning. But Michel, as his lawyers lost no time pointing out, still had 'unshakeable alibis' for 16 October. He was immovable, or was there nothing to move?

The same day as the interview in Bruyères, Maurice Simon issued a disclaimer from Dijon:

'Contrary to some people's interpretation of my statement, I have no set opinion on this case and no timetable has been set for its resolution.'

The judge's characteristically cautious remark did not stop the excitement continuing. After Michel and Ginette, it was the turn of the 'mystery witness' at Xonrupt to intrigue Grégory watchers when, after a 'frantic' car chase through the Vosges (journalist hunting gendarmes), a person was taken into the mountain headquarters hidden under a blanket on the back seat of the squad car. 'The witness who fears for his life.' Surely there was vital information in the offing? A journalist who ventured into upper Aumontzey to find out Michel Villemin's reaction was attacked and knocked down before he could even explain.

So who was the key witness? *Paris Match* had decided it was Marie-Christine Villemin, the wife of Gilbert. She was the missing link. Not only had Jean-Marie's discreet sister-in-law 'missed' the early handwriting tests, but in the first she took, Bucquet and de Ricci's, she came second only to Christine Villemin. Marie-Christine, remembered the magazine, had a younger brother who was arrested in 1983 for having beaten to death an old woman in Poulières. As for Marie-Christine, she was a frail leukaemia sufferer: 'She will probably never be able to have children.' Was hers another twisted, hate-filled existence?

But insinuations about Marie-Christine Villemin merely ended in another libel action, this time for the modest sum of 250,000 francs. In self defence, Marie-Christine had her employer make out a certificate proving that she was at work all through 13 September. You can never be too careful.

In fact, *Paris Match* had not been too wide of the mark: a few days later, it was revealed that the blanket-wrapped informer was Gilbert Villemin, her husband. He simply wanted to avoid getting involved in the case. Now, as perhaps he should have anticipated, it had caught up with him. Like everyone else.

The affair seemed to have recovered its old destructive vitality. Even Judge Simon seemed to be losing his serenity.

On 21 October, the magazine *Le Nouveau Détective*, a specialist in sensational crime, published a two-page exclusive interview with the judge. This time, Simon was a little more explicit.

'Bernard Laroche did perhaps abduct Grégory. But I am not prepared to say that he was his assassin. I have no proof it was him.'

It sounded, then, as if Simon had 'proof' of Laroche's involvement. Presumably, he had reached his conclusion about Muriel. And about Christine, too? Of the view that Grégory was killed later than 5.30 p.m., he admitted: 'For me, it is the most plausible hypothesis.' Christine was therefore innocent. As for the killers, Simon confirmed his belief that there were several of them acting together. 'But I refuse to charge or arrest anyone in the hope of making them break down.' The judge was a perfectionist.

Simon's interview also revealed that the case had not grown any less passionate in the apparent calm of his investigation. Like Lambert, he had had his share of hate mail – some four hundred letters filled with insults. Four of them were especially chilling. Not only did they contain death threats, but the writers were also capable of making detailed references to the investigation and knew about Simon's children and grandchildren, whom they also threatened to kill.

All these letters were posted in the same town. What especially troubled Simon was that 'only Albert and Monique knew about the existence of my family.'

Had not Albert and Monique always been the Crow's prime source of information? Once again, there had been too much talk in the Villemin household.

As for Simon, he had cracked under the strain. It was no use energetically denying that he had wanted to give an interview, that this was just a confidential chat. Although sensational in form, *Détective* is generally considered reliable in its content. The journalist involved had been following the case from the very beginning.

The prosecutor, Bruno Estrangin, felt it necessary to publicly insist that 'at the current stage of the investigations, we cannot reach any definitive conclusions'. And to give Simon a severe rebuke.

The most favourable conclusion was that Simon was playing cat and mouse: that his disclosures and his silences were intended for another person – the Crow. Like so many nods and winks. More likely, the judge had simply been taken in. His emotion had got the better of him after two and a half years on the case. He had spent too many hours studying the 35,000 pages of the dossier and going over the 180 interviews he had conducted since June 1987. Grégory had become an obsession.

'The image of the child is constantly before me. I have seen his birth. I have seen his personality take form. I have seen him grow.'

Perhaps, then, it was wishful thinking when Simon told *Détective* that he was hoping to conclude the investigation 'before the end of 1989'.

Clearly, though, the judge was beginning to form an intimate conviction. Earlier that summer, he had spoken to Muriel Bolle. The key witness had been inaccessible until late 1988 as *partie civile* against the gendarmes and defendant against Jean-Marie and Christine Ville-min. Then, once these cases had been resolved, Muriel got pregnant. Simon did not like to harass people. It was not until June 1989 that he summoned her to the gendarmerie.

Muriel had donned her smartest, most feminine clothes: a floating trouser suit in blue and high-heeled shoes had replaced her bomber jacket, drainpipe jeans and tennis shoes. Helped by a careful hairdo, a young woman was beginning to emerge from the tomboy whose existence had come to a standstill on 6 November 1984.

But this was no butterfly emerging miraculously from the chrysalis. Muriel and her child had been abandoned by the father. And Simon would be forcing her back into the nightmare of her adolescence. Before speaking to Muriel, he had been speaking to Jacqueline Golbain, the nurse who used to administer Jeannine Bolle's insulin until her death at the end of 1987. Golbain had told him that the syringe and insulin found by the Vologne just after Grégory's death were of the same variety as the kit she used in Rue de Maroc. She had told him that she used to leave insulin supplies and a needle at the Bolles' home, and that Muriel was the only other person she had taught how to administer them. And Golbain had insisted that the substance could not be detected in an autopsy – 'just look in Agatha Christie'.

What Muriel told Simon has remained a secret. But, as she left the station, observers saw her heading for the police van, instead of for Lucien's waiting car. Reflexes die hard.

Now, with Simon's interviews, Bernard Laroche's involvement was once again a public talking point.

The feverish hunt for accomplices could begin, with all the usual exaggerations and unfounded assertions. Just like old times.

A new name introduced by *Paris Match* was that of Bernard Laroche's uncle and neighbour at Aumontzey, Marcel Jacob. The two men were brought up together by Jacob's mother. The article in question claimed that Jacob was very attached to his sister, Monique Villemin, but could not bear Albert. According to the magazine, he had even made overt threats against his brother-in-law. *Paris Match* also suggested that Jacob's language was exactly the same as that used by the Crow.

Marcel Jacob has sued *Paris Match* for one million francs.

Days later, a radio station reported that Lucien Bolle had shot himself in the foot. He had been handling a rifle in the house formerly inhabited by Marie-Ange and Bernard Laroche, which had since become his home. But Lucien was not even there at the time of the reported accident. He therefore did not see the ambulance that some familiar and malign joker had sent for him.

Far from Aumontzey, Louisette Bolle was tracked down in her new home in Saint Dié: 'Marie-Ange threw me out of Bernard's house,' she explained. 'She said she wanted the money for her kids, but it was for her.' Besides this supplement of family hate, Louisette confirmed the rumour Judge Simon had helped to revive: 'Muriel told me she went in the car with Bernard. She went to fetch the kid with Bernard.'

To other reporters the following week, the word-chewing and retarded aunt of Bernard Laroche stated, with equal conviction: 'It's Christine who killed him. Why else would she have closed the shutters . . . She told me that when she had got rid of her son she would have a really good celebration.'

On their own, Louisette's words could not be taken seriously, but they gained weight from the declarations made by Judge Simon. Naturally, Marie-Ange Jacob, ex-Laroche, was outraged. 'It's as if they were murdering Bernard all over again,' wailed the tearful 'Merry Widow' of Christine Villemin's imagination. But Marie-Ange was going to do more than just complain. On 27 October, with Muriel and her brother Lucien, she went to Paris to lodge a complaint against Simon. Their aim was to get the case taken out of his hands. The Bolles were fighting back, and in the grand manner. Their bravado was short-lived.

Arriving at the Tribunal, the three plaintiffs were asked to submit to the routine security check. No one bothers with such precautions in Epinal, and the Bolles had come unprepared. The fear they knew was personal, not institutional. As she gave her handbag up to the guard, Marie-Ange went white. The reason was soon discovered. In the bag, the security personnel found a 357 Magnum revolver. By now Muriel and Lucien had understood. No search was required to make Muriel give up her pistol and Lucien his switchblade.

The Bolles' first official attempt to change the course of the investigation ended in tears, and three hours of police questioning. After five years of fear and grief, paranoia had got the better of them.

Maurice Simon's hopes of winding up the Little Grégory case in 1989 have been frustrated. More than five and a half years after the boy's death, the Bolles and the Jacobs and the Villemins continue to live in fear of accusation and of violence. It is said that Albert Villemin, the Crow's main target, has tried to hang himself. Still he and Monique are tied to the valley.

In the Essonne, Jean-Marie and Christine Villemin, the star of the affair, are leading a calm, contained life. Their greatest aspiration is to anonymity. They struggle by on an income eroded by regular payments to Bernard Laroche's widow. And Christine Villemin is expecting her third child for September. If she is lucky, her name will have been cleared before the baby is born, and Jean-Marie should know his fate before the autumn is over.

Marie-Ange continues to watch jealously and emotionally over the investigation and the good name of her first husband. Muriel Bolle continues to inhabit the mental prison that closed around her when she was fifteen. And if there are words that can be spoken to release her from it, Maurice Simon has still not persuaded her to utter them. Muriel's, someone has said, is the third 'death' in the affair.

Meanwhile, in the wider world, the attentive barristers in the case continue to make a name for themselves. Paul Lombard recently participated in a television 'trial' of Louis XVI, as part of the bicentenary celebration of the French Revolution. In this historical absurdity, the barrister acting for Grégory Villemin's grandparents found himself pleading against Maître Verges, the real-life defender of a Nazi torturer, Klaus Barbie. Lombard was against the king.

Henri Garaud, on his side, has also been involved in a highly symbolic case: defending the policeman accused of gratuitously killing 'Malek', the young student whose death in 1986 marked the turning point in the victory of French students against reforms threatened by a right-wing government.

In Epinal and Paris, while he continues his political career with the French Socialist Party, Gérard Welzer has been awarded the 'chocolate prize' for his public relations with local journalists.

And in Bourg-en-Bresse, the now less famous little judge has taken to running in local marathons: older, but still boyish.

The investigation he shared with the gendarmes and the SRPJ still manages to throw up the odd surprise. In January 1990, Maurice Simon chanced upon a letter given to Lambert by Monique Villemin – a letter in stick writing. Posted in Darnieulles, near Epinal, on 24 July 1985, the note said: 'I'll get you Villemins. Next victim, Monique.' Lambert had ignored it as a bad joke. But when Simon gave it to the graphologists, they told him it was the Crow's fifth letter.

The Crow continues to make his presence felt, perhaps unintentionally. For this fifth missive seems to prove that neither Bernard Laroche nor Christine Villemin could have been the Crow. Laroche was three months dead when it was posted, and Christine Villemin was under close police surveillance after coming out of jail.

It follows, then, that the Crow is still free. The letter had come back like a repeated provocation. A few days after this discovery, on 28 January, Maurice Simon suffered a heart attack while on holiday with his children. It was as if the crime had greater vitality than the judge.

'Perhaps he had spent too much time on the dossier,' commented François Robinet.

But Simon is continuing his work. Around him, the crime and its setting dissolve slowly into the decomposing present. The post office at Lépanges has been given a fresh coat of paint. The house on Paremont has been given a new finish and baptised 'Les Mille Fleurs' – the name being illustrated by abundant baskets of chrysanthemums. The owners have planted a hedge round the property and have built an extension. New *pavillons* are sprouting here and there on the slopes of Paremont, where the silence is disturbed only by the noise of tractors or dogs barking.

Even the River Vologne is changing, slightly, to accommodate a new stretch of road outside Docelles. There will be no more flotation tests.

Only the speckled pink granite of Grégory Villemin's tomb remains, regularly but unspectacularly decked with flowers, a score of marble funeral plaques cluttering its smooth surface. It stays, waiting to be carried away when the case is over.

And if you look long enough, you might say that the two parts of the headstone are like wings.